SON OF BIGFOOT

MICHAEL WALLACE

Published by Chapters of Life
Toledo, Washington
www.chaptersoflife.com

ISBN 978-1-939685-86-5 (print)
ISBN 978-1-939685-84-1 (ebook)

Cover design by Kathy Campbell of inkbooksdesign.com
Back cover photo of Ray Wallace as an older man by Dave Rubert
Back cover photo of Bigfoot by Roger Patterson and Robert Gimlin

Publisher's note: This is a memoir recounting events in the life of Michael Wallace to the best of his recollection. Some names have been changed to protect the privacy of those people.

DEDICATION

To Ray and Elna Wallace,
for giving me a loving and unique environment
where I could grow up and thrive,
and to Rose,
my loving and patient wife
of thirty-two years.

A NOTE TO READERS

This book is full of memories, mine and others'. While researching and writing my story, there have been numerous times my memory has not matched that of others. Sorting out the facts has been difficult at times. My goal has always been to remain as close to reality as I can.

I love history and could not help including some research rabbit trails at times.

There are far too many stories written about disastrous childhoods than there should be. It's a cold reality. Stories that are unthinkable, that no child should have to endure. Healing comes at a cost, if it comes at all. My story is not one of them. My wounds are self-inflicted but still need healing.

Writing one's own story can be very cathartic. Only by facing where you have been do you clearly picture where you are. From there, you gain a better perspective of where you are headed.

There are some complicated events from the past that I am not at liberty to divulge. Some are being faced, and others may never be. For me, my choice is to clean the closet to my best ability and be free. None of it is easy, whether you have brought problems on yourself or they were put upon you by others. Grace and mercy has prevailed in our family, which binds us together in the love of Christ, whether each is a believer or not.

Our children have achieved greatness in a multitude of ways, resting on their God-given gifts. Rose and I would trust our lives to any one of them and their spouses.

CONTENTS

Part One: Dreamland   **9**

Chapter 1: Where Dreams Begin   11

Chapter 2: The Sorensens   24

Chapter 3: The Wallaces   30

Chapter 4: The Fluckingers (Fluckigers)   36

Chapter 5: Merging of the clans   40

Chapter 6: Yellow Creek Logging Corp   45

Chapter 7: Pecwan   54

Chapter 8: Willow Creek (1954–1955)   61

Chapter 9: Willow Creek (1956–1957) Fishing . . . Bigfoot Style   68

Chapter 10: Hardy Creek   78

Chapter 11: Fort Bragg   86

Chapter 12: Bigfoot Country   89

Chapter 13: Riches to Rags   95

Chapter 14: Oakridge   97

Chapter 15: Sutherlin   99

Chapter 16: Back to the Beginning   102

Chapter 17: Toledo (Continued)   113

Part Two: The Good, the Bad, the Ugly   **123**

Chapter 18: Leaving the Village   125

Chapter 19: Off and Running Without a Village   128

Chapter 20: More Changes   137

Chapter 21: Bellingham   142

Chapter 22: Life in the Real World   148

Chapter 23: Keeping Busy   155

Chapter 24: Going for It   161

Chapter 25: A Mixed Bag   169

Chapter 26: The Cure   176

Chapter 27: Up, Up, and Away   180

Chapter 28: A New Path   185

Chapter 29: Welcome to Colorado   192

Chapter 30: Independent   198

Part Three: The Final Village   **203**

Chapter 31: A Different Course   205

Chapter 32: New Life   208

Chapter 33: A Better Life   216
Chapter 34: Growing Pains   221
Chapter 35: A Three-Year-Old   224
Chapter 36: My New Family   229
Chapter 37: Delayed Honeymoon   235
Chapter 38: Back Home   246
Chapter 39: Trinity Estates I   252
Chapter 40: Trinity II   258
Chapter 41: Bigfoot Rests   263
Chapter 42: A New Normal   269
Chapter 43: Dreams   273
Chapter 44: Growing!   280
Chapter 45: More Adventures   286
Chapter 46: A Trip or Two   293
Chapter 47: Like a Child   303
Acknowledgments   307
About the Author   308

SON

OF

BIGFOOT

MICHAEL WALLACE

PART ONE

DREAMLAND

CHAPTER 1
WHERE DREAMS BEGIN

IN THE BEGINNING

I'M HANGING OUT HERE JUST RUMINATING on the current situation. Ruby Fluckinger is in a pickle and trying to figure out what to do next. She and Arling have just broken up. They have been together long enough that this has created a very tough and emotional breakup for both of them. So, considering what's going on, decisions must be made. We're pondering the situation, thinking what would be best for all involved and know that Toledo is not the best place for her right now. Going to her sister's place in Oregon is the best option. It's a logging camp literally out in the sticks, in the middle of nowhere, west of Sutherlin, Oregon.

On the long bus ride, she has nothing but time to think of her next move. We discuss at great length what would be best for both of us and decide it will be good to go our separate ways in the near future. Having arrived at camp, we find seven married couples living in eight-foot by thirty-two-foot shacks and a bunkhouse full of single guys. In one of the shacks is Ruby's sister, Rosie, with Rube, her husband, and their two sons, Dick and Bob. They find suitable quarters for Ruby, and she settles in. The camp is overflowing with characters, most of them originally from the Toledo area.

Ruby and I develop a pretty solid plan that works well for both of us. Being around those interesting characters in camp and getting to know them, the choice becomes obvious for many reasons. I'd been hinting to Ruby that the guy running the logging camp and his really sweet wife would probably be a pretty exciting choice for parents.

For some time, Ray and Elna Wallace had been trying, without success, to have a baby. We both appreciate their character. Elna is a strong woman, born in Denmark. I love watching the way she treats others. Ray, her husband, is something else. When he was made, they threw away the mold. Wait, there was no mold; he was freehanded. Ruby agrees with me. I would adopt Ray and Elna to be my mom and dad. Months go by, and it's finally time for Ruby and me to slowly and lovingly part ways.

Elna and Butch, above, and Ray with Butch

So, when I arrive on July 29, 1948, in Roseburg, Oregon, about thirty miles from camp at "Mercy" hospital, I officially become James Michael Wallace. The "Mercy" part would explain many things later in life. I love Elna's choice of names right from the start. James, after the guy who wrote one of the later books in the New Testament; Michael, after one of the archangels; and, of course, Wallace after the guy leading the pack. Elna is responsible for the James Michael name choices. To reveal a little more of her character, she told Ruby, "If you ever decide you have made a mistake by giving up your baby and you want him back, it would be painful, but we would let him go."

Ruby stays in camp for some time. She often comes over to help Elna feed or bathe me or simply watches me if Elna had something to do. I'm off to a pretty good start.

By the way, after my first haircut at the age of three, I apparently earn the nickname "Butch." What might be called a crew cut nowadays was a butch

Ruby in camp

at this time. When this type of cut is finished, it's a down-and-dirty, getter-done, take-no-prisoners kind of a do with very little hair left and absolutely zero "do" to be seen. Apparently, golden curls before the "butch" didn't make it in a logging camp.

So here I am about twenty miles west of Sutherlin, Oregon, in a logging camp that has been running since 1946. At first I lived with Ray and Elna—my new mom and dad—in an eighteen-foot camping trailer, but they soon constructed an eight-by thirty-two-foot shack for us to live in and hauled it in on a log truck. The infamous Rant Mullins and his brother Joe built a cookhouse and bunkhouse for the single guys. Rant also has a talent for carving wooden feet. Some of the rest of the crew, especially the truckers, drive in each day from places around Sutherlin. Each building has an outhouse near it.

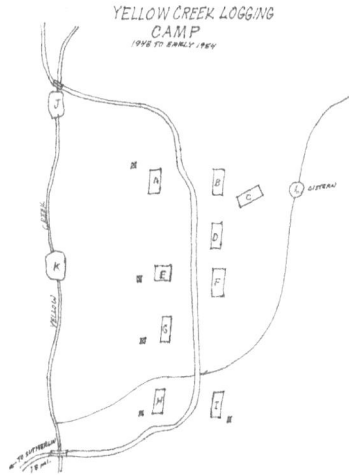

Yellow Creek Camp

Mom, the camp cook, feeds an average of ten men, mostly the single ones. There were rattlesnakes and, worst of all, no running water. If anyone outside of camp asked the women, "Do you have running water?" they would tell them, "Yes, you run to the creek, get your water, and run back." My guess is the running had something to do with rattlesnakes. At the beginning, with no electricity, the ladies used washboards for cleaning clothes.

Yellow Creek Camp

Billy near Cabin D, above, and the bachelor's bunkhouse

So here's the layout of the camp:

Cabin (A), the cookhouse, is equipped with a large wood cook stove, wall shelves for storage, and tables and chairs for eating and card games later in the evening. It has benches along the walls also.

Cabin (B) is for Uncle Les, Aunt Doris Wallace, and cousin Mick.

Cabin (C) is for Dick and Vey Brown with daughter Tere.

Cabin (D) is where the infamous Ray L. Wallace and crew live.

Cabin (E) is the bunkhouse (bachelors' pad) where fellows like Toad Washburn, Snoose Summers, Cayo Omeg, and Bud Snowsteen live. These guys, especially old Snoose, spit chewing tobacco farther than anyone I've ever seen.

Cabin (F) is the home of "Big" Rube and Rosy Turner and their sons, Dick and Bob. Rube, a timber faller, is way over six feet tall and all muscle. Rosy, a tough Swiss miss, can make man or child toe the line. Their son Bob was about five years old at the time. He told me later that Elna would make dresses

for the young girls in camp, plus some for cousins back in Washington. She uses young Bob for fitting the dresses. George Wilson, one of crew, started calling Bob "Susie." This gets around camp and irritates Bob. One day, my Uncle Wilbur, who was pure gold to me, tells

The Turner brothers, Dick and Bob

Bob, the camp model

Bob to call George "a lop-eared lard butt." That puts an end to that problem!

Cabin (G) is home for Lyle "Sam" Dew and his family. Lyle's also a timber faller and a good one. Later, Cabin (G) houses a trucker, Cy Awmiller, and his family.

Cabin (H) houses Big—and I mean "Big"—Jim Brockner and his wife, Lucille. Big Jim, a French-Canadian Indian, often speaks to Lucille in a very calm, low, and slow fashion, one word at a time, saying, "Oh, shut up, Lucille." This usually happens during the evening gathering at the cookhouse. Lucille is noted for speaking out of turn. But Big Jim's careful reproof seems to slow her down.

Cabin (I) is home for Jim Smith, an operator and hunter, and his family. The Upper Swim Hole (J), is where Dad and the guys dug out a hole in the creek with a bulldozer, surrounded it with logs, and backfilled the logs creating Bingo, a great swimming hole, although not particularly according to Fish and Game specifications.

The Lower Swim Hole (K) has the same design, but it's a little bigger and closer to camp.

Cistern (L) came a little later. Dick Brown, one of the truckers, fabricated a cement holding tank on the little stream east of camp close to his cabin (C), ran pipe to a bunch of the cabins and, bingo, we had running water. We didn't have to run for it anymore.

Each building has, of course, an outhouse nearby, but not too near. They weren't complete without the latest edition of the Sears catalog.

Our playground amounts to just about anything we can climb on.

Camp playground

15

THE TAKEOVER

So here I am, a little tyke standing in my office with a furrowed brow, deep in thought. Eureka! It comes to me. If Ray L. Wallace can make the big bucks, so can I. So, I get busy working up a business plan. It's going to be a semi-hostile takeover. I'm eyeing Yellow Creek Logging Corporation. This will be the mother of all takeovers, making those guys on Wall Street look like a bunch of two-year-olds. So, with plan in hand, I'm off to see my close friend. We've known each other all our lives (both years).

The office, above and venture capitalists

This buddy has hit it big with a thriving business that he named after himself. He's made a ton of money and lends out venture capital. I arrive at his mansion, the first double-wide trailer I've ever seen. I knock on the door and, lo and behold, there's Lionel. He says, "Long time no see, Butch. Come on in. Let me grab a couple of cold ones from the fridge." So we sit down and proceed to chew on a couple of cold ones. It takes us a couple of hours to catch up on things. After all, it's been two whole days.

Inspecting equipment TD-18

I present my business plan. It describes timber eight feet in diameter at the stump and plenty of it, only twenty miles away, which keeps transportation expenses down and profits up. We also have a crew of men, honest, hardworking, and tough as nails.

I tell him I can give him a 20 percent return on his money. After a full examination of my plan, with apple cores in hand, we shake on it. No paperwork to sign. A man's word is sufficient in those days.

With money in hand and an offer they couldn't refuse, we make the deal. The first thing I do is check out the equipment. I need to know it's all in top condition. The equipment needs to be suited for the high-production process I'm about to implement. This International Harvester TD-18 looks like it can do the job.

Second acquisition

Purchasing a loader

Although Dad's TD-18 works fairly well, I decide to upgrade and expand. So off to Portland I go. Dad has been getting pretty swell equipment there from Howard Cooper. I buy this new model from him. Unfortunately, I only have it for a year. They use it in one of Sutherlin's 4th of July parades on a low-bed to duplicate what a logging site looks like. They set everything up on Dick Moon's low-bed. Well, after the parade, everything is offloaded. My new dozer is behind the low-bed when Dick proceeds to back over it and flatten my dozer.

With the insurance money, I purchase a better log loader and, with ongoing profits, buy another dozer.

With my first load of logs, I didn't need to invest in trucks. Plenty of guys would haul for so much a load. It's a short haul to the mill with big timber,

A better log loader

Atop the supply truck, left, and consulting with my secretary, above, while my log scaler is below

which produces big bucks.

I buy a badly needed supply truck. We're expanding rapidly. Our need for supplies must be met.

While doing fuel inventory with one of my secretaries, I realize Oops! Somebody forgot to pick up the empty bottles after last night's celebration.

The logs fly out of camp. I'm rollin' in deep clover. I have Dad scaling logs for me, so we won't get taken to the cleaners by scalers at the mill. It's been known to happen. Also, besides running equipment for me, he's a top-notch timber cruiser. A good cruiser can walk a patch of timber and tell you how many board feet are in that stand with great accuracy. It's critical to know before purchasing someone's stand of timber. That's where the profit is made or lost.

I'm doing so well logging that I figure I can splurge and buy myself some wheels. I purchase a brand-new two-cylinder with white sidewall tires. One

The Lemon

cylinder for my left foot, the other for my right. I can actually write it off as a business expense, for the simple fact, I can take it up through camp to the logging sites. Anyhow, I climb in the sucker but can't get the lousy speedometer to do more than two miles per hour. I'm taking this thing back to Roseburg. The dealer there sold me a lemon. Forget this. I'm headin' to the cookshack for lemonade.

Just before quitting time, I ask my other secretary to check the cooler to make sure it's full, so we can have a cold one together. She wasn't seeing anyone else at the time. Lucky me!

I buy the guys a few rounds also. After all, it's Friday. Everyone had worked their fingers to the bone. We all need to unwind.

Here I'm advising Uncle Wilbur not to stop netting salmon. I tell him I'll fix it with state Fish and Game. In fact, I advise them to leave all my relatives alone. We're all doing it, especially the ones up in Washington State.

I have a great deal of experience with wildlife. In my spare time, I hire out as an

Kickin' back with the secretary, above, and having one with the men

Fish and Game Department with Wilbur

advisor to the state Fish and Game Department. Pictured on the next page is "Billy," a forked horn friend of mine who was abandoned as a fawn. Dad rescues Billy, goes to a local farmer, and buys a nanny goat to provide milk for the fawn.

BRIEF INTERLUDE

Unfortunately, a trucker by the name of George McGill tells us he "accidently shot Billy," my deer friend. I'm so bummed. He was one of my closest buddies for most of my life (two years and counting). This kinda thing can put you in a dark hole. I need something or someone other than the logging business to pull me out of this funk. Lo and behold, it comes in the shape of a cute little curly-headed blonde.

Feeding Billy

When I spot her in camp, it's like, "Wow, I've only heard about angels before." I scramble as quickly as I can to find my cute little kitty and head for that gorgeous little thing sitting in the grass. So I sit down beside her with Kitty. She says, "That's the coolest kitty I've ever seen. I've always wanted one like her."

She says, "Can I touch her?"

Me with the cute little blonde and a kitten

"Sure, but please be gentle with her," I say. "She cost me a small fortune. I had to trade a piece of logging equipment for her."

She says, "You know, Butch, if we were engaged, I could help you raise her. What do you think?"

She didn't waste a second. She kisses me.

I tell her, "Please be gentle; I've never been kissed by a young woman before."

I can't take the pressure. I cave, right then and there. With Kitty in hand, I'm up and out of there. I can't get into Sutherlin's only jeweler quick enough.

The next day, I say to her, "Here, take this ring. We're now engaged."

She says, "Oh, it's so beautiful."

There went another piece of logging equipment sold to buy that ring. She says, "Meet me here tomorrow with Kitty."

I'm pretty juiced at this point.

The following day, over by our favorite grassy spot, I experience a very memorable moment that turns out to be a "love 'em and leave 'em" situation. My kitty and the ring just walk away, never to be seen again.

NAVY HITCH

If losing Billy the deer wasn't bad enough, I also lose the cute little curly-headed blonde. She flies the coop with my awesome little kitty and my big diamond ring. This hits the heart and the pocketbook big-time. Being a tough logger, I don't share my feelings with the camp. I just tell Dad to take over for a while. I must clear my head. So, with a burlap bag full of diapers and my thumb sticking out, I catch the first truck coming through camp for the mill. I end up in Roseburg, the nearest place to a Navy recruiter. After spilling my guts

21

to the poor guy, he says, "Butch, you'll fit right in nicely." I sign on the dotted line for the longest hitch they could give me, four weeks. I'm off to San Diego for training.

First year to Canada

BACK IN THE SADDLE

Dad, my foreman, and I decide that all work and no play isn't a good example to set for a bunch of hardworking loggers. I call him into my office, knowing he's up to his eyeballs with creative things to do.

"We need to put out the money," he says. "We've had a good year, so we can take the crew on an all-expenses-paid moose-hunting trip to Canada. I know of a top-notch guide in Prince George, B.C., Canada. He has this awesome cabin on the McGregor River."

I say, "Let's do it."

It's time to go hunting. I'm still kinda struggling over the loss of my first love and exhausted from a tough year of logging. I'm just going to hunt around here.

So they're in Canada, having great success. Knowing they'll be heading back soon, I think I'd better get out and see if I can bag a big buck. When he sees it, Dad's jaw drops. I've done quite well. All the men gather around and take a photo.

Me and the buck

22

Second year to Canada: Dad, me, and five others

A NEW ADVENTURE

So, after another successful year of pumping out the timber, it's time for a different kind of adventure. We're off to see Herb Simmons in Prince George again. After a day's hunt, we sit outside the cabin at night. Some nights we hear five different packs of timber wolves in different directions. Herb always says that when a pack makes a kill, one wolf at a time quits howling and starts eating the prey until the whole pack goes quiet.

With an amazing event behind us, we head for home. One of our stops along the way is south of Toledo to drop off Uncle Forest. He owns a large ranch that begins just under what's now the I-5 bridge. The ranch, on the east side of the Cowlitz River, runs south for about a mile.

Behind me in a photo insert with my prey is a large barn that still stands to this day. We take the large photo after we're done hunting in Prince George.

Returning from Canada

CHAPTER 2
THE SORENSENS

L IFE IS A COMPILATION of people, places, and things that touch our lives and make us who we are. As an adult looking back, I realize how fortunate I am to have three special families involved in shaping who I am: the Sorensens, the Wallaces, and the Fluckingers. As this story evolves, you'll see how many of these family members play a special part in my life. But we need to dip into the past (and past tense) for a little background first.

THE SORENSENS

Ray Wallace and Elna Sorensen met in Toledo, Washington, where both their families owned farms. Grandpa Nels Sorensen was born on March 7, 1887, in Nore, Denmark, and came to the United States in 1906 aboard the *Lusitania* (nine years before it was sunk). He worked on a farm in a Danish community in South Dakota for two years before returning to Denmark in 1908, where he was employed as a bricklayer.

In 1911, he married Anna Marie Christiansen, who was born on February 12, 1892, in Denmark. In 1912, they came to the United States. After waiting in line to board the *Titanic*, they and others were turned away because the ship had become full. As most of you know, that was the *Titanic's* maiden voyage, heading from England to New York City, but it struck an iceberg and sank. With a great shortage of lifeboats for the 2,200 people aboard, only 705 survived, mostly women and children. Most of the others died of hypothermia or drowning.

Elna and her Sorensen brothers. Pictured from left are Ernie, Richard, Harold, Elna, Cliff, Arling, Aage, and Bill.

By the way, the *Lusitania*, which Nels sailed aboard earlier, was torpedoed and sunk by a German submarine on May 7, 1915, killing 1,195 people. Only 764 survived. Nels liked to move around. In 1919, he and Anna moved to Denmark, where they stayed for three years, during which time Elna was born. Then, in 1922, they returned to the United States. On the way over, an explosion in the ship's boiler room killed two sailors. The rest made it safely to Ellis Island. They returned to South Dakota, farmed, then went to Minnesota to farm in 1932. In 1939, they finally settled on a farm in Toledo, Washington, never to move again. Nels and Anna raised eight children.

AAGE

Aage, being the oldest, was gentle and kind. He was born on January 11, 1913, in South Dakota, and worked as a farmer and school bus driver. He married Anne Brekhus in 1935. They lost their one and only child during the first year of marriage, which was a real heartbreaker for them. They were two wonderful people.

WILLIAM (BILL)

Born on March 26, 1915, also in South Dakota, Bill always seemed like the serious type. He married Aunt Gertrude "Gerti" from Holstein, Iowa, in 1936. They moved to Ephrata, Washington, and later to the Toledo area. My clearest

Elna with Gerti, Bill's wife

memory of Bill was being hired by him to ride behind his hay baler. Bill was all about efficiency. So instead of having hay bales scattered all over the field when the baler was finished, he made a sled using three very large planks about ten feet long, spaced six feet apart. The sled was attached to the baler by a chain. I was given a six-foot iron bar. The idea was that as the baler spit bales of hay out at a breakneck speed, I had to arrange the bales in an interlocking manner, producing one large rectangular stack on the sled. The trick was, after arranging the last bale on the stack of hay, I had to very quickly grab the iron bar and stick it into the ground between the planks at the front of the sled. This would cause the rectangular stack to slide off the sled before the baler spit out the next bale. It was a challenge to pull off and somewhat satisfying to know I could. The pay was decent too.

CLIFFORD

Born on March 20, 1918, in South Dakota, Clifford married Blanche Rindahl from Rindahl, Minnesota. Cliff was involved in logging and road construction, while at the same time running a chicken ranch, which will come back into my story later. Cliff was a very kind and thoughtful man with a good soul.

ELNA LILLIAN SORENSEN

My mother, Elna, was born on September 21, 1920, in Blenstrup, Denmark, when Nels and Anna returned to their native homeland for three years. Being raised on a farm, just over the bridge east of Toledo, she was no stranger to hard work. Up at daylight, Nels would send her and a couple of the oldest boys to milk the cows. Nels said, "After you're

Elna farming

finished with that, get back in here and help your Mom with her housework." Little did Mom know at the time, all of this was boot camp for what would come down the road for her later. It prepared her for a life with Ray L. Wallace. She needed to be strong and able to hold her ground. With a good dose of Danish DNA, she was well prepared.

HAROLD

Harold was born on December 5, 1922, in Wagner, South Dakota. Soon after his family moved to Toledo, he married Edith Lampitt. Harold worked mainly on road construction, eventually owning many gravel trucks and several very productive rock pits. When we lived in Oregon and California, we stayed with them a lot while visiting relatives in Toledo. Edith and Harold were wonderful to be around. This was definitely a strong family trait that ran through all of Mom's siblings.

RICHARD

Richard was born on July 15, 1925, in Wagner, South Dakota. He married Verna Holland in 1944 in Woodland, Washington, where they lived out their lives. Richard worked as a shop foreman. He was excellent to work for. It was always wonderful spending time with their family in Woodland. Pictured here with Richard is brother Larry and myself.

Richard

ARLING

Arling was born on April 25, 1928, in Wagner, South Dakota. He moved to Woodland and drove log trucks.

Now here the plot thickens. Sometime between 1946 and 1947, Arling dated a pretty young lady by the name of Ruby Fluckinger in the Toledo area. For reasons unknown to me, they broke up sometime between Thanksgiving and Christmas of 1947. Arling later met and married a wonderful lady by the name of Harriet Apling on June 17, 1949.

After her breakup with Arling, Ruby, being an attractive young lady, was quickly pursued by another man. I have zero information on him, but this relationship lasted for only a short time. Ruby quickly realized she was pregnant with me and left Toledo to live with her sister, Rosie Turner, who was with her husband, Rube, at the Yellow Creek logging camp near Sutherlin, Oregon. Rube felled timber for a guy named Ray Wallace, who later became my dad.

Unfortunately, Arling was killed in a logging accident on March 22, 1961, just outside of Toledo. He was checking a load of logs to see if any of the binders that held them tight had loosened, but the load broke loose and rolled down on him. To understand how this happened, especially if you haven't been around logging, after a load of logs is piled onto a truck, the driver wraps cables around the logs with and tightens them with binder chains. He then proceeds down an often rough logging road, which can cause the load to shift and move. With too much movement, the binders can come loose and topple the load. When Arling stopped to check the binders, the load rolled off the trailer and crushed him. He died instantly.

Arling left behind Harriet and seven absolutely wonderful children. The kids were blessed to have a mom like Harriet. No one could have done a better job raising those kids, considering the loss she suffered.

ERNIE

I slipped in a photo of Ernie for a good reason, because it's one of those pictures worth a thousand words. He was always a character.

Ernest Anton Sorensen, who was born on May 24, 1929, in Wagner, South

Ernie, back row, second from left

Dakota, was a lighthearted log truck driver, not the serious type, the kind of guy who made you thankful we're not all born alike. He enjoyed goofing around and being silly, maybe a little mischievous. I loved being around Ernie. He married a girl by the name of Freda Mae Stanfield, originally from

Oklahoma. She was a no-nonsense kinda gal who worked in the county superior court as chief deputy clerk.

Thanks to Kathy, their daughter, the Sorensens to this day have a yearly family reunion at the Toledo park, normally late summer. It always started off with a prayer from Uncle Harold who lived to be just over a hundred.

Most of the Sorensens played a much larger role in my life once our family moved back from Oregon to Toledo in 1961, although we had visited during holidays. In the last photo, I'm bottom left with the crooked hat, my two bare-chested twin brothers, Larry and Gary, are bottom right of center, with little brother Ricky behind Larry. All of us were adopted.

One thing in those days that wasn't always so cool, depending on who you were around, was being adopted. Sometimes we were teased and made to feel like second-class citizens. Other times we were just the brunt of busybodies' tales. But not in the Sorensen family. We were always treated as one of the family.

The Sorensen clan

CHAPTER 3
THE WALLACES

JAMES HICKLIN WALLACE WAS BORN in a small unincorporated town called Wallace, Missouri, in 1867. He married Emma Huber, who was born on April 10, 1876, in Minnesota to parents originally from Germany. I'm not sure where they met, but at some point, they moved to Montana before returning to Boliver, Missouri. They lived on a farm in Clarksdale, Missouri, just east of St. Joseph, Missouri. The family raised many kinds of vegetables and grains and hauled them to the farmers market with a team of horses six days a week. All of their children except the youngest were born in Missouri: James Forrest in about 1903; William Lester about 1905; Cora about 1907; Mary about 1908; Carl about 1911; and Ray (my dad), on April 21, 1918. Their youngest, Wilbur, was born in about 1922 in Washington.

Being an avid hunter, James would track different kinds of game. On one trip, looking for squirrel with a friend, he was accidentally shot in the leg and ended up losing it. This event, down the road, had a negative effect on his disposition.

His brother Will wrote James a letter from Washington state, telling him it was a better place to raise vegetables and grains. Will described the riverbottom soil as rich and said the rain aided in producing abundant crops.

Taking Will's advice, James and Emma sold their farm, its machinery, and all of their livestock. With their furniture loaded on a westbound train, they landed in Vader, Washington, on October 20, 1919. Uncle Will met them with his team of horses and a wagon to ferry them across the Cowlitz

River to a forty-acre piece of property he then rented to James for four years. During this time, Uncle Wilbur was born in 1922, the last of their seven children. The family, after several moves, ended up with a large farm that ran from what is now the I-5 bridge over the Cowlitz south for some distance. It is still owned by family cousins.

When Dad was twelve and Wilbur eight, he remembered the two of them plowing a large cornfield. At the end of the field stood a pear tree where they would stop and rest the horse. They could hear whistles from a distance from a logging operation where a steam engine pulled logs out of the woods. One of Dad's older brothers explained later to Ray that those whistles signaled the steam donkey to stop and go.

This was when Ray told Wilbur, "When I grow up, I'm going to work for someone and learn how to log timber and save money and own a logging company." That was exactly what they ended up doing together.

FORREST

The most memorable thing about Forrest was his love life. He dated Lou Calvin, but her father, Lacy, didn't take a liking to him. One day after hunting, Forrest stopped to see Lou. He got into it with her father and ended up shooting him in the leg. Forrest disappeared for quite some time, but later returned and married Lou.

Being the oldest, Forrest took over most of the ranch after James passed and continued to expand his holdings His expansion methods included netting salmon on the Cowlitz River, right outside his front door, and making moonshine. Uncle Forrest built a smokehouse, which I remember always being full of salmon. I spent a lot of time there whenever we visited. I always thought it was so cool, those huge cornfields with silage to feed cattle and crops of potatoes to sell.

Later, I found out the corn wasn't just to feed the cattle, and the potatoes were definitely for more than human consumption. Consuming much of that produce was something called a "still," tucked away in the woods behind the farm, one of the largest producers of moonshine in Southwest Washington.

I remember coming up to visit Forrest from California one time. Mom, Dad, and I were at his place, just the three of us, waiting for him to return home. I saw at least several dozen quart jars on the counter filled with water. All of a sudden, I hear Dad tell Mom, "the sheriff is here." The lower cabinets in the kitchen had curtains for doors. The back door, which everyone used, was right next to the kitchen counters with all the quart jars of water. I watched Mom and Dad scramble to hide all the jars behind the curtains. The back door had a half-light window with no curtain. I kid you not, the last jar went behind the cabinet curtains just as the sheriff knocked. Dad opened the door, and the sheriff said he was looking for Forrest and wanted to know who we were. Dad told him Forrest was his brother, and we had just come from California. Dad let the sheriff know Forrest would be back soon, if he wanted to wait. The sheriff said he would check back later and left.

Years later, I was informed that the quart jars contained not water but a part of Forrest's latest batch of moonshine. And, while researching this book, I discovered Forrest had an arrangement with the sheriff, one of his good customers.

He liked salmon to go with his liquor, so under arrangement number two, he warned Forrest whenever Fish and Game wardens were coming. See, Forrest regularly strung salmon nets across the Cowlitz from his place on the east side of the river to Uncle Carl's ranch on the west side. When Forrest heard from the sheriff about Fish and Game wardens coming, he passed that information along to Carl so he could pull the nets before they showed up. This worked pretty smooth for a long time.

Back to the moonshine; eventually, the wrong person got wind of the still's location. But Forrest sent someone up there to hide the barrel of moonshine sitting by the still. He rolled it down the hill to a safe place before the authorities showed up. Our theory is the sheriff was forced to act but tipped off Forrest. The authorities found the still and demolished it but found no liquor as evidence. But that wasn't the end of the moonshining.

Forrest's brother Ray, my dad, had done well logging in Oregon. With his profits, he bought ranches farther down the river from Forrest. One was the ninety-acre Cruser ranch, which had a two-story stucco home with a basement containing one of those old octopus-type furnaces. Forrest talked Ray into letting him set up a new still in the basement. This way, any smoke or smell would float up and out through the chimney. The smoke looked normal, and nobody could smell anything suspicious. Bingo! Forrest was back in business. He remained successful for many years. They were never caught.

RAY

Ray, my dad, didn't fare as well as Forrest did with James, their father. Ray had no problem working long hard hours around the place. What he did have a problem with, however, was the lack of fun mixed in with the work. Ray couldn't go long without pulling a prank or concocting a story to amuse whoever would listen. At fourteen years of age, Ray spent as much time away from home as he could. His dad did not appreciate his humor at all. It was

Ray on a cougar hunt and with his '41 Chevy below

so bad at one point that James chased Ray into a large cherry tree with an axe, threatening to kill him. From that day on, Dad kept his distance from his father, spending most of his time trapping. He always had other kids with him. He'd tell them stories or say the game warden was after them, so they needed to keep quiet. It was a more effective way to capture and keep their attention. Often he left early in the morning before school to check his traps.

One morning, he had an altercation with a skunk. Needless to say, Ray spent the entire rest of the day in the hall at school by himself. Ray, at an early age, was good at finding ways to make and save money. He started out trapping, hunting, and fishing. At eighteen, Ray started his lifelong career in logging, working as a "whistle punk." This person signaled direction to the steam donkey, otherwise known as a yarder, that pulled logs out of the woods. At twenty-three, Ray bought a new 1941 Chevy coupe. Then in 1945, at twenty-eight, he sold his Chevrolet and used everything he had to buy a TD-18 bulldozer and arch to start his logging company and keep his promise to his brother Wilbur.

LES

Les, another hard worker and gentle soul, was a couple of years older than Dad. You couldn't find a better brother. He knew right from wrong and always leaned heavily into doing the right thing. I always had a great deal of respect for him. Les married Doris Turner,

Uncle Les and Ray

Rube Turner's sister, an important connection I'll make later. Doris was a tough no-nonsense kinda gal but very easy to love, and not just because she always had a small dish of the most awesome pieces of candy available.

Uncle Les and Dad always had something going together. For a while, Dad helped Les raise an excellent line of bloodhounds used for all kinds of tracking. They later became partners in a logging business in Oregon with Uncle Wilbur.

WILBUR

"Shorty" was Wilbur's nickname, which was interesting, considering how tall he was. Wilbur was born December 10, 1922, in Castle Rock and raised on the Wallace ranch by the Cowlitz River. A good athlete in high school, he was offered a four-year scholarship to college. Instead,

Uncle Wilbur and Ray

he chose to stay on the farm and care for his mom. In 1947 he came down to Yellow Creek to partner with Dad and Uncle Les, logging. This is where Wilbur met Bessie. After they were married in Vancouver, Washington, in 1950, he continued working with his brothers.

I always loved being around Uncle Wilbur, a kind and gentle soul unafraid of hard work.

CARL

Born on August 31, 1911, in Boliver, Missouri, Uncle Carl was another good man. He married Lillian "Toots" Calvin from Toledo. They had a sizable farm on the west side of the Cowlitz River, opposite his father's farm. Along with raising four wonderful daughters, they tended to cattle and crops. Carl also loved raising his hounds; they were excellent trackers. I remember going over there and playing board games upstairs with the two youngest cousins. Carl lived a good life on his ranch and passed October 20, 1998.

CORA AND MARY

I'm sad to say that I never spent much time with either Cora or Mary. I do know Mom and Dad thought highly of both.

I truly wish that I had more time and resources to dig deeper into the Wallace history. I'm pretty sure I'm not connected to Mel Gibson, but maybe the Toledo Wallaces are descendants of Sir William "Braveheart" Wallace. However, the one who most caught my attention was William Alexander Anderson "Bigfoot" Wallace, who was born in 1817 and died in 1899. He was a big man, six-foot-five, and weighed 240 pounds. He worked as a Texas Ranger and fought in five different Mexican wars as well as a Comanche war and the U.S. Civil War. Needless to say, he had large feet, hence the nickname "Bigfoot." It would be quite ironic to connect him with my father, Bigfoot himself.

CHAPTER 4
THE FLUCKINGERS (FLUCKIGERS)

THIS FAMILY WAS FASCINATING TO RESEARCH. In most cases, the Swiss/Germans kept excellent records. Churches or parishes were responsible for births, baptismal, and death records. The Fluckinger clan is easily traced back to 1348. One man I found most fascinating was Ulli Fluckinger (1600–1653). Ulli's father Caspar Fluckinger died when he was 16. He and his brother Kaspar inherited the family farm, which was fairly large. They turned it into a huge estate. They divided their now vast holdings around the time Ulli married Barbara Wynistorffen (1621). Barbara's parents passed away just a few years later, and she inherited her parents' estate, which was the size of Ulli's.

What had been happening in Switzerland from the time they were married to 1653 was similar to what happened in the United States before the Revolutionary War. Also the same thing in France before their Revolution. There was very little middle class at all. Ulli and a handful of powerful men were not

The Fluckinger estate in Switzerland

supporting the government's abuse of the poor, that is to say peasants and serfs, as they were referred to. This didn't sit well with most government officials. All of a sudden, this whore, as the court records have it, accuses Ulli of adultery—no proof was brought to light. But the only problem in those days was that extortion was rampant with the judges. It was a lucrative business. In Ulli's case the judges could impose fines simply for taking up the court time. The fine was very large for Ulli.

This happened several times with different accusers. In 1646 Ulli commissioned Ulrich Fisch II, a well-known glass painter, to create a leaded panel, 23.1cm by 39.5 cm, divided into two themes. The upper central theme is a story out of the book of Daniel in the Apocrypha. These are books that did not make it into the Bible. It's a great story about the chaste and beautiful Susanna being falsely accused by two judges. Above her depiction reads: Spread both your wings, O Jesus my joy, and accept your little chick. If the enemy wants to devour me, let the angels sing: This child shall be unharmed. At the bottom third of the panel is depicted, both Ulli and Barbara's coats of arms. Ulli's commissioned art undoubtedly expressed trust in Heavenly protection against false accusations and corrupt judges. Ulli's wife Barbara testified to the bitter end of Ulli's innocence

Susanna and the Elders

pertaining to all the false charges brought against him. The injustices were continuing to mount for the poor in Switzerland, each year growing worse.

THE PEASANT WAR OF 1653

Things came to a head. Ulli and two other influential allies stand with federal chairman Niklaus Leuenberger who becomes the leader of a revolt against the government. Ulli, Emmanuel Segisser, and Bernhart, Duke of Langenthal, each lead an army. To keep this short, they were defeated. What happened next was brutal. Ulli and the other leaders were tortured. They were pulled up by ropes and their legs were loaded with weights. First twenty-pound weights, then fifty, then a hundred, until a satisfactory confession was made. As they confessed, one by one they were brought before the high court, consisting of three judges.

Ulrich Fluckinger, one of Ulli's relatives, should have been one of the judges, but the government rulers were not about to risk a ruling of not guilty. The way the law worked was that the property of every criminal and every executed person went to the state. This had absolutely nothing to do with justice. It did have much to do with the rich gaining more wealth and giving them more power. But they had their debts too. The government had hired mercenaries and foreign troops to defeat Ulli and the rebels.

Ulli and the other three leaders were quickly decapitated by the sword, not hung like many others. Supposedly, out of respect for their position. Their property, which is what the leaders were after—not justice—was quickly seized. Ulli had fought and died for what he thought was right. Ulli's wife Barbara was able to hold on to much of what was given to her by her parents, only because of the way the law was written. Some of the Fluckinger family moved outside the borders of Bern. Barbara and others stayed. I'll describe later visiting the Fluckingers in the same area still held by the family. This visit occurred in 1994.

Fluckinger (USA)

Adolph Friedrich Fluckinger, who was born in Switzerland on November 15, 1852, trained as a locksmith. In 1886, he brought his family from Switzerland to the United States. He chose to settle in Woodburn County, Nebraska, where he farmed. The family, which included seven children, later moved to Grants Pass, Oregon, and then to Winlock, Washington. In 1908, Adolph moved to Seattle and settled on Beacon Hill. He died in 1926.

Adolph had five brothers and one sister who followed after him to America, most settling in different areas. Those related directly to me moved to Seattle. Rudy, my

Bertha Fluckinger

biological grandfather, moved to the Toledo area. He was a farmer and meat cutter. He married Bertha from Winlock, just west of Toledo. They had three daughters: Mary, the oldest, then Rose, and last Ruby, my biological mom.

Mary met and married Merle Rogers in Toledo and had a son, Jerry.

Rosie met a bigger-than-life man named Rube Turner in the Toledo area. They married and had two sons, Dick and Bob.

Ruby Jane later married a man named Gerland "Jerry" Norman Mathias, and they had three daughters—Kathy, Mary Ann,

Ruby Fluckinger

Lorrie—and a son, Jerry. They are my half-sisters and half-brother.

Most of these characters end up converging at a place called Yellow Creek, which is west of Sutherlin, Oregon. This, in turn, produced what I call the Yellow Creek Gang. Now you know their background, I can go back to my story.

Lil Butch with cousins

CHAPTER 5
MERGING OF THE CLANS

LATE IN 1941, while Ray is driving his new 1941 Chevy coupe from who knows where to Toledo, he spots a cute blonde, Elna, walking down the street. The first thought that comes to him is, "I'm going to marry that woman" (his words, not mine). Ray asks around Toledo, which didn't take long, knowing the size of Toledo.

He finds out she belongs to the Sorensen family. They have a farm on the east end of the bridge leaving town. Ray learns Elna has been married for a year and a half, but her husband, Art Rindahl, died of tuberculosis on June 3, 1941. It had only been months since she lost her husband, and she later told us how difficult it was when her mellow and loving husband passed away. At twenty-one, Elna returns to the farm, unable to stand being alone. Even harder, though, was her mom's absence; she was in a sanatorium with tuberculosis and died two years later.

After getting the scoop on Elna, Ray spots her in town again. Without a shy bone in this guy's body or brain, he is this polar opposite of the reserved Art Rindahl. Ray doesn't know what reserved means. In a nutshell, Ray saw life as one opportunity after another for humor, spinning yarns, telling tales, entertaining, or promoting whatever he was presently focused on, and—oh, I almost forgot the best part—a puller of pranks.

So, he catches her alone and introduces himself. To make a long conversation short, let me interrupt myself here: Ray seldom engaged in short conversations with anyone. Ray finally asks her out, and she accepts the offer.

On their first date, Ray doesn't waste time. He asks her to marry him. A little taken back, she says, "But Ray, I don't know anything about you." His response was, "What better way to get to know someone than to marry him."

World War II is raging after the Japanese bombing of Pearl Harbor on December 7, 1941, just months earlier. Ray enlists in the Army and is immediately sent to Camp Haan in Riverside, California, a training camp for Coast artillery antiaircraft where prisoners of war were housed. The camp was four miles by three miles, 8,000 acres with mostly tents. After training, he's sent to guard the Douglas Aircraft facility on the coast at Long Beach, California. There he manned a

Top left photo shows Ray at his post and right at ease with a buddy. Center photo shows him in the middle while peeling potatoes, and the aerial photo at left shows Camp Haan during World War II.

fifty-caliber machine gun. During the war, Douglas aircraft built C-47 transports, SBD Dauntless bombers, and the A-26 Invader. At one point, Douglas employed 160,000 people. The facility was one of the main targets on the West Coast for the Japanese. Ray doesn't see much action there, but occasionally a Japanese zero passed through, and they scrambled to do their best on their guns to deter any damage.

Earlier during his training at Camp Haan, things were a little slow for him. Knowing his personality, I doubt he liked peeling potatoes on KP duty as seen in many of the two dozen photos from that time. I have a feeling his sergeant didn't have any more of a sense of humor than his father had.

Elna's still living at the Sorensen ranch, surrounded by great siblings and a good father, but she struggled after the loss of her first husband and now with an absent boyfriend, Ray. So Ray, having been sent to Riverside, sends for Elna. She's all too happy to answer the call. They find a safe place for her away from Douglas aircraft in Santa Monica, about thirty miles away. She quickly makes friends with other ladies with boyfriends or husbands in the service. One owns a coupe they drive around, which works out great for them because they have the mobility to be with their guys when they are off-duty. They really enjoy dancing. Roy Rogers autographed a photo for Dad on the back: "I got this picture from Roy Rogers in person, at the Venice Pier Barn Dance, about two miles from Santa Monica, California." Roy Rogers was a class act. I grew up loving to watch his western movies. The

Elna at Santa Monica, Ray on the beach, and Elna's nice ride in a coupe

Ray and Elna dating, above, and an autographed photo of Roy Rogers at right

characters included Roy with his wife, Dale Evans, and sidekick Pat Brady, who was always kind of a "Yayhoo," adding plenty of humor to the show. I mention this only because I ran into Pat Brady about twenty years later, a story I'll share when the time comes.

I specifically remember Mom telling me, "Your dad was getting very upset with a lot of the servicemen flirting with me all the time." So, he tells her he thinks it's time to quit fooling around and get married. As the story goes, California had a waiting period for those who wanted to get hitched, probably for good reason. Ray finds out Arizona doesn't, so he and Elna hop a bus filled with other servicemen and their brides from Los Angeles to Yuma, Arizona. They could get a license there, get married, and be back on a bus headed for L.A. the same day. Matrimony set up factory-style. Not taking any chances at this point, Ray tells her she would be safer to wait out the war back home. I think he was more concerned over his comrades rather than what the Japanese would do. Ray spends all of his leave going back to Toledo until his discharge. He couldn't return to his bride back home fast enough.

For the next several years, Ray works and saves. I'll never know how he pulled it off, but he hatches a dream of starting a logging company. He comes up with enough equipment to start and somehow connected with some log buyer near Sutherlin, Oregon. After the war, the nation saw a huge demand for lumber and a shortage of men willing to do the dangerous part. Dad's timing was good; he could work as much as he could handle. So, with everything set, he's off to Oregon.

Hitched

CHAPTER 6
YELLOW CREEK LOGGING CORP

IT'S BEEN STATED MANY TIMES that it takes a village to raise a child. In my case, it took a logging camp, and a crazy cool one at that, filled with nothing but characters, yet people you felt safe with.

Here I am, in a logging camp, away from someone else's version of civilization. I'm part of a family tree rooted with righteous rebels. I'm referring to Ulli Fluckinger, going back seventeen generations in Switzerland, and Sir William Wallace of Scotland, twenty-eight generations ago. Both ancestors, rebels against injustice and tyranny, were beheaded for rebellion. Our camp consists of milder forms of rebellion. If they need fish or game, the men don't track down a game warden to ask if it's okay. They take what they need only when they need it.

The camp also rebels against boredom. Working long hard days in the woods isn't enough for these guys. With no televisions, radios, or video games, they don't have any problem amusing one another.

Ray Wallace (Dad), being a master prankster from an early age, leads the pack when it comes to amusement. One of my favorites happens one night after dinner in the cookhouse. Dad must have thought of this one all day. Probably giddy with anticipation, he waits until some of the men settle down at a table near the wood-burning cookstove to play cards.

Earlier, he had strategically placed a wooden ladder behind the cook shack to give him access to the roof. He had also purchased some M-80s on his last trip to town. An M-80, for those not familiar, is an overgrown firecracker. He

Cook shack, right, with ladder

wraps the M-80 in a large amount of wet toilet paper, then grabs the ladder stashed behind the cook shack, quietly leans it against the eaves, and slowly climbs to the chimney, then drops that baby. Knowing he has time, he descends the ladder, returns to the cook shack, and lies down on one of the benches along the wall away from the card table, mumbling something about being tired.

As soon as the last word leaves Dad's mouth, boom goes the M80! The lids fly off the cookstove followed by a great deal of soot and ash. The men are obviously surprised and wondering what happened. Dad, now off the bench, walks over to the men after the soot settles and says, "What the heck's going on over here? Are you guys using that wood with a lot of pitch in it?" Dad never pulls a prank without thinking it through to the finest detail. He's so good at his pranks that victims seldom figure out he's the culprit. Ray never seeks credit for his creative abilities; he just loves the moment. This is true for everything he did.

For another of his pranks, Dad uses brevibacterium (Limburger cheese). He finds out its unusual odor resembles smelly feet or sweaty gym socks, so he somehow procures a chunk. He decides to put this pungent cheese on some of the men's pickup truck engine manifolds. After driving a distance, the engine manifold grows hot and melts the cheese, causing the odor to fill the pickup's cab. It smells so rotten the drivers stop and try to pinpoint the smell. It doesn't take them long to figure out the source of the problem.

After they marry, Mom and Dad try to conceive a child but without any success. Mom mentions adoption from time to time, but Dad never receives it well. Finally, when it happens, the results are more than wonderful, especially for me. Forget the thousand words, this picture is worth a million with clear bonding going on. In researching this book, I interviewed 102-year-old Don Buswell who tells me, "You know, Butch, your dad took you everywhere he went, right from the start." After mentioning that to me, Don goes over to the stove, opens it up, and pulls out an apple pie. After I figured out what he was up to, I say, "Wow, Don, your granddaughter baked you a pie?" Don looks at me like he's saying, get a grip young fella, and tells me, "I baked this pie; you want a piece?" I kid you not, that was a great piece of apple pie; it didn't even need ice cream.

Pictures speak volumes

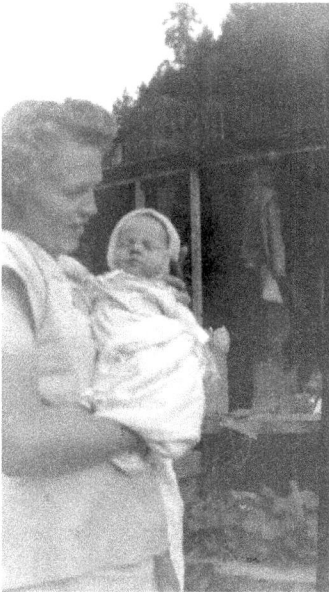

Homecoming in 1948,
Yellow Creek Logging

Don and his brother Anor, also from Toledo, owned Hardly Able Logging and logged near us. I love the name they chose for their company. Those two guys were more than capable in all they did. Hardly Able merged with Yellow Creek Logging after we finished in the Yellow Creek Camp.

Clearly, my adoption works well for Elna who's a keeper. Her heart draws a constant stream of friends and relatives to our home regardless of where we live. She has pretty cool sayings. A couple of my favorites are: "If you can't say anything good about someone, don't say anything at all" and "It takes the same amount of energy to be a jerk as it does to be nice to people." She prefers the latter, to be nice. I always remember at bedtime seeing her through the open door on the far side of the bed, down on her knees, praying silently for me and others brought into her life.

Her forte is baking. Every kind of pie and pastry you could think of, she could make it and do it well. Most mornings, someone visits at our kitchen table, sipping a cup of coffee and eating cookies or a slice of pie. The biggest draw is that she's an excellent listener. Everyone feels safe with her, and she always offers sound advice that trickles down from her faith.

One thing Ray and Elna are not is helicopter parents. Dad takes me on just about every piece of equipment he owns before I'm three years old, including his cars. This is so important in forming who I become and how I make decisions throughout my life. It gives me a calm and a focus even in crisis situations.

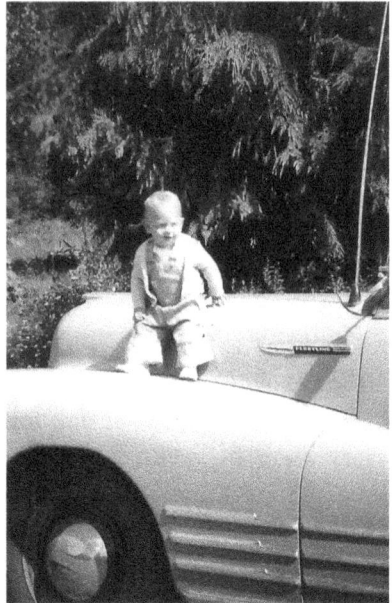

No helicopter parents, but an injured father

As many of you know, logging is not a sport for the weak-hearted. You must be heads-up at all times. Danger always lurks around the corner. As careful as you try to be, accidents still occur. Sometime around October 1948, when I was about three months old, a tree hit Dad and put him in a body cast for a short time. Less than a month later, he was back to work and hard at it.

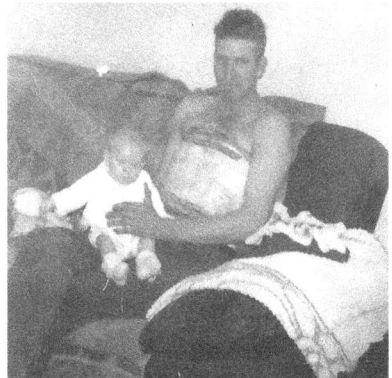

Baby on a bulldozer

A logging site in those days consists of many pieces of heavy equipment. First, bulldozers punch in roads to the timber where none exist. Second, a log truck hauls in a yarder mounted on two logs. A yarder is basically a motor that turns several large drums filled with heavy cable. It's

48

used in conjunction with a spar pole to pull logs to an area where they can be loaded on trucks for transport. The spar pole is a large well-rooted tree in a calculated spot. Once the tree is picked out, someone brave, strong, and fearless dresses the tree. He dons climbing gear and lugs tools to limb and top the tree. I've seen climbers, more than eighty feet above the ground, saw the top off a tree,

Top left, the yarder at work in the woods and at right hauled on the truck, while at lower left, two men work on a spar pole and at lower right is the log loader

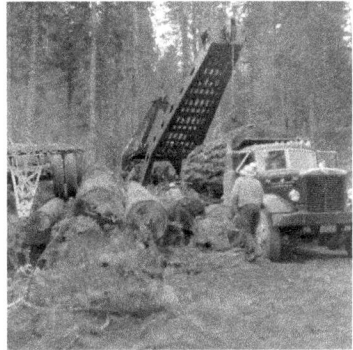

then stand on it. I witnessed world champion high-climber Danny Sailor do a jig on a spar pole in the mid-1950s at a Toledo Cheese Days celebration.

Once this is done, they attach guy wires to stabilize the tree, then affix a pulley to the top of the spar pole. Cables from the yarder run through the pulley in different directions to stumps with pulleys on them. To make a long story short, this enables the yarder to pull logs onto the landing from all different directions, mainly up steep hillsides inaccessible to bulldozers.

Once the logs are in a pile near the yarder, which is called a landing, a third piece of equipment is used, a log loader. Using a large set of tongs and cable, it loads the trucks with as many logs as it can haul—sometimes even only one huge log, something you'll never see again. Mills are not geared to take anything near that large anymore or even the second log with Uncle Wilbur on the left pushing it.

Uncle Wilbur's huge load at left, and a one-log loader below

From day one, through all my years in logging camps around rowdy loggers, I always felt safe. Their kind of rowdy never provoked fear in a young child, which speaks to their character. Even the Yellow Creek Gang, my four cousins, had my back from the beginning.

The Yellow Creek Gang in 1948, left; Ray holding Butch and feeding Billy, center; cousin Bob still camp model in the bottom photo

It was more common for us kids to keep a deer for a pet than a dog. For two years, I had Billy, my deer that Dad weaned from a nanny goat, for two years. He would eat right out of our hands, no matter your size.

Cousin Bob Turner, part of the Yellow Creek Gang, is probably one of the most useful in camp. Bob's a person who takes his work seriously. He always gets the job done right. Size-wise, he fits the bill of Elna's dressmaking skills, and he sees the job through to the end. Just a few short years later, Bob packs gas in the woods for his dad, Rube, to use in power saws. I can't begin to tell you how thankful Bob and I are for the experiences we had. Sorry, Labor and Industries, glad you weren't there. You'll never convince us our parents

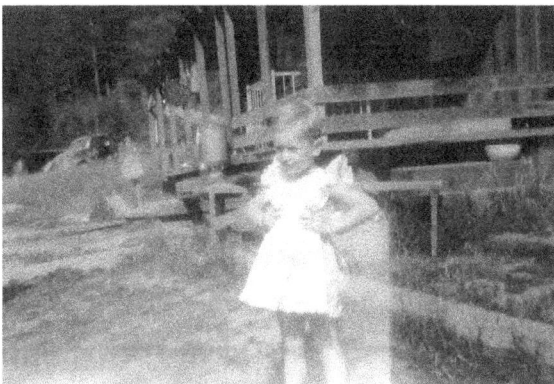

are negligent or uncaring. We see it as getting a big jump on life, building character while taking a little fear out of the dangerous side of life. I'm not sure what other young ones our age were doing, but we didn't miss much.

The men around us work hard and play hard. Uncle Ted Fluckinger plays a little too hard one evening. Being over the limit with hard beverages, he decides to swim in one of the camp's man-made pools. Clear thinking is not on the menu that night. Without hesitation, he dives in, but there's only two inches of water in the pond. If he asked, someone would have informed him the pond recently washed out downstream. So after he lands, he finds himself missing skin on his chest. A lesson to look before you leap. Ted, a good man, is younger brother to my biological mom, Ruby.

Uncle Les and Wilbur are partners with Dad in Yellow Creek Logging Corporation. Les and Aunt Doris buy a place in Sutherlin and commute, while Wilbur and Aunt Bessie live in camp. It's truly great how well everyone works together. I always appreciate having them in my life.

Mom, the camp cook now for four years, also raises me for two years and reaches a point of exhaustion. Not realizing the real problem at the time, Dad takes her to the doctor who tells Dad if he doesn't find a cook to take her place, she's in danger of having a nervous breakdown. So right away, they increase the size of the cook shack, making it easier to use, and add lodging for a hired cook.

On top of this, because a woman in camp makes things difficult for Mom, she and Dad agree to buy a small house in Sutherlin. Mom and I still go back and forth to camp when we want. At times I go to work with Dad at camp. The cook watches me when Dad can't. I love being at camp, closer to the action and to my cousins.

In December 1951, I'm about three-and-a-half years old when logging shuts down. It's time for a break. Each winter Dad takes those who want to go on a hunting trip. I believe this was his second or third trip moose and deer hunting in Canada, but it's my first trip. At the time, I have no idea how special and unique this was for someone my age to join in an adventure of this magnitude. Like I've mentioned earlier, Dad didn't go many places without me, just more crazy cool building blocks he brings into my life. Yes, it's cool, even with all the wolves around us at night.

Seven months later, on July 4th, Mom and Dad adopt twin boys, Gary and Larry. We drive all the way up to Centralia, Washington, to adopt them at birth. They are descendants of Chief Imboden, whose traditional homeland was an area between Toledo and Castle Rock, Washington, where I live today.

The twins, left and center

I'm not sure how the connection was made, although Dad had purchased property in the area adjoining Imboden Road.

It's unusual to have twins but at the same time pretty awesome. In a small logging camp, it's like living in a tribe, the more the merrier. So having twins is a bonus, even though it's a little tricky at times for moms of twins. Often the twins need certain things done simultaneously. So, Mom and I divide and conquer. I take one while she takes the other. I learn how to bathe, change, and feed those little guys. Mom and I work well together. I love and appreciate her. Gary and Larry are welcome gifts.

In 1952, toward the end of our stay at Yellow Creek, Dad drives into the big city of Roseburg to buy a movie camera to film the logging they were doing. Also, he wants home movies of our family. He finds a sixteen-millimeter Bell and Howell movie camera, but it doesn't have sound. Nobody sells those available for home use at the time. The salesman says a company in Hollywood can modify one with sound, but it'll take a few months and cost a lot. Dad says, "Have it done." We've formatted some of his movies to DVD. It's special to visually go back in time. Dad always does things outside of the box.

CHAPTER 7
PECWAN

WORK PRETTY MUCH WRAPS UP at Yellow Creek. Dad acquires a large patch of timber in a place called Pecwan in California, along the Klamath River eighty-five miles north of Eureka. This is our next stop.

Dad always juggles several things at once. Logging and road building aren't enough to hold his interest. He raises parakeets to sell and later chinchillas. Upon leaving camp, Dad decides to give his remaining parakeets to Rube and Rosie Turner. Cousin Dick found it funny. I don't think his parents did.

Because of the size of the new job, the Wallaces decide to merge with Hardly Able Logging Co. owned by the Buswells, Don and Anor, who are also from Toledo. They've been logging near us for several years. Both men trained as bomber pilots in WWII, although Don trained other pilots stateside. Anor, however, flew bombing missions and returned home a decorated lieutenant. They own a small single-engine Piper airplane, not just for fun but also for hauling in smaller equipment parts. The Buswells were a great fit with our crew, sense of humor and all. Hardly Able proved more than able.

Don and Anor Buswell, owners of Hardly Able Logging Co., joined the crew

THE ACCIDENT

On February 4, 1954, Anor drives Dad and two others in a crew bus along a nasty old narrow road to check out a potentially lucrative logging job near an old Indian site called Pecwan. The hard part of the drive began at Orick on the Northern California coast. From there it was a forty-mile treacherous drive, especially in bad weather, to Pecwan. If they had driven that road before, they probably would have waited for better weather. They left Orick, but the weather kept getting worse the farther they traveled. They knew along

The Army surplus bus that slipped off the road

the way that, if they took the job, they'd need to repair the road before hauling in their large equipment. Close to their destination, the yellow Army surplus bus slips off the road, then rolls over and down a steep bank. When the bus stops, Dad is the only one thrown out. He finds one of his shoes twenty feet up on a tree branch. The other three have bad cuts and bruises, but Dad's in bad shape with a broken pelvis, five broken ribs, a damaged spleen, and injuries to vertebrae.

Quite fortunately, at the time, a Native American comes along and quickly gathers blankets and water to bring back for Dad. This act of kindness keeps Dad from dying from exposure. Someone else finds the nearest phone toward Orick and calls for an ambulance, which took quite some time. The ambulance hauls him eighty-five miles over rough road to the nearest hospital in Eureka. There, doctors stabilize him. Anor and the other two fortunately are treated and released.

Mom and the others finally show up late that night. The surgeon does all he can. He tells Mom the next twenty-four hours are critical, and Ray may never walk again. The next twenty-four hours pass slowly. Dad, who's thirty-six and healthy, begins to respond in a positive way. He's eventually released and sent home with a hospital bed. With Mom providing his care, he has the best. Three weeks later, after being told by the doctors that he may never walk again, Dad, his brothers, and the Buswell brothers set up Camp Pecwan. See it however you want, but we call it miraculous.

NEW CAMP

The new Yellow Creek Logging Corporation is in full swing. Camp is set up. A large building that looks like a lodge belonging to the Native Americans has been abandoned, but it's perfect for our needs, much better than anything we had at Yellow Creek. It provided a good kitchen, eating area, and sleeping quarters for those without a camp trailer.

For us kids, the great part is there are more of us. The Pecwan gang is more like the Pecwan army. Pretty neat. Now being older with experience under our belts, instead of our diapers, it's time to build our own camp and roads. We scrounge sticks, limbs, or any kind of building materials we can find to make forts in our camp. We also clear many trails in and around the fort. Most of the time we are too busy having fun to get into much trouble. The majority of us work well together.

The Clark family joins us. Darrel, David, Jerry, and Mary June are my new friends. Darrel is six, a year older than me. David is my age, while Jerry is a year or two younger. Mary June is the same age as my twin brothers, Larry and Gary. Frosty, their father, was Dad's mechanic. He works wonders in the middle of nowhere with few resources. He's also a great dad. Silvia, their mother, is a beautiful woman in more than one way.

We've known the Clarks for a short time, but already Silvia plays an important role in Mom's life. She's become Mom's best friend and confidante. Mom has borne the brunt of a particular woman's tale-bearing. In the first round, she accuses me of not

The Pecwan Army, above, and Silvia with Butch

sharing my toys with the other kids. When those kids were asked if that is true, they said, "Mike always shares his toys with us." For round two, she accuses Mom of not taking good care of the twins, leaving them in dirty diapers. The fact was they aren't even in diapers anymore. Third round, she accuses Mom of receiving special favors from the camp cook. Even if she did, is it any of the woman's business? Fourth and last round, she accuses me of taking things that are not mine. Having enough of this, Silvia straightens out the woman. As much as they could figure, it's a runaway case of jealousy.

The camp, located close to the Klamath River is a very short haul for the trucks from each landing site, which is a huge bonus. Instead of driving a long treacherous road with loads of logs, the men haul their loads for a short distance to a drop site along the Klamath River, where they are offloaded into the river.

The logs are then made into huge rafts by tying them together with wire cables and special spikes. The spikes have round holes at the head of each one. They are driven into the logs at each end. The cable is then carefully strung through the spike. With the cables fastened at one end, the logs are drawn together, then the other end of the cable is secured. With both ends of the logs secured, it's just a matter of waiting for the tug boat to return.

Klamath drop site, above, and offloading logs below

Tying the rafts together is not a job for the faint of heart. It's dangerous. Men lose their lives doing this job. If you're out there and the log rolls and you lose your balance, you could plunge into the water between two logs. The logs then close together, leaving you underwater with no escape.

The tug returns from the mill near the mouth of the Klamath for the next

Making log booms

raft of logs. I'm seven when Dad takes me out across one of the log rafts for a ride on the tugs, which is really exciting. He takes me from one unique experience to another.

Dad collects quite a few interesting sayings while working on logging and road building jobs. One often heard when a piece of equipment broke down was "Why, this dirty hay-wired son-of-a-gun." To translate: "Dirty" means someone is upset at a piece of equipment that's not doing what it's intended to do. Also, you know you're a long way from civilization, where equipment parts are found, so it's often MacGyver time when the "hay-wired" part comes into play. This means bringing Frosty Clark, our mechanic/operator, up as soon as possible with baling wire or whatever parts he can find with welder in hand. The "son-of-a-gun" is just added for intensity.

ELK TAILS

As intense as the Pecwan job is, Dad still knows how to take breaks. The key for him is to work hard and play hard, always. He knows how to do both quite well, packing us to head for Toledo during elk season in Washington.

One particular place Dad never fails to stop on our way up is Kalama, Washington, to visit the famous master totem carver and storyteller, Chief Don "Lelooska" Smith (also known as Chief Lelooska). The chief loves telling stories as much as Dad does. He carves the totems in front of the restaurant at the north end of Kalama. The two of them sit in a separate booth next to Mom and us boys for at least two hours, usually the minimum visit. We learn the meaning of the word patience. This is common for us; it happens every time we go anywhere with Dad.

The totem carving initially grabbed Dad's attention, but it's definitely the storytelling that keeps drawing him back. Hours later, we are back on the road to Toledo. We stay with Uncle Cliff on his chicken ranch.

The plan for the hunt is to head outside of Raymond, Washington, near the coast with sixteen people in the group, including Marie, the camp cook. It rains the day before, making their journey to the campsite difficult. The last portion of their trek is on a muddy road. Dad drives the repaired 1942 Chevy Army surplus panel crew bus that they had wrecked. One of the Pecwan crew brought it up to haul in all the camp supplies.

The men come to a muddy and wet portion of the road in a draw. Dad is following behind when they all halt. The guys are gathered around, wondering how they can pass through the draw without getting stuck. Dad says, "I'll give it a try." The others say, "You'll get stuck." Dad tells them to move aside. "I'll show you boys how to do it." So, he takes a run at it and gets stuck right in the middle of the draw.

He talks the guys into pushing him out by hand. So, Bud Snowsteen and John Byers position themselves at the back while the rest grab something on the side. They all push as hard as they can for several attempts but go nowhere. Dad says, "Now one more try. Give it all you've got!" So Bud and John are all in, pushing as hard as they can. But unknown to them, they had been set up. Dad slips the truck unto four-wheel-drive, leaving Bud and John lying in the mud. Everyone, except those two, laughs. They did later, after they spend more time around Dad.

Bud, a unique fellow, is quite a character, always with a cigarette hanging out of the left side of his mouth. The cigarette would hang down so the smoke constantly drifts up into his left eye, causing it to close more than open. The funny part is, he cocks his head slightly to the left, making him look lopsided. When you add his red hat with its dramatically clipped bill that points almost straight up, you have a sight to behold.

Each night they all return for dinner and share their hunting stories for that day. Dad waits until everyone finishes telling how their day has gone before sharing his. He starts describing a scene where two bull elk locked horns, going at it with each other. It's rutting season, of course. Dad continues his tale as a nephew comes in the tent and asks Ray if he's seen anything today. "No" came out of his mouth before he could reel it back in. Having been caught spinning his yarn, he turns to his nephew and says, "Why, you goofy harebrained screwball." They all laugh, including Dad. No one is ever bored around Ray L. Wallace for long. He's a constant source of entertainment in and out of the woods.

MORE CHANGES

September soon arrives and, for the first time, I'm going to school. I've never been far from Dad for very long. With first grade descending upon me, Mom, the twins, and I move to McKinleyville, which is seventy miles away, about fifteen miles north of Eureka on the coast. We stay in a trailer court on the outskirts of town. It's not a good trade for camp, but I accept the lot given to me. The logging is intense at this point but going well. Dad can come to us only one weekend every two weeks. Winter closes in with much still to be done. If the job is finished before the bad winter hits, they won't need to winter-over there. All goes so well they even get all of the equipment out before the prohibitive weather hits. They head for the next job, which is in Willow Creek about seventy miles south, near the Hoopa Valley Reservation.

At the same time, Wallace cousins from Toledo move equipment into Hoopa. Dale Lee, Don, Ron, and Gail Wallace are all in their twenties. I'm quite a bit younger than most of my Wallace cousins, more the age of my second cousins. Gail ends up with a clothing store in Hoopa while Dale Lee, Ron, and Don build roads and log. As they bring their equipment onto the reservation, it's raining so hard it causes flooding. They arrive at their destination when, behind them, the bridge they crossed washes out. Dale Lee and Don later work for Dad on several jobs.

CHAPTER 8
WILLOW CREEK (1954–1955)

A T CHRISTMAS 1954 IN WILLOW CREEK, CALIFORNIA, our new place for the next couple of years, I receive the best Christmas present ever. Our family is back together again! Dad isn't just visiting us anymore. It must have been a difficult time for Mom, especially after almost losing Dad in the accident. Then, months later, she's separated from him at McKinleyville for long periods at a time. It doesn't make it any easier that his work is potentially dangerous.

We're in our trailer house outside of Willow Creek on a flat, roughly five-acre piece of land against a hill to the east and a farmer's orchard to the north. At the base of the hill, up roughly twenty feet, stands a huge oak tree. From one of its branches dangles a big thick rope. I can swing way out about fifteen or twenty feet off the ground.

One day, with cap pistol in hand, I pretend to be Roy Rogers or maybe the Lone Ranger; both are pretty cool. I back up the hill with the rope in hand as far as I can, then, positioning myself on the knot tied at the bottom, I proceed to swing out as far as I can, holding the rope in one hand and my gun, shooting at the bad guys, in the other. I fly out in space. Apparently, with my focus a little overcooked on the bad guys, down I fall!

Next thing I know I wake up next to what looks like a twelve-inch boulder. I sit up, somewhat regaining my senses, and look down at my hand, which appears really weird with my hand displaced about a half inch higher than normal. Someone must have seen my attempt at flying. The next thing

I know, Mom's checking me out. She calmly says, "I think we need to visit the doctor," mumbling something about a broken wrist.

The orchard, twenty feet behind our trailer, provides a great deal of fun for us kids. The farmer has all kinds of fruit trees and grapevines. When the cherries next to our trailer are ripe, I spend a lot of time trying to figure out which I like the best, the Bings or the Royal Anns. For the next two years, I sampled them but never decided.

When the grapes ripen, a cousin and I decide to raid the enemy's storehouse (grapevines). So, with pretend wooden rifles in hand, we soldiers go on a mission. Crawling on our bellies near our target, we sit to enjoy the fruits of our enemies' labor, when boom, a shotgun blast goes off. Leaving a trail of dust, we dash out of there for the trailer. That farmer must have wet his pants, laughing and watching us beat feet. He must have been a pretty nice guy because he never said one word to Mom or Dad.

Larry and Gary are not quite old enough to go on any of our dangerous missions yet. But they like their new digs at Willow Creek and especially having Dad home every day.

CAMP SUPPLIES

First grade at Trinity Valley in Willow Creek is finishing up for the year. All has gone well, but I'm anxious for summer to come to go more places with Dad. He's been working a great distance north of Willow Creek but is moving to a job closer to us sometime soon.

By this time, Dad and Anor Buswell are good friends who do quite a few things together. They take the crew bus, which was called a crummy for a reason, for supplies in Eureka, a winding sixty-mile drive. If this happens on a Saturday when I'm not in school, I go. The guys remove the rows of seats to maximize the amount of supplies they haul. On the way to Eureka, I sit on a small box behind them, listening to endless tales, mostly Dad's.

Anor is a terrific guy who always wears a big smile. Anor never talks about being decorated or about his exploits in the South Pacific during WWII as a lieutenant, flying the B-24 Liberator. Anor flew forty-seven successful missions. After Anor's transfer, the B-24 he had flown was shot down during its next mission.

I enjoy being with Dad and Anor. We arrive at the warehouse and give them a list of what we need. The process always takes a lot longer than it should. Not because of anyone at the warehouse, but Ray slowed things down with his knack for finding someone to listen to one of his yarns. They are never short ones. Anor, always patient with Dad, stands there with that smile, watching the reactions of listeners.

Finally, when the talking finishes, we pay for the supplies and head for the crummy. This is the cool part. The men in the warehouse arrange the supplies, leaving about a twelve-inch space on top with one of those family-size Hershey bars on top, waiting for me. Dad slides me in on top of the supplies and hands me that monster Hershey bar. So we are on our way back, listening to more stories and munching on that endless chocolate bar. What a way to go!

FIRE

A big fire breaks out on one of the mountains close to Willow Creek where the Wallaces and Buswells were logging. The U.S. Forest Service immediately shuts down all logging in that district. Loggers are enlisted to help the Forest Service's firefighters. The Forest Service sets up headquarters on top of an adjacent mountain. Dad takes me to the headquarters, which is an amazing sight to see. The best part for me is watching the Army helicopters (H-19 Chickasaws) coming and going with supplies. They haul in barrels of cooked beans, corn, water-melon, and whatever

U.S. Army supply helicopter

else firefighters need. Two other young boys about my age are up there also. The pilots are really cool. When everything is unloaded, they let us climb into the back of the helicopter. That is a memorable day.

HIGH TIMES

It's late summer when I turn seven, and school hasn't started yet. I'm with Dad and Anor as they meet up with their fuel supplier, either at Arcada just north of Eureka or at Orick, farther north. Anyhow, Anor has his plane nearby. I think it was a Piper Tri-Pacer. He says, "Hey, Butch, you want to go for a ride?" My answer is something on the order of "Why are we still here?" Dad obviously trusts Anor tremendously. He picks a great place to fly. We soar down this narrow canyon with mountains close on each side and follow a river. I'm beside myself; it is so exciting! I can't wait to go home and tell as many people as I can what I did with Anor. That experience at such a young age is pretty special.

Dad is now working in the Bluff Creek area building a four-mile road for logging access. Bluff Creek happens to be the place where Bigfoot tracks are found a few years later. Hmmmm! This is about late 1955, when rumors of these big tracks float around. Uncle Wilbur and Dad along with some of the other men make the tracks, but the only problem is, nobody spots them—at least not then.

LOST CHOPPER

It's winter break now for logging and road building. Anor and Ray are at their shop by themselves, amusing each other as usual. Both are filled with an inordinate amount of sunshine. The big shop door is open, and they sit there doing their thing when a young man and his boy walk up. He asks if this is Yellow Creek Logging, and they say, "It is."

The young man asks, "Who does your hiring?"

Dad says, "I usually do."

"Are you hiring?" he asks.

Dad tells him that they just shut down for the winter and sent everyone home. As the young guy is telling them how he desperately needs work for his wife, boy, and himself, Anor elbows Ray in the side. Now, the next thing that happens shows how fast Ray thinks on his feet. Dad proceeds to describe to the young guy something that happened here a week ago. Dad tells him their mechanic was under the hood of their helicopter, messing around with the throttle when the linkage got stuck, and the next thing that happened, it just took off. "Still haven't found a trace of it," Ray adds. "Why, I've been to six county fairs and ten hog stickin's, and I haven't seen anything like it since."

The young fella stands there like a deer in the headlights.

Dad says, "I'll tell you what I'll do. I'll pay you to go find that goofy hay-wired son-of-a-gun."

The young man comes back by himself the following day to commence his search. For three days, this guy is coming and going. Anor and Dad are there each day to make sure he stays safe. The area he's working is steep and rugged.

Finally, on the third day, the poor kid shows up. It appears he's fallen over everything that could remotely cause a person to do that. All wore out, he comes up to Dad with the bad news. He has found absolutely no trace of their helicopter.

Another one of Dad's favorite lines pop out of his mouth. "Good guyish shakes man, if that isn't something." It's his way of saying "good grief, man." Dad then reaches for his wallet, pulls out a hundred dollar bill, gives it to the young guy, and thanks him for all his effort. The young man appears pretty grateful as he leaves.

I think this is up there as one of my all-time favorite Ray L. Wallace stories. That young man might have been chasing an illusion, but the $100 was as real as it gets. He walks away with what nowadays would be the equivalent of $1,200, feeling like he earned every penny of it while keeping his dignity intact while searching for a figment of my father's imagination.

MOONLIGHT CANOE

Dad pays quite a few visits to the chief of the Hoopa Valley Reservation. Many of his nephews are on the Res, still building roads, logging, and running one of the stores there.

One particular evening sticks in my mind. Late in the evening, the sky is clear above us with a full moon. Apparently, just the right time, according to our Indian friend, to be in a canoe stringing nets across the Trinity River, which runs right through the Hoopa Reservation. The water is calm where we cross as the net is strung across the river. No one says much. All you hear is the paddles dipping in and out of the water. My eyes flash back and forth between the moon and the net. I don't remember much else about that evening, but it's enough for me, one more unique experience under my young belt.

Dad has been unusually quiet. If he didn't say it out loud, he's thinking, "Boys, boys, boys, now if this isn't somethin'."

WHAT A TRIP

It's mid-December now, time to head to Toledo for the holidays and visiting all the family. I don't know when Dad finds time to work; he always has some side thing going. This time it's propagating bullfrogs. Somewhere he discovers a pond of very large bullfrogs, so he collects a bunch of tadpoles (baby bullfrogs) in a five-gallon bucket with about four gallons of water in it.

Mom has the car packed; we are ready to roll. I normally sit in the back seat behind Dad with the twins at the center and right of me. We're all in the car, a four-door Cadillac, waiting for Dad, which is nothing unusual. Here he comes with his bucket of large tadpoles. He opens my door and says, "Butch, I want to put this bucket on the floor between your legs. What I want you to do is take this stick and, about every half hour, stir the water to get oxygen to the tadpoles."

I'm like, You have got to be kidding me.

Mom says, "Ray, what on Earth are you doing?"

Well, he says, he's taking them to a pond a couple of miles south of Woodland, Washington, which looks to him like a good place to raise bullfrogs. So it's about an eight- or nine-hour drive, 450 miles to Woodland, then another forty miles to Toledo. So, off we go on another adventure, stirring tadpoles on the way.

There's one problem about sitting behind Dad in a vehicle. He develops a habit, from many hours of operating a bulldozer, of spitting up dust. If my window is down, and I'm not paying attention, Dad hocks a loogie out the window and the wind carries it back into my face. So, if you're stirring tadpoles or intently focusing on a comic book, you're in trouble.

I can laugh about it now; but then, I am so ticked off. Mom just shakes her head. I think she does a lot of that. The part I love about being in the back seat is when evening arrives, and the sky is clear, I can do something very special. Some of the bigger cars back then have a space about the size of a twin bed, starting at the top of my seat back to where the rear windshield drops down. As soon as the stars shimmer, I crawl up into that space, lie on my back, and watch the stars. I always love looking out into all those twinkling lights and wondering what's out there. Sometimes I just simply drift off into a wonderful sleep. For the moment, the tadpoles are on their own.

It's well into the evening now. The car comes to a halt, waking some of us. We are now a couple of miles south of Woodland by a pond beside Highway 99 (now interstate 5). Dad carefully takes the bucket of tadpoles down to the pond and slowly releases them into the water; mission accomplished. We are back on the road headed to Uncle Harold Sorensen's. We normally stay with one of Mom's brothers. We are welcome at any of their homes.

SANTA IS COMING TO TOWN

We settle in now for several days, having a great time visiting, laughing, or playing board games. If the weather is good, we're outside exploring.

It's Christmas Eve. One of the places we always go to is the house of Dad's mom, Emma. Along with her kindness, she offers all kinds of great Christmas goodies.

Being seven years old, I still buy into the Santa thing. The grownups sit us boys on Emma's sofa that faces the big picture window in the front of the house. It's evening and dark outside. All of a sudden, one of the grownups says, "Did you hear that?" We're thinking, hear what? Suddenly, as clear as can be, we hear sleigh bells outside. Shortly after that, "Ho, ho, ho!" Following the hearty laugh, we see the head of what looks like a reindeer with antlers walking past the window. Then a knock resounds on the front door.

Lo and behold, when the door opens, in struts Santa with a large sack of presents. We sit there speechless. One by one, we are all given gifts. Santa then says he would like to stay, but he has many more children to visit before the night is done.

Gramma Emma, Butch, and Elna

Quick as a flash, he is out the door and gone, leaving us with pretty cool gifts. Mine just happens to be a long narrow package about thirty inches in length. I tear that baby open with intensity. Unbelievable, the gift of all gifts for a seven-year-old, a Red Ryder BB gun. I am beside myself. The weird part is most kids don't get one of those until they're eight or nine.

Anyhow, when the dust settles, Dad strolls out of the kitchen and asks what all the commotion is about. I hadn't even noticed he had been gone quite a while. Mom's only comment is, "Now, I want you to be careful! You know you could shoot somebody's eye out with that thing!" I'm pretty sure this present was not her idea.

After a great Christmas, it's now time to head back to Willow Creek. I've traded tadpoles for a BB gun. I call that more than fair.

The long drive back is somewhat uneventful, until we hit the fog! It's evening, and we just crossed the northern California border, heading for Highway 1 along the coast. We're about twenty miles from the coast on a long winding stretch of road with a steep bank on our right. The fog grows so thick that Dad opens his door to try to find the center line. He can only go five to ten miles an hour for fear of ending up over the bank.

Dad has me open my window with my head out to help him watch for the white center line. Mom keeps the twins occupied, praying for our safety. Dad's doing a great job keeping the car on the road. He's no stranger to danger. The fog finally clears before we hit the coastal highway heading south. Only a few more hours to home.

CHAPTER 9
WILLOW CREEK (1956–1957)
FISHING ... BIGFOOT STYLE

IT'S THE SPRING OF 1956, and I'm still seven. Anor Buswell and Dad decide we all need a great salmon feast. So after work, armed with flashlights, gaff hooks, and trojan lures, the three of us head for the Trinity River. The Trinity, which runs past Willow Creek, is one of the most beautiful rivers I've ever seen, pristine, winding its way past steep rugged mountains and eventually dumping into the mighty Klamath River.

We park as close as we can to the river on a logging road about a mile or two from the Trinity, then on foot we follow a gradual descent on a steep hillside that turns into nothing but a goat trail. In the last quarter mile, the trail is more than twelve inches wide and the hillside looms almost straight up above and below us. I mean, serious goat trail! Probably like a freeway for a goat. But I'm not much feeling like a goat at the time. Dad keeps telling me, "Stay between us and don't look up the bank or down toward the river. Just concentrate on the trail and where you step, and you will be just fine." Piece of cake, right?

So, we make our way down to the fishing hole. Dad knows of this place because of his good friendship with the chief of the Hoopa Indians. They spend a lot of time telling each other stories. Oh, to have been a fly on the teepee's wall! Anyhow, back to the fishing trip, we reach this spot, and oh my gosh, it's so amazingly beautiful. We are just below the rapids where the river bends and widens, creating a calm hole where fish can rest from their journey upstream. The perfect place to catch fish. It has a small sandy beach, and the river is so clear you can see the salmon above an almost sandy white bottom as you look through the faint turquoise water.

Before I say more, for those of you who don't know what a trojan fishing lure is, I'll explain. It's strictly a time-saving device used only when you want to catch a lot of fish in a hurry. The trojan part is a dead giveaway already to some of you. In building many logging roads, you often come into nasty boulders too large for even a bulldozer. A company called Trojan has an age-old solution called dynamite.

So Dad, armed with half a stick of dynamite and a short fuse, proceeds to fish: boom! Up to the surface float four stunned salmon. You see, the explosion doesn't kill or damage the salmon; it only stuns them. So, with gaff hook in hand, they quickly harvest the four giant salmon. Minutes later, with the sun already set, here we are making our way back up the goat trail in the dark. It was bad enough coming down the goat trail in daylight; imagine trying to navigate this thing in the dark.

Dad and Anor both hold a salmon almost as big as me in each of their hands, positioning me between the two of them. Dad tells me, "Just keep your penlight and your eyes on the trail in front of you." A little nervous with my penlight in hand, away I go. Having been raised on bulldozers since I was one-and-a-half years old, the goat trail didn't seem that bad in the end.

Good buddies, bottom row, second from left, David Clark with Butch to his right

BIG MONEY

The second grade is great. David Clark and I have each other's back. We have a nice teacher, and our class seems to lack bullies.

School's out, and I'm pretty excited to see what the summer brings. In another couple of months, I'll be eight years old. At this time, Yellow Creek

Logging Corporation is doing a big road job. Dad, being its president, does most of the hiring. He asks me if I'd like to have a job picking up limbs off the new road they're building. I couldn't get yes out of my mouth quick enough. He tells me that I will get fifty cents an hour.

Dad also purchases a small pocket-size time book for me to track my hours at work. My office is his pickup. He explains how important it is to keep a road free of anything that may rot later and damage the integrity of the road. I'm ready to roll. Mom packs my favorite food into my own lunch box with pictures of the Lone Ranger on it. Inside is a peanut butter and jelly sandwich, an apple, and a small bag of potato chips.

Things go well with the roadwork. I'm not sure who the rest of the men are on that job, but I do know that Uncles Les and Wilbur work there with Dad.

Every once in a while, when I catch up with the road debris, I head to my office. Grabbing my time book, I attempt to forecast what this summer will yield financially. I've heard the grownups talk about a savings account, saying you could put your money in a savings account, and the bank pays interest on your money. After the first payday, I ask Dad to take me to the bank so I can set an account up, which he does.

UNCLE WILBUR

All goes well on the road job. The men make great headway with the road. I'm picking up my limbs along the road when Uncle Wilbur comes along with one of the TD-24 bulldozers. He tells me they are moving this dozer out. He's taking it down the road to a wide spot where a low-bed waits to haul it out. Wilbur tells me he needs my help as it's getting toward the end of the day. He says, "It's been a long day, and I'm really all wore out. Get up here. I want you to steer this thing down the road to where the low-bed is. I'm going to take a nap."

After climbing up on the dozer, Wilbur sits me on the seat between his legs, right behind the steering levers. He instructs me on what to do with the levers. Then he says, "Just keep this thing in the middle of road. Now I'm going to take a nap. Wake me when the low-bed is in sight." So, off we go. I'm a little nervous about the steep drop-off on the bank to the right. With the low-bed in sight, I turn and shake his arm. It never occurs to me until later in life that he isn't napping. I love that guy.

These men working with Dad are golden. I firmly believe to this day that all of them helped instill confidence in me, giving me the ability to tackle tough situations.

UNCLE LES

Here we go with the "It takes a logging camp to raise a child" thing again.

It's the weekend. Uncle Les stops by for something. Unbeknownst to me, he has not yet knocked on the trailer house door, but his timing isn't good for me at the moment. I'm just inside the door in the middle of a dispute with Mom. Les hears me say, "My dad said I don't have to mind you." Without knocking, Les opens the door. He tells Mom he needs to borrow me for a minute.

He grabs me by the back of my collar and trousers with both hands, my feet barely touching the ground on the way to

Speech lesson for Butch

wherever. This little journey takes me to the far side of one of the TD-24s near our trailer house. Sitting me up on the dozer track and looking me straight in the eye, he proceeds to set the record straight.

"What your father may or may not have told you is not going to happen," he says. "From this day forward, if I catch wind of you sassing your mother, I'll see to it that your hind end will deeply regret it. Do you clearly understand me?"

I had only one word to say. "Yes."

I never tried that one again.

THE DOUBLE

The summer—in fact, the whole year of 1956—is pretty hard to forget. I'm able to play Little League baseball for the first time. Little did I know how special the sport would be to me for years to come. Mom has a little problem finding a mitt for a left-hander. She finally comes up with one before the season starts.

I'm working on Dad's road job during the week and making it to practice after work; Dad sees to it. Games are on Saturday. It's a little ironic the coach from the start put me in left field, which became my predominate position through college. I'll never forget my first game. I'm in left field and lift my glove just a shade too late. The ball hits me right in my forehead. I do the only thing left to do, grab it as quick as I can and throw it to the third baseman. That is the only part I got right. As the season progresses, I start to get the hang of it. I find out later that if I hadn't improved, I would have been sent to right field. Usually, at that age, right field is the last stop before the bench.

The end of the season draws near. We have only a few games left. Our coach gathers us around his car. As he opens the trunk, he shows us this big box. He reaches inside and pulls out a beautiful royal blue baseball cap. Up to this point, there's been no money for caps, let alone uniforms. This was the case for most teams. Coach informs us that if we win this game, he will give each of us one of those beautiful blue hats.

Each game is six innings long. The only part of that game I remember to this day is the sixth inning. The score is their team two, our team one. We have two outs with a kid on second and one on first, and yes, it's my turn at bat. I don't know what the count was on me, but I remember hitting that sucker over the shortstop's head into the outfield. It lands somewhere between the left-fielder and the center-fielder. By the time those two in the outfield decide who is going to pick up the ball and throw it in, our two guys have scored, and I was standing on second base, not sure what would happen next. Coach calls us in. He motions us over to his car, and in no time, we all wear beautiful blue baseball hats. I'm thrilled about the timely hit but even more excited about wearing that beautiful royal blue baseball hat!

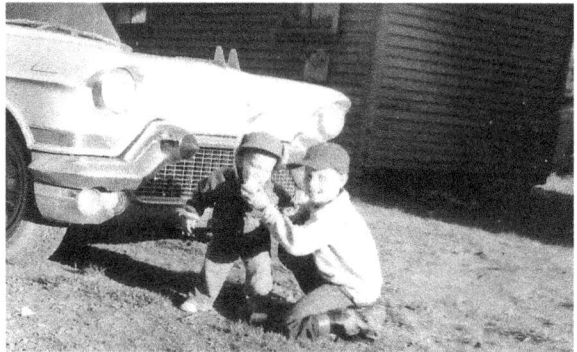
Royal blue hat

LITTLE RICKY

It's the second week in July 1956. Mom gets a call. Someone on the other end of the phone is telling her the baby is coming soon. It's due at the end of the month. All the paperwork for adoption is in order. All we need now is to drive to Centralia, Washington, before the baby is born. No drive to Toledo is complete for Dad without a stop at the large pond south of Woodland to cheer on the large pollywogs that are now bullfrogs and another to spend a couple of hours spinning yarns with Chief Lelooska in Kalama. We arrive in Toledo and stay with relatives until we receive word. On July 28, little Ricky arrives. He's now all ours, and we head back to Willow Creek.

Bouncing ahead, Rick is a few months old now. Mom is a little concerned after finding a penny in Rick's diaper. She's trying her best to keep little things out of his reach. The next morning, she changes his diaper and finds a marble in it.

This starts to upset her. She wonders how on earth he got a hold of one of Butch's marbles, which are stored on his shelf. To make matters worse, the third morning when changing

Little Ricky completes our family of four boys

him, she finds a tiny padlock in his diaper. Now she's visibly shaken, afraid she's going to find him choked to death. Dad confesses that evening after getting home from work and hearing her tale. All I can tell you is, if she'd had a frying pan within arm's reach, he would have been knocked out cold on the trailer house floor!

MRS. SHORT

I'm eight years old, still attending Trinity Valley School in Willow Creek, California. Now in the third grade, I face a few challenges. My teacher's name is Mrs. Short, appropriately as she's stout and commands respect. She attempts to teach us penmanship.

She marches up and down each row, making sure we do exactly as we're told. A bit of an authoritarian, you might say. Anyhow, my problem is I'm left-handed and, according to Mrs. Short, "One does not write with

Mrs. Short

one's left hand." But, according to me, "One only wrote with the left hand."

So, every time she catches me using my left hand, she knows the only rebel is me. She comes up behind me, nails my left hand with her ruler, and tells me to do as I'm told. As soon as she moves on, I go back to using my left hand. You see, I view being left-handed as being among the privileged few. I always have. I never earned a great grade for penmanship, only a passing one. And no, folks, I never feared for my life because of that ruler or the lady who wielded it. I'm still left-handed. Actually, it came in real handy when pitching on a baseball team. I liked Mrs. Short, outside of penmanship.

My second adventure with Mrs. Short takes place during lunch period. We get our hot lunch trays and find a spot at the big, long table. Wow, hot gravy over turkey and mashed potatoes, applesauce, a roll and, yuck, spinach.

Well, according to Mrs. Short, "If one doesn't finish one's lunch, one will be unable to go to recess." I'm sitting there thinking, this really sucks being "the one" all the time. I'm beginning to think it has something to do with being raised in a logging camp. Am I the only challenged kid in this school?

I need quick thinking here. I must get out of here to the tetherball pole for a rematch with that turkey who beat me yesterday. Got it. I eat almost everything on my plate and drink my small carton of milk, ha! Small carton. I grab the empty carton, stash it between my legs, and each time Mrs. Short looks elsewhere (which was rare), I slip a large spoonful of spinach into the carton. Having stuffed it with spinach, I close the lid and carefully wipe any trace of green from it. With a smile on my face, I drop the allegedly empty carton in the garbage and the tray where it belongs and head out to do battle on the tetherball court. I doubt "Popeye the sailor" or even my mother would be impressed with my notions. But Dad thought it downright creative!

MOM AND SILVIA

Mom's relationship with Silvia deepened as time passed. The two get all gussied up, as they would say in those days, then go to church or do a little shopping together, always looking like a million bucks, well, a billion nowadays. Always there for each other, they're both beautiful inside and out.

At times I'm not sure if Mom would have survived so well without Silvia's support. Dad, the ultimate multi-tasker, provides a constant barrage of work and fun (mostly pranks on the fun side). I guess his motto is "Getter done while having

Out on the town

fun." But Mom is no wimp either. Having been raised by a tough old Dane, she never shies away from hard things, including Dad.

So, dealing with Ray, being the boss's wife, handling occasional blowbacks from one of the other men's wives, and raising four boys can be taxing at times. This is where Silvia is golden. Mom always receives the support she needs when she needs it. Our families do a lot together. It's always fun playing with Darrel, David, and Jerry. One of our favorite things to do after work is head to the nearest swimming hole.

One particular time at the swimming hole turns out slightly different than the rest. My cousin, Mickey Wallace, Uncle Les's boy, apparently grows fed up watching me wade around in the water, not swimming like the rest of the kids. We're at a large creek where the water comes down the rapids from above and makes an

The Clark family with Gary in the middle

S-turn, with the upper portion of the S a bit wider. This creates a whirlpool where the water circles, then proceeds on down the creek.

Well, the thing is, you don't want to get caught in it. The whirlpool can suck you under, so you have a difficult time escaping unless, of course, you're a pretty good swimmer. I'm messing around in about eighteen inches of water, pretty happy with myself, when Mickey comes over and says, "You need to learn how to swim like everyone else." I'm thinking to myself, "No, I don't." He's standing there, describing with his hands something he calls a dog paddle, telling me how easy it is, saying you just kick your feet and move your arms at the same time. I'm thinking, "Easy for you to say, big fella; you're five years older." I think he takes my silence as a "get lost." But then he picks me up and bodily throws me in the deep end.

I find myself flying through the air, hearing, "Don't forget to kick your feet." As I'm in the air, it appears I will land on the outskirts of the whirlpool. Fear of that thing causes adrenaline to kick in as soon as I reach the surface. I quickly figure out which way is the opposite direction of the whirlpool, saying to myself, "Don't forget to kick your feet!" I set a personal dog paddle record. Looking back, I don't think I ever broke the record. Thanks to Mickey, I'm now an official swimmer. I don't hold that against him. He's the kind of guy who's really hard not to like.

AVERT YOUR EYES

Fall arrives and it's back to school for me. The worst part is no more paychecks and no more baseball. I'd fallen head over heels for that sport.

For some reason, Mom and Dad need to go to Eureka. We all pile into the Caddy and head out of Willow Creek, driving in and out of patches of fog. It's not a problem for Dad, but it is for another guy. All of a sudden, we come upon a California Highway Patrol (CHIP) officer. He informs Mom and Dad of a helicopter crash on the highway just ahead.

"Ma'am," he says, looking her directly in the eye. "You and your four boys need to drop to the floor and keep your heads and eyes down. You're not going to want to see what has happened here."

I feel sorry for Dad's driving through, but I didn't know the worst until I asked him years later and he tells me the road was littered with body parts from the helicopter crash. I feel the tension in the car heading to Eureka and keep quiet. No one says much. Fortunately, the drive back is much easier.

We find out the purpose of the trip. Brother Gary has a speech problem. Well, let's put it this way, it's not a problem for Gary, just everyone else. Actually, I think it's pretty cute. Instead of saying, long, lean, and lanky, he would say "Yong, yean, and yanky." Mom is concerned he'll be teased when he starts school. On some occasions, we're teased for being adopted. I guess they want to make us feel like second-class citizens. Mom and Dad pick up this package containing LP records and instructions to help brother Gary. Within six months, his speech problem disappears.

ELK HUNT

When the fall elk season opens, Dad takes me and a couple of other guys to Eastern Oregon for the hunt. I don't remember what towns we pass, but we end up in a huge field with tall grass surrounded by forest timber. A wide trail used by elk crosses the field, and the men do well with their hunting. I don't know how they pull this off, but Dad positions me, with my Red Ryder BB gun, about thirty feet downwind, just off the trail, not far from where the elk trail left the forest. Dad's with me in the tall grass and tells me to just be quiet and keep my head down when the elk come out to feed. Eventually, they come just like he predicts, and he says, "Wait until they are right across from us, then stand up and fire." Following his instructions I pop up when they pass by and shoot my BB gun.

Writing this book, I think often of my out-of-the-box dad and all of our crazy experiences. It's just plain weird. I never thought much about the whole thing before writing this book. I wish I'd expressed my gratitude more when Dad was alive. All these weird experiences, I guess, become normal. All the crazy things Dad, my uncles, and my older cousins do in this business, they're never short on humor. As hard as all those men work, you wouldn't think they'd have anything left at the end of the day. But they did. I spoke recently with Don Buswell, who's 102, and he says, "We knew how to have fun."

Gary and Mary June eyeing each other at a birthday party

CHAPTER 10
HARDY CREEK

JUST AFTER DAVID CLARK AND I FINISH third grade at the Trinity Valley School, we're told we're moving again soon because Dad scored a state road job on the coast about twenty miles north of Fort Bragg on State Highway 101. The state is having problems with rocks and debris falling off the cliff onto Highway 101 along the ocean, creating hazards. Dad presents an innovative idea to solve the problem. He plans to stairstep the mountain above the road, similar to terracing done for agricultural reasons on steep mountainsides worldwide. Preferring his solution, officials award him the job. Now, the first order of business is to find two Caterpillar scrapers to lease for five or six months. Scrapers are more efficient at moving large amounts of loose soil faster than the dozers. But, when it comes to dealing with rock and making cuts in

Ray on the bulldozer

78

a mountain, dozers win the day. Dad already has six bulldozers but needs about a dozen men to do the work. He needs two scraper operators, six dozer operators, two surveyors, one mechanic, and himself as the boss/operator. Two of the workers are my older cousins, Dale Lee Wallace and Gail Wallace, also our mechanic/operator Frosty Clark with his family, yes! That means Darrel, David, Jerry, Mary June, and Silvia are moving with us.

Hardy Creek solidifies deep lasting friendships and memories. Dale Lee, for one, grows close to Mom and Dad and enjoys making Bigfoot tracks with Dad, now and for many years to come. Although at this time the tracks pretty much go unnoticed, his appreciation for Mom's love and patience for that wild and crazy guy she married wins her great favor in his eyes.

Mom's appreciation for Silvia grows, especially as this is the only job in the last eleven years with only one other woman around. The rest are mostly bachelors. With her special confidante, Mom can get all gussied up and go to town or church. We live pretty rural again in two tarpapered shacks, about twelve feet by forty feet. An old overgrown building sits up on the hill, a remnant from 1902 to 1915, when R.A. Hardy operated a small post office and a wharf used for shipping lumber from a now-burned

The photo above of cousin Dale Lee Wallace holding the footprints Ray used to create the Bigfoot hoax appeared on front pages worldwide, including The New York Times, where it accompanied an article by Timothy Egan. At right is a photo of me with the feet. Both photos were taken by photographer Dave Rubert of Winlock, Washington.

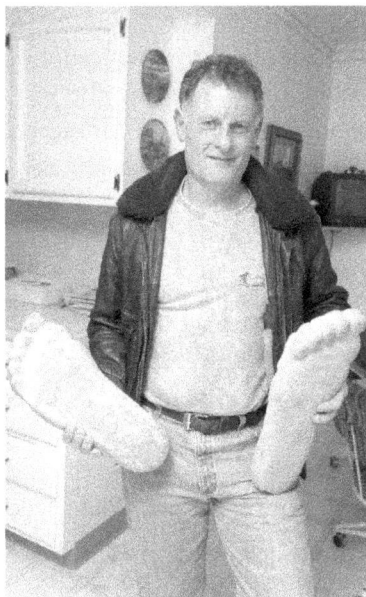

mill at Hardy Creek. An abandoned railroad trestle sits about a quarter mile up Hardy Creek, which runs east to west between two small mountains toward the ocean. Highway 101 crosses a small bridge a quarter mile from the ocean, just down from the bridge and the two tarpapered shacks about twenty feet from the stream.

From there toward the ocean a grove of small deciduous trees about twenty feet tall runs for a ways and then opens up onto a large pond. On the north side of the pond looms a steep rocky cliff. Beyond the pond lie sand dunes fronting the Pacific Ocean. I can't speak for any of the others, but this place is Dreamland for me. To this day, I hold Hardy Creek as one of the top ten places I've lived.

I simply can't remember a day fighting or arguing with the other kids. I'm sure we must have at some point. Each day is so packed with adventure, we have no time for quarreling. We have the old railroad trestle to explore or Hardy Creek itself with its small trout. The next day, maybe the small cave on the mountainside to the south. We find old bottles and miscellaneous junk. I remember Mom's clothesline set up between the shack and creek. With much to do and the bigger kids exploring, she tethers little Ricky with a rope tied to the clothesline and hooked to a comfy little harness he wears. Little Ricky spends time howling until he figures out it's fruitless. She gives him just enough rope to reach the water but not drown himself. I doubt the harness and entire setup would have won approval from the State of California; it's too early for OSHA (Occupational Safety and Health Administration) regulations.

The six of us boys spend a great deal of time in the grove of small trees below the shacks. By the way, each twelve- by forty-foot shack has two rooms, a smaller one for our parents and a larger room with a small kitchen and table with chairs. The rest of the larger room has an old sofa and four cots on the floor.

THE GROVE

The creek runs through the grove of small trees off to the southside with a small deer trail that we begin to widen. Then we clear areas large enough for each of us to build a fort. We end up with four. This does not go quickly. It takes time just to gather the tools we need. We forge ahead. Eventually, by using the small trees we cut and a few boards, we finish our little city. But it isn't quite complete. Dad suggests a telephone system. He heard that if you string blasting wire tight from one tin can to another for a short distance, you can faintly hear sound by talking into the can. The men blast a lot of rock on the road job, so they have a great deal of old blasting wire available. Dad brings us kids so much wire we not only had our phone system from fort to fort but plenty of wire left over for other projects. The three of us older boys are well prepared for Hardy Creek. By this time, we've gained a great deal of MacGyvering practice in previous camps. We learned how to do a lot with a little. Here again, with no stores close to buy whatever we want, like our fathers, we MacGyvered things together with wire or whatever we could find.

THE POND

The pond, about a hundred and fifty feet wide, runs from the grove of trees roughly a couple hundred feet to the sand dunes. The north side abuts a steep cliff with goat trails close to the top. Occasionally we catch a glimpse of them defying gravity. The pond has fish under the water and snakes on top. After completing our city, we construct what we call the mother raft, big enough to hold six of us. The shallow pond enables us to use two long poles for propulsion. We supply the ship with a pile of cannonballs, rocks two to three inches in diameter, and war against all kinds of imaginary enemies, including evil snakes.

Later, we construct four smaller rafts with smaller cannonball piles. Under the rules, we cannot hit the enemy ship. We can only get the ship and its occupants wet. Only snakes are not off-limits. It's amazing; I can't remember anyone getting hurt. Any injuries might have cut our seafaring days short. Life is pretty special at Hardy Creek.

THE BEACH

Just beyond the pond, the sand dunes lead to the beach, offering its own delight. We collect shells and driftwood, mostly while exploring north and south. You can see the goats from there also.

The beach is exceptionally awesome with the tide out. Low tide exposes many wonderful things. My favorite are the little spiny sea urchins, especially the purple ones. If you find one just the right

The twins and little Ricky at Hardy Creek Beach

size, you can make a really cool lampshade with it. You must empty the shell, remove the spines, then dry the shell. The hard part is the long wait for someone to drive into Fort Bragg. I need a lamp cord with a switch in the middle, a male plug on one end, and a tiny light socket on the other. This fit a small bulb like the size for a night-light. Once I have everything I need, the little bulb goes inside the urchin shell. I put my homemade light on my nightstand, which is a wooden box. When you flip the switch at night, you get this beautiful purple glow.

Another beach bonus is abalone. Dad waits for low tide when he isn't working, grabs a crowbar and gunnysack, which is most often a large burlap bag, and heads for the beach. For those unfamiliar with abalone, they are an edible mollusk with shallow ear-shaped shells. The cupped interior is a beautiful Mother of Pearl. You use the crowbar to

Abalone

pry off the critter inside, attached like a large suction cup to the rock.

After all of us enjoying a great time at the beach, the sun sets, and we head back to the shack for Mom's first shot at preparing abalone. She thinly slices the meat and pan-fries what she has before serving it. Most all of us liked seafood. With knife and fork in hand, I cut off a piece and chew, and chew, and chew. I'm sitting there thinking the taste is unique and pleasant, but I'd prefer eating shoe leather to this thing. Mom didn't know at the time that cooking abalone is a delicate and timely process with a short window between raw and overcooked. Once you figure out how to prepare abalone, it's a rare seafood delicacy. Well, at least we have beautiful shells. When all else fails, we can always eat peanut butter and jelly sandwiches.

Dad's nickname for Mom is "Kitty" or "Kitty Cat." Whether returning from work or collecting abalone, he comes through the door and the first thing out of his mouth is "Kitty Cat, come here." He hugs and kisses her. If we are in the room, he gazes at us and issues one of his many sayings regarding Mom. "Boys, boys, boys, she's no toy!"

GOOD FRIENDS

For my ninth birthday, there's nothing better than having really good friends to celebrate with, and the Clark kids always fit the bill. Jerry Clark, six years old at the time, does a great job of showing how we all get along with one another. Jerry is quite a happy-go-lucky kind of guy. His sister, Mary June, ends up dating brother Gary for some time in the 1970s.

I'm not sure why brother Rick, not shown in the picture, isn't with us. Mom may have forgotten to unhook him from the clothesline out back.

CASCARA SAGRADA

With autumn and school fast approaching, Dad reads somewhere that

Jerry, Butch, Gary, Larry, and Mary June in November 1957

companies are buying cascara bark. Cascara is a deciduous broad-leaved tree or shrub that grow up to fifty feet tall. The bark is processed as a laxative for constipation; oh boy, she's no toy! I'm not tempted to chew on the stuff. Dad discovers a large grove of cascara trees in the direction of his road job. He informs me that companies pay fairly good money for cascara by the pound. That sounds great for my savings account.

With a knife and large burlap sack in hand, Dad takes me to the grove. With peeling instructions complete, he tells me how many hours it'll be until he returns. This goes on for a week or so. Sometimes Dad peels with me for a little while when dropping me off or picking me up. It's a great spot to harvest the bark because I hear the ocean. It's a win aesthetically and financially.

WESTPORT

No more footloose and fancy-free for me. September means time for school again, bringing our adventures to a dull roar. The yellow bus travels six miles north during the week to pick us up, turns around at Hardy Creek, and heads back with three of us—Darrel, David, and myself. I feel little anxiety in going to a new school. After all, we have each other's backs, bullies or no bullies.

The white schoolhouse sits on the uphill side of Highway 101 overlooking the Pacific Ocean, with a parking area in front and a small playground with a tetherball pole and set of monkey bars in back. The only other building, other than a few houses, is a small post office. The school has one big room, kind of like in *Little House on the Prairie*. Front and center is a large blackboard on the wall next to the teacher's desk, followed by five rows of desks, one specifically for each grade, first through fifth. You hang up your coat, if you have one, just inside the front door and set your sack lunch on the shelf just above your coat.

With Darrel in the fifth row, and David and myself in the fourth, we settle in among the twenty-five or twenty-six kids in the school. The teacher and the kids are nice. At lunchtime we grab our sack lunches and sit at our desks. My favorite is always peanut butter and jelly sandwiches with an apple and a small bag of chips. Recess is great because I love looking out on the ocean where there's always something to watch, mostly boats, but we left before the whales started coming through in February.

Temporarily rolling things forward to 1966, Hollywood producers used the beach in front of us to film a comedy with Alan Arkin, Brian Keith, Carl Reiner, and others called *The Russians Are Coming the Russians Are Coming*. The movie, meant to be a spoof on Paul Revere's cry of "The British are coming," used the little post office for a scene where the Russians hung the proprietor on a coat hook inside the door and left him there thrashing. This was Westport's five minutes of fame.

WRAPPING UP

I have Dad's old time book for the Hardy Creek Highway 101 road job. It's a special keepsake for me, mostly because of where we lived at that time. I couldn't have wanted a better place to live for five months with all the irreplaceable awesome sights, smells, and adventures we had as kids. Hardy Creek will always be special.

The bonus for our family is Dad made serious money on that job, which he finished on November 1, 1957, just ahead of schedule. All twelve of the men worked a ten-hour day on that Friday. Only Edward von Schillinger, our surveyor, and his assistant returned in mid-January to wrap up their survey.

We all prepare to move to a road job not far south, around Juan Creek. Goodbye sweet Hardy Creek.

During our time there, Don and Anor Buswell, still under Yellow Creek Logging Corporation, worked on a road job quite a ways east of us outside of Corning, California. Don recently told me both he and Dad did extremely well financially on both the Hardy Creek job and the one near Corning.

This is where the Buswells part ways with Yellow Creek Logging Corporation. Don made it very clear nothing negative brings about the decision to part. I know Anor is to Dad what Silvia is to Mom. Distance never changes that for any of them. The Buswells go off to a road job near Covelo, forty miles east of Hardy Creek, while we head to Fort Bragg, just down the beach twenty-plus miles.

Recently, during numerous informative and entertaining visits with Don, I've filled gaps of information for my book. The best part is his sense of humor, especially with regard to the occasionally PG-13 description of how he's feeling at 102. Those visits remind me of how much I appreciate knowing and being around Don and his brother, Anor.

I'm not sure of the timing, but sometime after Hardy Creek, Mom and Dad give Frosty and Silvia money to buy a home. My parents appreciate so much what they both meant to our family, and Dad makes it clear the money is a gift not intended for repayment.

CHAPTER 11
FORT BRAGG

BUSY MEN

DAD'S NEW ROAD JOB is not far south of Hardy Creek. But Mom and Dad decide it's time to leave the tarpaper shack, which is a little uncomfortable in the middle of January. They choose a trailer park outside of Fort Bragg. Moving into the trailer is like living in a mansion compared with what we had in Hardy Creek, especially for Mom. I don't feel the same about the situation. It doesn't take me long to start missing Hardy Creek.

Uncle Wilbur and Dad don't waste time making more new Bigfoot tracks. The freshly turned dirt from this long road job provides a great opportunity to make the prints. They operate thirteen to fourteen bulldozers at a time. A couple of Dad's nephews work on this job. Years later, after Dad passed, one of them tells me he earned enough working for Dad to buy himself an Oldsmobile. Dad always pays his men well. He's never tight, but he does expect a hard day's work out of all the men.

Dad loves his sixteen-millimeter camera, especially now as he experiments with making Bigfoot films. He has a suit made up for Big Jim Brookner to star in one of his attempts. This one, like most, has flaws, but he persists, believe me.

NEW DIGS

Speaking for Mom and us boys, even though accommodations are better here outside of Fort Bragg, we all miss Hardy Creek. We're in a nice trailer house, but we're piled on top of twenty others. What I would call cramping, not camping. The one bright spot is that I apparently graduate to a real cool big guy's bicycle. The downside is trying to learn how to ride it. This particular trailer court has never seen fine gravel. It's hard enough learning how to ride, but even more difficult when you throw in, what seemed to me, boulders to navigate. I'm just a little fearful of falling off that bike, and fear drives me to be a quick learner.

DONT BE A BOAR

Every once in a while, after a day's work, some men stop at this tavern on the way home. Inside, hanging on the walls, are mounted game heads of whatever happens to be prevalent in the area. This tavern, in particular, excels in wild boars, displaying many heads with huge tusks. The bigger the tusks, the bigger the trophy. Ray asks the owner where the boars come from. He tells Dad they're all around here, no particular area.

A couple of weeks go by, and Dad and some men stop in again. They find a table and sit there enjoying themselves. A little while later, Bob Doxy, a friend of Dad's, limps through the front door with a cast on his leg. They ask him what happened to his leg. Bob tells them he was attacked by one of those wild boars and had a horrible time getting away from it. He and Dad engage in a lengthy discussion as to how you stop one of those critters. It almost becomes an argument. Each has his own opinion on what to do or what type of gun to use.

A local man sitting at another table, originally from Oklahoma and a good hunter and tracker, introduces himself and tells them a bit about himself. He says he can track down the boar, so Dad hires him to find the animal before anyone else gets hurt.

At this time, a nephew plans a trip to Hoopa to see cousins. Dad asks him to pick up a sack of pig manure and two pigs' feet from one of the dead pigs on a farm there. His nephew tells him, "No way, I'm not carrying pig manure in my new car." So Dad drives to Hoopa himself and comes back with what he wants. He creates what looks like an area where a boar has bedded down, scatters pig manure around, and drops the pigs' feet to make it look like a dangerous boar had killed its own.

Dad set up the whole thing with Bob Doxy ahead of time. He knew the hunter but pretended not to when Bob limped through the door. They timed it so the hunter, a tavern regular, would be inside the tavern. All goes as planned.

The hunter searches several times with no success. Dad tells him later he might have a better idea where the boar is from talking to Bob. So, Dad takes him to the spot where he spread the manure. The Oklahoman starts to realize he's being had. A few days later, he invites Dad to go deep-sea fishing. They set up a short distance offshore below a cliff. Dad's getting all these bites, but he's not bringing in any fish. This continues until the hunter, now a fisherman, tells Dad, "Let's try it again tomorrow; we will probably have better luck." Dad goes home and asks his nephew to come with him. He might have better luck.

The next day the same thing goes on. Dad feels a bite, and the fisherman gets excited and tells Dad to play the fish and not jerk too hard on the line. Pretty soon, Dad notices this odd but familiar smile on the fellow's face and finally figures out he's been had. All this time they've been fishing over a kelp bed, which causes his hook to catch in the kelp. Along with the action of the tide, it feels like he has a fish on. The fisherman gets quite a kick out of it.

Dad tells his nephew later, "I can't believe he did that to me." It's like the pot calling the kettle black. He's shocked someone would give him a dose of his own medicine.

The Juan Creek roadwork goes well. The guys have fun, being up to their usual tricks and hard work. We prepare to move back to the Hoopa area after Dad finds another job around Weitchpec, just a couple of miles north of the reservation.

I'm excited about getting back out in the wilderness.

CHAPTER 12
BIGFOOT COUNTRY

WEITCHPEC

HERE WE ARE IN WEITCHPEC, several miles north of the Hoopa Reservation. Things are looking up again, back to more comfortable surroundings.

Before we move from Fort Bragg and the Juan Creek job, Dad gives a warning to one of my cousins and some of the other young guys going with us to Weitchpec. He tells them they need to watch out for maulcats, which hang out in the tall timber. Ray tells them the maulcats get really irritated with anyone working around where they live. Dad describes them as similar to a mountain lion, only with different tails consisting of a bushy ball of spikes. When they swing their tails, they can rip the bark right off a tree. Dad starts a rumor about how a timber faller attacked in that area saves himself only by waving his chainsaw at the cat and chasing it back up a tree. After the cat scurries up the tree, the faller throws down his saw and runs like crazy. Dad never lacks details.

When they set up for work at Weitchpec, my cousin and the other young guys ask Dad to show them where the maulcats hang out. Dad says he'll show them in a couple of days.

He finally takes them quite a ways into very tall timber, then tells them to stop and says, "Did you hear that? There, way up there in those tall trees, just out of sight?" The boys are still convinced after leaving, never having seen one. Another one of Ray's tall cat tales.

HONING ONES SKILLS

Ray, with a few others in the crew, always goes to a jobsite ahead of the others and clears an area for a campsite. This leaves soft dirt everywhere for families to haul in their trailers. Dad doesn't waste any time making Bigfoot tracks with the wooden feet that he commissioned Rant Mullins to carve. Mullins also had a long history with Sasquatch in the Great Northwest. Dad straps on the wooden feet and goes to work. This time he makes tracks up to a trailer window like he's Bigfoot having a curious moment. Pretty soon several women in camp express concern. Rumors fly, but nobody makes anything of it. Dad never tells anyone what he does because some consider the prints real. If he confesses, they'd be embarrassed, so my cousin stayed tight-lipped.

Dad hones his skills at more than road building. Brother Rick and I reminisced recently over Dad's antics. I love how he summed it up, "Dad was outstanding in his field, not particularly the ones with cow dung."

WORLD GOES APE

Working next to us in the Bluff Creek area just north of Weitchpec in late August 1958 is another road building company constructing road for Granite Lumber Company. Among that group is Jerry Crew, a bulldozer operator. After vandalism to equipment on jobsites in our area, Ray figures he can deter that activity by making more tracks around equipment.

On this day, Dad is supposed to be looking at a job a hundred miles east of us, but instead of heading east, he goes to Jerry's job next door. That evening, he parks out of sight and waits for Jerry Crew to park his dozer for the day. After Jerry leaves the site, Dad starts up the dozer. With the machine's heavy blade, he crushes a partially full barrel of diesel oil and pushes it over a steep bank. Then, after parking the dozer, he uses limbs to cover his and the machine's tracks. Next, he dons his big carved alder feet and proceeds to make tracks around the machine, then strides to where the barrel had been initially. From there the tracks lead to the bank, then just wander away and disappear.

Jerry comes to work the following morning only to discover all these big footprints. Being more than concerned, he informs the rest of his coworkers. He runs into Uncle Wilbur nearby on our job and tells him what he saw. Wilbur tells him not to worry too much, just stay heads-up for any unusual activity. The only problem is that the footprints continue for days around Jerry's job. Dad and Uncle Wilbur put in a little overtime, but not on their dozers.

Jerry finally reaches a point where he must do something. So he makes plaster of paris casts of the footprints he finds, measuring roughly eighteen inches long

Huge Footprints Found On Wilderness Road

Cutten Seeks Single Family Residential Zone At Meet Slated Tuesday Night

Thurmond Calls On South To Defy Supreme Court

Atomic Energy For Blasting

2 Men See Bigfoot--Mystery Deepens

Eye-Witnesses Tell Standard Reporter Story Of Sighting Hair-Covered 'Creature'

Venezuela Plane Missing Today

In October 1958, The Humboldt Times *ran several articles about the sighting of Bigfoot and his prints in dirt near Bluff Creek, and Ray Wallace denied making the prints and threatened to sue the sheriff.*

by seven inches wide. The prints are about fifty inches apart. Jerry then takes his castings to Eureka, California, to *The Humboldt Times* newspaper about fifty miles away. He shows the feet to one of the newsroom's lead reporters, Andrew Genzoli, who observes the evidence and writes an article. The headline reads, "Giant footprints puzzle residents along Trinity River." The article, published on October 6, 1958, states that Jerry Crew and his road construction squad found Sasquatch footprints in the Bluff Creek area. It also mentions for the first time the word "Bigfoot." The article goes on to say the creature visited the area from time to time and details other sightings. The only ones I'm sure of are the who, what, when, where, why, and how the tracks Jerry Crew saw came into existence.

"I'LL SUE," vows Ray Wallace, of Willow Creek, referring to accusations allegedly made by the Humboldt sheriff's office that he was the perpetrator of a hoax in the Bigfoot prints found on the upper Bluff Creek road project, which his company is constructing. Wallace is a firm believer there is a creature making the sixteen-inch-long tracks. He plans to attempt to trap the beast.

A closer look at Ray denying involvement

On October 15, 1958, reporter Bill Chambers of *The Humboldt Times* reports that the Humboldt County Sheriff's Office thought it discovered the man responsible for the tracks found in Bluff Creek. They half-heartedly attempted to arrest him but soon turned Ray loose. The headline reads, "Sheriff's office ends up with Bigfoot in mouth." Below the headline is a photo of Dad pointing his finger at the sheriff while supposedly being arrested. Both men are smiling in the photo.

After Andrew Genzoli's article hits the Associated Press wires, it quickly runs in *The Los Angeles Times* and *The New York Times*. After that, it quickly circles the globe and—voila! Bigfoot is born! Of all the pranks Dad pulls in his long illustrious career, his timing can never have been better. The world appears quite ready for Bigfoot and so is Ray L. Wallace. All of a sudden, he morphs from prankster to promoter, offering stiff competition for the Ringling Brothers Barnum & Bailey Circus.

For you younger folks, P.T. Barnum, an American showman who lived from 1810 to 1891, was a businessman, politician, and promoter of hoaxes—

one of the best when it came to promoting. Ringling Brothers Circus still operates today.

The whole Bigfoot thing starts to go ape. Shorty, Uncle Wilbur, happens to have Dad's carved feet. Don Buswell borrows them to make tracks while being slowly pulled behind a pickup. By doing this, impressions from the feet are deeper and farther apart. The man in charge of keeping down the dust on the logging road drives a truck with a large water tank on it. While doing his job the next day. he spots those eerie tracks. He's so scared he takes the door handles off his truck so whatever it is can't get in. He works one more night and quits.

GOLD RUSH

After the world hears of "Bigfoot," the area around Bluff Creek and Weitchpec looks like the '49er gold strike. Men pour in from all over creation. Streams of backpackers and strings of mules loaded with supplies seek evidence of Bigfoot. After a time, it becomes a nuisance for the road crew, including Dad, at times making it difficult to safely do their work. One particular fella by the name of Roger Patterson hangs around too much. My cousin says Dad finally tells the crew not to talk to any of the Bigfoot trackers, possibly for multiple reasons. I give Roger Patterson and Robert Gimblin a lot of credit for their movie-making abilities in 1967. It's definitely not one of Dad's gifts; he has his own fields of expertise.

As far as to what Patterson did or didn't do or as to what's real or not real, our family's opinion has always been the same. We can't attest to a yeti, Sasquatch, wendigo, grassman, abominable snowman, or any similar creature. We can tell you precisely who Bigfoot was. We can also tell you he had a Mrs. Bigfoot, his wife, and four Littlefeet. They roamed all around Northern California, Southern Oregon, and Southwest Washington. He's particularly fond of Southwest Washington in his later days.

Another interesting man Dad doesn't mind communicating with is Tom Slick Jr., who inherited a great sum of money from his father, Tom Slick Sr., the "King of the Wildcatters." He made his fortune during the early 1900s Oklahoma oil boom.

Tom Jr., well-educated, uses his fortune for scientific research, oil drilling (like his father), cattle breeding, exploration, and art collections.

Although this is where things get a little fuzzy, I bring him up because I believe that at one point, Dad, having communicated with Tom, receives an offer of a million dollars for the capture of a Bigfoot along with an iron cage to contain the critter. But I'm not sure. One thing I do know is Dad enjoys his conversations with Tom during that time.

A huge upside to all of this activity is Willow Creek, California, became the Bigfoot capital of the world, creating a regional economic boon. Dad should have received a medal instead of the at times not-so-friendly correspondence. We have no argument or ill will toward anyone seeking what may or may not live in the vast wilderness of this planet or any other.

Bigfoot becomes big economic boon to California town

TOURIST LURE: *Leaders in remote community hope Sasquatch seekers will find way to Trinity River area*

By Ralph Jennings
Record Searchlight

WILLOW CREEK, Calif. (AP) — This Trinity River town is staking its fortune on what could be a hoax.

With five lumber mills closed in response to federal logging limits, the 1,000-person community is turning to a tall, hairy, apelike guy for prosperity.

That's Bigfoot.

Town leaders hope he'll make people stop to shop in town along forested Highway 299 between Redding and Eureka.

"There was never a big push on it until we lost our lumber industry," said Max Rowley, a volunteer with the 90-member Willow Creek Chamber of Commerce. "We had to grab ahold of something else. As far as the chamber is concerned, (Bigfoot) is our slogan."

At the town museum, open Friday through Sunday, travelers can buy $10 casts of Bigfoot's alleged foot. Or they can snag a "Bigfoot Country California" cap for $5.49, a "BIG FOOT" mock license plate for $5.99 and three books about the human-ape hybrid's suspected sightings in Northern California.

DON'T FORGET the postcards and the miniature Bigfoot statues — starting at $3.99 — sold at Bigfoot Lumber.

paper ad that "Bigfoot loves our fajitas."

Every Labor Day weekend, Willow Creek celebrates Bigfoot Days with a parade. In Humboldt County near the border with Trinity County, Willow Creek also serves as a staging area for Bigfoot seekers.

PEOPLE COME from all over the world to look for Bigfoot, merchants say. This year a film crew came from Germany and researchers came from Reader's Digest.

About five times a week, visitors ask the Chamber of Commerce about Bigfoot's vital statistics and history. The chamber hands out a brochure and tallies the requests.

About once a week someone stops in at the U.S. Forest Service ranger station to ask about Sasquatch. The station recently ran out of Bigfoot brochures, said receptionist Marilyn Meza.

Bigfoot seekers may stay at the town's three motels and six bed-and-breakfasts, and patronize the stores and restaurants.

"You'd be surprised. Over the years, we get a lot of people in here," said Al Hodgson, who has lived in Willow Creek since 1933. "I get disgusted. We get so many who are there to catch them overnight, and it gets old."

Hodgson believes in Bigfoot and knows its entire unconfirmed history. Most people never see a mountain lion, but they all believe in mountain lions, he noted. He can't ignore Bigfoot evidence, including famed 1967 video footage and consistent reports of oversized humanlike footprints.

Bigfoot in Willow Creek, California

94

CHAPTER 13
RICHES TO RAGS

FOSTER MOUNTAIN MINE

DAD IS INTO EVERYTHING. As far back as I can remember, we always find huge piles of every kind of magazine, along with responses from people he's written to, on both sides of his easy chair. This drives Mom crazy because she always keeps tidy all the shacks or houses where we live. The articles he reads address oil drilling, logging, medical cures, mining, UFOs and, last but not least, making LP records.

At this time, we're near Willits, California, near a place called Foster Mountain. He has a road job and also reads somewhere about magnesium in the area to be mined. Here we are mining, road building, and still making Bigfoot tracks. The downside is that just as he hits a good vein of magnesium, the price drops bad enough he discontinues his mining. They finish the road work around June. This is one of the first times he goes backward financially.

From Willits, we move back to Oregon for a short time and find ourselves in Canyonville with no job.

Dad finds out his accountant, John Frankeur, is embezzling money from Yellow Creek Logging Corporation, our company. He's eventually convicted of tax evasion and sent to prison, but we don't get any of our money back. However, it explains why the bank account is lower than it should be. This, coupled with his earlier generosities, the mining misadventure, and, oh yeah, corrupt log scaling at a particular mill puts things in a temporary tailspin.

We were sure that the log scaling was not adding up to what it should have at the mill but had no way of proving it. Dad had a good idea of how much they should be getting for the logs we shipped from our landing site.

Ray isn't handling it well. He often comes home upset and takes it out on Mom. Nothing dramatic but definitely troublesome to her. Patience, though one of her gifts, is definitely strained at this point. She talks to Uncle Wilbur, who tells her, "Don't put up with that. Tell him off!" So, after several more times of his less-than-kind behavior, he's in the middle of a rant when she calmly says, "Don't you dare yell at me because you're having a bad day." He stands there looking like a deer in the headlights.

This is around Christmastime again. Mom isn't sure how this will pan out. She has a habit of dumping all her small change in a quart canning jar, which she keeps way up on a shelf above their bed. One day, as she's sitting on her bed counting what she has in the jar, I happen to come in and ask what she's doing. She says, "Just trying to see what we can do about Christmas presents for us." Mom mentions how, during the Depression one year, she was absolutely thrilled over receiving an orange—and only an orange—for Christmas. That helps put things in perspective and keeps it there.

CHAPTER 14
OAKRIDGE

IT'S LATE AUGUST, AND DAD HAS SECURED a ten-mile road job that will help us recover from our financial problems. Dad's been wise over the last fourteen years in that he slowly purchased six hundred acres back home in the Toledo area. So, we are land poor and working to protect what we own at this point.

Speaking for myself as a kid, it's not about what we had or didn't have; it's about where we've been, the great experiences we shared, and the people we lived and worked with. I'm thankful for the way Mom and Dad raised us, even during the hard times, which they never took out on us. We always felt secure and loved. What more could any kid want? Not bad for being adopted, huh?

Here in Oakridge, we are fortunate to be with Uncles Wilbur and Les, along with Ed von Schillinger, a cousin, and a few others, all with their families. The state just cleared a large area for a new dam, and Dad's been given the contract to build a new road around one side of what would soon be Hills Creek Lake and Dam. Construction starts in 1956 and finishes in 1961.

I'm in the sixth grade and having no issues in class. Gary and Larry are not doing well after being separated by their teacher for the first time. I think for talking too much. Larry struggles the most, grappling with his temper, while Gary's a teaser, not a great combo. Most of the time they play well together.

My issues are outside of class. Playing marbles is the thing, at least at Oakridge, at this time. I end up with a decent collection of marbles. Not everyone takes losing well. This tough-acting boy a year younger than me loses his marbles in more than one way.

One day after school, I'm standing near blackberry bushes, practicing my quick draw with my imitation pearl-handled Colt .45 in its holster, with the bottom of the holster tied firmly to my leg. The younger kid walks up and starts picking a fight. At this point in my life, I've never been in a fistfight. All of a sudden, I am! We end up in the blackberries.

I don't remember at all what he looked like when we finished, but when I got home, after explaining to Mom what happened, I pull off my shirt to clean the bloody scratches caused by wrestling in the blackberries. That kid must have landed twenty good punches to my midsection. I'm black and blue from my waist to my upper chest. This incident is so weird for me, never having been in a fistfight. I found it to be number one in a string of life-altering events, but this one has a very positive effect. There and then, I knew for a fact, I wanted to be a lover, not a fighter. Prizefighting was definitely out.

FAREWELL

Life seems back on track again. Wilbur, Les, my cousin, and Dad finally make good headway on the Hills Creek Dam project. The first quarter mile of the ten-mile road is brutal, nothing but solid rock, which means a lot of expensive dynamiting. This causes problems with the profit margin, but fortunately, the rock fizzles out and, from there on, nothing but dirt.

Fortunately for the men, it's a short drive home after work. Dad is back just before dark. Much of the time, he's late after dealing with problems at work, and Mom keeps his dinner warm in the oven. We all just finish eating, including Dad this time, when a knock sounds on the door. Mom opens it to see cousin Mickey, Uncle Les's son, with tears in his eyes, trying to speak. When he finally can get out the words, he says, "My dad's dead." It's hard to wrap our minds around what we hear. Mom brings Mickey inside, sits him on the sofa, and tells Dad to go over to Aunt Doris's to check on her. It's a horrible night and a huge loss. Uncle Les was one of the best.

The following day, Dad determines that when a tie-rod for the steering shook loose, Les lost control of his pickup, and it plunged over a steep bank. This is off the road they're building that runs along a cleared hillside where the dam and lake will be. When Les and his passenger went over the bank, the passenger stayed in the pickup, but Les decided to jump. As he was leaping out his door, it hit one of the hundreds of stumps on the cleared hillside, slamming it against Les, killing him instantly. The passenger survived. Later, we discover Les had worked on the tie-rod just days earlier. Dad suspected he forgot to tighten the nuts. No one really knows what happened. All we knew for sure is we just lost a great human being.

CHAPTER 15
SUTHERLIN

COUSIN MICKEY

AFTER THE DEVASTATING LOSS OF UNCLE LES, Doris, Mickey, and his sisters, Netha and Darlene, find a house close to the trailer park where we live in Sutherlin, Oregon. Our Fleetwood, now a twelve- by sixty-foot trailer, has two sets of bunk beds, one set for the twins and the other for Rick and me. It's a big step up from the smaller trailer we had. This is one of the nicer trailer parks we've lived in. It actually has fine crushed gravel to ride your bike on. This is where I upgrade my Schwinn Panther bicycle, which is unique because between the two upper crossbars running from the front of the frame to the seat it has a fancy cowling or cover where I painted a large firecracker with a lit fuse. I install tassels in the handlebar grips and two rearview mirrors, a horn, and a portion of my Yankees baseball trading cards attached to the front and rear

Butch with his Schwinn Panther in April 1960

99

frame that stick into the wheel spokes to create a cool sound. Mom's clothespins hold the cards to the frame. Mom lets me take my bike to cousin Mickey's. You would have thought I'm driving a Lamborghini with that bike pretty tricked out. I pedal over often to see Doris and Mick and the girls.

Something I've never forgotten about Mick; he's very good at playing baseball. After his baseball practices end, he has me come over to his house. Mick says to me, "You're left-handed. I want to teach you how to pitch a baseball." Up to this point, opportunities to play baseball are few and far between with moving from camp to trailer court so often. I jump at the chance to learn. After all, Yankees pitcher Whitey Ford was left-handed. How could I go wrong?

Mick is patient like his father, Uncle Les. After some time, I'm pretty comfortable pitching. I don't have much of a fastball, but I manage a decent curve. Left field, still a favorite, is where most of the outfield action takes place. I think educators try to get most of us to be right-handed; maybe not!

WHAT IS IN A NAME?

At the start of seventh grade, being officially named James Michael Wallace, I want to no longer be called "Butch." What self-respecting wonderful young girl wants to go out with someone named after a haircut. It works well in the logging camps, but here we are in the big city of Sutherlin, Oregon. So, I figure Jimmy works well with my pursuits, but that doesn't last long.

Midway through seventh grade, our teacher, with a tight jaw and pursed lips, marches into the classroom (now, we're talking about a woman who looks like she should have retired when Oregon became a state). She commands, "Of the five Jimmys in this classroom, four of you will, in no uncertain terms, show up in the morning with a new name!" So, here we go again. I come to school the next morning with the short version of my middle name, Michael. I'm now Mike. All is well, or so I thought.

Sometime later I start dating this babe named Roberta—smart, good-looking, what more could a seventh-grader want? So, my friends gibe me, giving pre-dating advice, saying, "Now this is what you want to do: ask her to go to the movies, but it has to be one of those scary ones. Your timing has to be just right. You wait 'til it comes to one of those real scary parts, and when she starts cringing, slip your arm around her to protect her. If she lets you keep it there, bingo, you've made it to first base. Also, don't forget to sit in the back row. One of two things may happen. She'll let you keep the arm there, or you may get punched for gettin' fresh. In that case, you may want a quick escape route." My friends at school are nothing short of pure genius. I'm sure at least one of them will turn out to be a rocket scientist.

So I ask Roberta if she wants to go with me to this Saturday matinee to see *The Pit and the Pendulum*. Without hesitation, she accepts the date. Awesome! I can't wait to tell my buddies. Each of our parents drops us off in front of the theater. I buy our tickets and immediately proceed to the back row of the theater after loading up on popcorn and Coca-Cola. After about a half hour into the movie, it starts getting scary. I'm more scared of my next move than what's happening on screen. Here it comes, the scary part of the movie. Noticing her cringing, I make my move. I stealthily slide my arm around her. To my amazement, she just kinda snuggles right in. By the end of the show, I no longer have any feeling in my right arm.

So, the show is over. We are holding hands outside, standing on the sidewalk, feeling pretty optimistic about our date! All of a sudden from the other side of Main Street, across two wide lanes of traffic, I hear my dad yell "BUTCH!" I immediately cringe, embarrassed by the name.

Knowing it was going to either be a long walk home or a second time of him yelling BUTCH, I acknowledge my dad. I offer a sheepish wave, and he gives both of us a ride home. After that, I'm sure our first date will be our last date. To my shock and awe, we date in a steady fashion until I'm informed we're moving for the twelfth time in my life. This is a tough one.

By the way, I inform Mom and Dad that, as long as they call me Butch, I will not, under any circumstances, answer to the name. It took about six months for the situation to become livable. This is the toughest move I make. Between Roberta and this crazy guy by the name of "Lucky," a good friend, I'm not eager to give up this place. Lucky is a character, sometimes a little too much of a one. Let's put it this way, hopefully he becomes a lawyer. I'm beginning to think he may need one on a steady basis.

At this point, just about all of my aunts, uncles, cousins and those we grew up with decide to move back to Washington, mostly the Toledo area.

So, it's the summer of '61 and we head, Fleetwood and all, back to where "Bigfoot" was raised: Toledo, Washington.

CHAPTER 16
BACK TO THE BEGINNING

BEFORE I TALK MUCH ABOUT TOLEDO, I want to mention something about my cousin Dale Lee. I appreciate him so much. He epitomizes so many of the men I grew up around in the logging camps—good, hardworking men with a sense of humor. He continues, to this day, telling me how much he enjoyed Dad, work or play, especially his good heart. He put a smile on a lot of faces and still does today.

Ray purchases an empty corner lot in Toledo for our home with wheels. This particular lot comes with a problem. If you look out our kitchen window at the front of the Fleetwood, you can see, kitty-corner across the street, an unoccupied house. Mom spends a fair amount of time standing in front of the kitchen sink, fantasizing about our family occupying it.

The eighth grade starts for me, with Larry and Gary going into the fourth grade and little Ricky hanging out at Mom's clothesline. Just kidding, Rick.

I don't know what it is about city life, but with a thriving metropolis of 499 people as of the last census, it seems like the four of us boys get into a little more trouble than usual. Or maybe we just like being amused by Dad's responses to Mom informing him of problems with us. Response No. 1 is, "You goofy little knothead." Response No. 2, "Why, you goofy harebrained screwball; you don't have a lick of sense." He offers response No. 3 when we are supposed to have done a chore a particular way, "Why, you goofy sucker;

you couldn't run a duck to water on a tiny island." Dad is always kind of loud but never mean to any of us.

WATER FOUNTAIN INCIDENT

I haven't been in Toledo long and just started the eighth grade. Unknown to me at the time, I'm in this new village and won't move again soon. Gary Springer, the principal, turns out to be a wonderful man. For me, personally, and for many others. I'm slowly getting to know my classmates and spend four-plus years with most of them.

One day, I'm in the hall drinking water before class when a girl walks up to me, and in a very angry voice says, "You're the ugliest guy I've ever seen!" It's like, Whoa, dudette. For the life of me, to this day, I don't have a clue what I did or said to ruffle her feathers. I've speculated on the incident but never came up with a good answer. There's probably a good reason why I can't remember anything about her other than what came from her mouth. I do know one thing. It was humbling, and I carried those words with me for a long time. My confidence is really good in a lot of things, but occasionally, when looking in the mirror, I'm haunted by that incident.

Speaking of Gary Springer, he's also the eighth-grade basketball coach. I know what a basketball is but have never picked up one much. Now, baseball is a different story, having weaseled its way into my DNA much earlier. With basketball season approaching and practice starting soon, Mr. Springer recruits players and asks me if I've played before. I tell him, "Not on a team, only shot a few times in my cousin's barn." I mostly watched my cousin practice and play against others. He even played against the famous Harlem Globetrotters once. Anyhow, Mr. Springer says, "Why don't you give it a shot?" So I say "Okay." I just want to be with my friends.

I'll never forget the first day of practice. I'm over by one of the baskets, trying to put the ball through the hoop, and Mr. Springer comes up and pulls me to the side. In his loving and calm manner, he says, "Mike, you shoot like a frog. We need to work on that." So, he spends a lot of his spare time trying to get me up to speed with a basketball. I really appreciate his patience and kindness. My skill level lags behind that of my friends, but I try my hardest to catch up.

I'm just thinking, maybe that unimpressed young girl at the water fountain saw me trying to shoot a basketball. Oh, well!

Being in Toledo in the eighth grade and realizing Mom and Dad are sinking their roots here feels great. We have two huge families of Sorensens and Wallaces around. What more could we want?

Eighth-grade Toledo basketball team in 1962

EASY MONEY

Ray is no longer logging. He either clears land or does what he's a master at, road construction. Some road jobs involve stacking timber along the road.

Dad finishes a small job near Pe Ell, west of Chehalis, Washington, and prepares to haul the bulldozer home. He happens to stop at a cafe in Pe Ell and overhears a conversation between two men sitting at a table next to his. One, who happens to be a contractor, tells the other to fulfill his road contract agreement and finish a certain stretch of road within the next two days.

Dad, who apparently knows the area he's talking about, pops up and asks the guy what he would pay to complete it in time. He says, "I'll give you $5,000 to get it from point A to point B." Dad says, "I'll get it done for you." They shake on it with plenty of witnesses around.

What looks impossible to the contractor really isn't. Dad, who is more familiar with the area, knows about an old railroad grade running through the area. He just needs to connect point A to one end of the railroad grade and point B to the other end. Clearing the old grade is easy because it's mostly covered with brush and young trees. Dad moves his dozer out there that night and goes home.

At sunrise he's topping the dozer's tank with diesel and checking the oil. He finishes at sunset. Just a little thinking outside of the box does the trick. He has one happy customer.

ALMOST HOG HEAVEN

Entering my freshman year, I find out Toledo High School offers woodshop and mechanical drawing, all-in-one. I just know I'll love it. Our teacher is Mr. Roeder, a no-nonsense kinda guy. It wasn't long before three of us find out Mr. Roeder doesn't like repeating himself. We talk multiple times when asked not to. I think Mr. Roeder is curious to see if the three of us appreciate his woodworking talents.

He pulls this menacing-looking wood paddle full of holes out of his desk, lines us up, and explains the structural dynamics of his piece of art, telling us the holes allow his artwork to move faster through space, with a stronger effect on what it contacts. "Now bend over and grab your ankles." Next thing I know is whammm! Talk about an efficient board of education; I just met one. We become model students from then on. It doesn't take long before I don't want to be anywhere else but shop and drawing—well, maybe the baseball field. What a way to finish the day.

I'm not going to dive into the whole discussion of disciplining a child. All I know is that in that era with parental support and administration knowing their staff, it works well. Mel Roeder is one of the best and most respected teachers I ever had. Partly due to this man, I built a wonderful career designing and building homes.

The first year of design covers mainly the basics. Our sophomore year, our first big design project is to measure and draw floor plans and elevations of the home where we live. Thank goodness I didn't need to draw up our Fleetwood

Elna's dream home

trailer anymore because Mom's dream came true. In December, with the home kitty-corner to us still available, Dad strikes an amazing deal with the kind widow lady who owns the home.

We move in just before Christmas. It's like moving into a castle, skeleton keys and all, with only one big thing missing—no shrubs or flowers around the outside. It takes a few years to mature what Mom plants, but later she wins first prize in Toledo's yearly contest for the best yard in town. If they still held the contest today, my sister-in-law Donna, little Ricky's wife, would win it with her eight-foot Bigfoot statue included in the landscape. They put a Santa's hat and lights on Bigfoot every Christmas.

Speaking of little Ricky. In our new castle, we enter through the side door, which opens up to the kitchen. If you walk straight ahead, you come to the hall. If you take a left, you'd need to take another left into the main dining area, then another left to end up back in the kitchen. My point being, this could be used as a racetrack, which is exactly what we use it for from time to time.

More often than not, the race includes Dad chasing me down with his Army belt in hand, saying, "You goofy little screwball; you don't have a lick of sense!" or one of his other forms of verbiage.

It never occurs to me that the reason I never get caught is something other than my great speed and agility. A light bulb finally goes off in my brain one day when little Ricky is the "goofy harebrained screwball," and Mom and I watch the race from the kitchen table. It sounds like Dad actually corners him in the bedroom off the hall. We just figure little Ricky panicked and took a wrong turn. We begin to hear Rick howling in the bedroom behind its closed door along with the sound of the belt.

We get concerned, and I follow Mom as she carefully cracks open the bedroom door. Mom peeks in, then turns and motions me to look. There they are. Rick's sitting on the bed making these mournful sounds as loud as he can. Dad stands next to him, beating the snot out of the bed. Both wear these big smiles on their faces. I'm obviously not the track star I figured I was. Past all the bluster, Dad has a mighty soft heart for everyone.

CAVALRY TO THE RESCUE

Being a freshman at the high school is awesome with all these new people to meet. The best part is that I have backup and don't think I need such a thing. We eat hot lunch down at the grade school, and I'm on my way back, climbing the last thirty yards or so of a fairly steep hill to the side door of our high school.

Unknown to me, a welcoming committee of two waits for new students in town. These two call me out and threaten to beat the snot out of me. If they hadn't spent so much time mouthing off, they might have had a chance to do their thing, but their long-windedness apparently gave someone time to send word to two of my Sorensen cousins, who are on the football team.

They charge out the side door at those two yayhoos. They don't say a word. Those two bullies, not knowing the tribe I belonged to, crawl away, never to bother me again. My advantage in Toledo is I had to go only about thirty feet before running into a relative. One of my cousins happens to be the top rusher in our league with 11.6 yards per carry. Four of the league's top five rushers are Toledo boys.

TOLEDO INDIANS

On October 12, 1962, I keep statistics for our football team and, after each game, call *The Daily Chronicle* sports desk with results. The bus is all loaded and ready for the forty-five-mile trip to Pe Ell. I'm sitting up front with the coaches and cheerleaders with the team behind us. The wind grows stronger the farther we drive. We're more than halfway there when the wind blows seriously. The bus enters a long straight stretch of the road with tall fir trees on each side.

All of a sudden, about two hundred yards beyond us, a large fir falls over the road, a frightening sight. Being in front, we have a good view of what happens. By this time, the cheerleaders are not doing well. Coach Hippi tells the bus driver to turn around as soon as possible, which he does. I still can't believe no trees fell down behind us as we turn around. That part is like slow motion.

We don't realize we're in the middle of a category 3 hurricane, which turns out to be the worst recorded windstorm in the Pacific Northwest's history, now called the Columbus Day Storm. By the grace of God, we return to Toledo unscathed.

The last game of the year, we always play our rival neighbors, the Winlock Cardinals. Rumor spreads that one of the Cardinals swiped our victory bell mounted on a post at the end of the football field. I'm contacted by two of my Sorensen cousins. At the time, their father owns a chicken farm. They want to know if I'll help with something.

The boys pick me up and head back to their place to fill the back of a pickup with chicken manure. Late at night, when we have it loaded and ready, we head to Winlock. Someone helped them sew together what looks like a large stuffed cardinal bird. The plan is to stealthily pile the manure on the fifty-yard line in the middle of the field.

We are off to Winlock, giddy with anticipation. With lightning speed and great stealth, we spread the manure in place. We then grab the stuffed cardinal and put it head-first in the center of the pile. Mission accomplished! Fortunately, not a creature was stirring, not even a cardinal, as we left the metropolis of Winlock.

Friday night, it's time to take on the Cardinals. It's a sloppy, muddy game, and we do what we came to do. At the end of the night, the score is Toledo 19, Winlock zip. We finished second in state that year. At this time, it's a ballot rating system, not playoffs.

The crew in our castle

OUR CASTLE

We settle into our castle, where Gary, Larry, and Ricky share the large bedroom. I call it the barracks with three twin beds and a small closet. None of the three complain about being in one room together. It's much more space than we're used to. For the first time in my life, I have my own room, a small bedroom next to the barracks. It's so cool to have my own space. Being the concrete sequential type, everything needs to be tidy.

Mom and Dad's bedroom is at the far end of the hall on the other side of our one bathroom. Every evening, as we head to bed, Mom and Dad's bedroom door stays open. If you happen to pass by their door, you "always" see Mom down on her knees, praying. Dad comes to bed later. Most evenings you find him sitting in his easy chair in the living room. On both sides is the usual scene. He reads something from his enormous stacks of magazines, newspapers, journals, and letters, perhaps trying to find a homeopathic cure for someone. Or he's writing a letter to the US president, telling him how to fix a certain problem, or another letter informing Rockefeller he could help him drill for oil in Washington. Sometimes, he simply sits there, contemplating where he and my cousin will make more Bigfoot tracks.

Mom sees to it now that we all attend church on a regular basis. I remember a couple things about church well. The first is Kenny McEwen, my Sunday school teacher, and our class. Brock and I are the only two boys in Kenny's class. Brock goes on to be lifelong friends with me and my dad. Later, Dad becomes a constant source of entertainment for Brock. Our teacher, Kenny, is a real special guy, a patient and caring person, almost like a second Dad. Kenny cares about character building. The second thing I remember is going on a date with the pastor's daughter. I don't remember where we were, but she kisses me with conviction. Being the first time, I don't know what to do. That kissing stuff catches me off guard. After all, I've only just gotten used to holding hands with girls.

Elna's kitchen

ELNA'S KITCHEN

Mom's kitchen is a special gathering place for relatives and my friends. After 10 a.m., with her pies, cakes, cookies, and warm heart, she welcomes whoever feels like dropping in. One or two at a time, uncles, aunts, or cousins show up on a steady basis. Mom is not only a fabulous Danish baker; she's a great listener.

In contrast to Dad, I took to heart all her sayings, like, "Waste not, want not" or "Eat what you put on your plate; just think of those kids who don' t have anything and are starving." My favorite all-time one is, "It takes just as much energy to be nasty as it does to say something nice." I remember coming home one day from school and telling her one of my relatives says I'm not a real Wallace because I'm adopted. She says, "You just thank the good Lord you don't have any of his genes." That helped. I'd been teased before over simply being adopted, but not by family. She took the bite out of it for me, offering a better perspective and several of her cookies. She is one fine lady.

WILD ANIMAL FARM

Ray's love for children led him to open what may be the area's only free zoo. He begins collecting animals from all over the world and throughout the United States. He owns white African fallow deer,

White African fallow and Japanese sika

Japanese sika deer, reindeer, buffalo, and a Rocky Mountain bull elk from Wyoming (called Mr. Ed). He also has black deer from India and tame rabbits running around everywhere. He lets parents take a small rabbit home since they're so prolific.

The animal farm is on twenty-five acres, surrounded by twelve-foot cedar fence posts painted alternating red, white, and blue. A large barn contains feed and hay storage. Dad has a large wooden box attached to a post with small paper sacks filled with oats that a child or parent can grab to feed the animals. He puts up a small donation box if anyone feels like dropping in a coin. The idea in Dad's mind is that all children, rich or poor, need the opportunity to see and feed exotic animals.

Dad buys a small burger bar at the mouth of the Lewis River north of Kalama and moves it to the animal farm. He adds a dining area facing the animals so families can shelter out of the weather if it's raining. Mom cooks a dynamite burger and earns enough to pay the feed bill during the year. She also gets us through the winter when Dad can't work.

Unfortunately, I have only a few limited pictures of the wild animal farm, which isn't a "happily ever after" story. A dozen years later, the head of Washington's wonderful Game Department decided to take Dad to court, accusing him of keeping an elk native to the state of Washington in captivity. Both sides argue their case.

Later, we return to court. I remember sitting on an aisle seat about halfway up on the right. This particular case has drawn attention, so the courtroom is reasonably full. I turn to look back as the Game Department official walks by. All I remember is his bloodshot eyes peeking out of a stern-looking face. The judge comes in a few minutes later, and we all rise. The judge says he has reached a decision: "I find the defendant, Ray L. Wallace, not guilty." The crowd cheers.

Although I have a theory as to what happened over the following year, I'll keep it to myself. Dad receives a notification from the State of Washington's Department of Transportation (DOT), saying they're constructing an overpass with no on or off ramps, which will cut off access to the free zoo. Dad contacts the DOT and offers to build the on and off ramps at his expense, which he's quite capable of doing. Their answer to him is simply no. A real headshaker.

CASTLE INVASION

By the summer of 1963, Bigfoot is in full bloom for Ray L. Wallace. A constant stream of Bigfoot seekers visit our home. Mom grows pretty tired of it. Just about every kind of humanity you could imagine shows up. Dad

Reserve buffalo on Dad's ranch in 1988, above, and Dad feeding critters at the animal farm

fills them full of sunshine and sends them on their way, happier than they were before they came. Mom often hears, "Elna, fix these guys something to eat." She feels like she's running a restaurant.

If not visitors, the phone rings with a constant stream of phone calls from disc jockeys from the Pacific to the Atlantic. Calls for Bigfoot info usually come from 6 p.m., when Dad normally returns home from work, to sometimes 3 a.m. (call from St. Louis). This 3 a.m. DJ likes having Dad on his talk show and knows how to encourage him. This guy's talk show starts at 6 a.m., St. Louis time. He wants Dad live, I guess. During many interviews, Dad leads that DJ down more rabbit holes than there are rabbits.

Dad not only lights the "Bigfoot match," he also feverishly fans its flames with an industrial-size imagination.

In the fall, with football season starting, I thought I'd have more fun playing than keeping stats, so I sign up. The practices are an eye-opener. It's much different than basketball or baseball, all new to me. After the first few practices, it's time to do hitting, lineman on lineman. I'm a newbie sophomore lined up across from a senior. Next thing I know, I'm lying on my back with no oxygen in my lungs. Coach Hippi looms over me, grabbing me by my belt. While he's trying to pump air back into my lungs, he says, "You're not going to die." I seriously need to hear that. Things get much better from then on. I eventually learn how to hold my ground, mostly.

CHAPTER 17
TOLEDO (CONTINUED)

THE UNEXPECTED

THE SUMMER OF 1964 ends with an interesting twist and starts with a job. Mrs. Cattermole, who runs the Toledo funeral home, needs someone to completely clear the hillside below the funeral home so it can be planted with ground cover. She offers me $2.50 an hour, which is top dollar for a fifteen-year-old country kid. Mrs. Cattermole is great to work for and always brings me lemonade and treats me with kindness.

During this time, it's also Babe Ruth baseball season, and our team does great, due to the fact that Rob Hippi, our high school coach's son, plays on our team. We have some good athletes, but Rob is gifted in all three sports. He has the best fastball in the county. Having to bat against him in practice definitely hones my hitting abilities. We are both picked for the Lewis County all-star team. I clearly remember going to Aberdeen for a game. Aberdeen, a large town supported by sawmills and logging, has a large stadium. I remember coming out of the locker room onto the field, never having seen

o, Rob Hippi, Mike Wallace, and Jerry Chastain.

PITCHING RECORDS					
	W	L	Pct.	I.P.	E.R.A.
Mike Wallace	1	0	1000	18	2.10
Robin Hippi	8	4	.800	70	0.69
Arne Sippola	1	1	.500	16	2.48
Dan Wallace	2	3	.400	29	2.40

Rob Hippi, Mike Wallace, and Jerry Chastain

anything like it before. It resembles walking into Yankee Stadium. Speaking of Yankee Stadium, Rob was drafted by the Yankees his senior year after winning the national championship with Central Washington State College in Ellensburg, Washington.

Another surprise that summer, which seemed to already be full of them, occurs in mid-summer when Dad comes up to me and says, "Your birth mom, Ruby, is downtown. Do you want to meet her? She's down at Engers Grocery." I clearly remember my response, which was, "I don't know; do you want me to?" With that he said, "Let's go." So, off we went. I remember walking through the front door, seeing this pretty blonde lady off to the right, not knowing it was Ruby. Dad directs me to where she stands. I remember being comfortable and positive, mainly due to being raised by two awesome parents. It doesn't upset me or leave any negative ramifications. Ray and Elna never hid anything from us boys as far as being adopted. They couldn't have handled it any better.

I didn't know until recently that Rudy, Ruby's brother, worked as the meatcutter at Engers Grocery. I'd seen him many times working there, never realizing how we were related. The world can be pretty small at times.

Sorry to say, I never see Ruby again. She died in an auto accident several years later.

In the fall of '64, I'm a junior and loving Toledo High School. My favorite classes are still woodshop/drawing (industrial arts) and baseball. I make it through football relatively unscathed, but now it's basketball season. I don't shoot like a frog anymore but still look like I'm pretty new at the sport. Same with football. The cool part is being part of the team. I love that camaraderie.

After one of our basketball games, usually a home game, a bunch of us head up the freeway to the Skyline Restaurant for a soda. That's a popular hangout in our part of the county. If you remember, back in 1942, Dad met the TV western star Roy Rogers. Well, we're all sitting around, laughing, having a good time when in walks Roy's sidekick, Pat Brady. It creates quite a stir. Pat walks in with a fella who was driving—what else but a Jeep, similar to the one he drove on the television show? We quickly determine that (1) it's a good thing he's not driving and (2) he's in no condition to sign autographs. We have a lot of fun talking to him, though. He was a pretty happy-go-lucky type of guy headed to Seattle. Hopefully, he made it in one piece.

Being the youngest in my class doesn't help when it comes to sports. I'm still glad I didn't start a year later in the first grade because I wouldn't have this great class.

Driver's ed is fun because our instructor is our coach, Mr. Hippi, a Little All-American collegiate football player. He knows his business when it comes to coaching. We drive all around the countryside, talking sports nonstop. It makes the time pass quickly and works well for us. Most of us already learned to drive a hay truck on someone's farm.

LIFE IS GOOD

The spring of '65 means baseball is here, which is really fun. I'm getting my batting average up over .300 and relief pitching after Rob Hippi wears out the other team's batters. My slow roundhouse curve is my specialty. The trick is to just give me one inning. Batters soon realize all I have is a pretty curve, and nothing but a slowball compared with Rob after that. One or two innings pitching is enough. I'm happy to be back out in left field, waiting for my next at bat. I meet my goal to finish over .300. Can't wait for next year.

I spend the summer working for Mom at the wild animal farm burger bar. I love working for her. I still have the guest book Dad kept in the restaurant. We greet regulars from Southern California and the East Coast. My cousin David puts up a small glass-blowing shop next to our restaurant that tourists also love. I remember one day this couple from Germany comes inside, places their order, and while at the window waiting, see my brother changing the fryer grease. When he spills hot grease on his foot, the German lady immediately says to my mom, "Grab some fresh potato peels and put them face down on that burn!" Fortunately, Mom uses fresh potatoes for her French fries. She grabs the peelings and applies them to Gary's foot. We can't believe how quickly it draws the heat and pain from of his foot with no scarring later.

Another time, Dad returns in the afternoon from work. First thing he normally does is check the large box with the small bags of feed to be sure it contains plenty. For some reason, Dad walks out in the middle of the field. We don't know he's out there, but Mom happens by a window and yells for me to come over. We watch Dad being chased by a bull buffalo. He just makes it to the ten-foot fence and up far enough as the bull rams it, no exaggeration here. He climbs up and over the fence. Dad's a big guy. I still don't know how he made it up that fence that fast.

Another incident at the animal farm involves Mr. Ed, our enormous bull elk. During his rutting season, being kind and docile isn't up there on his to-do list, and for the first time, Dad becomes concerned for the safety of some of the smaller deer. He entices Mr. Ed into a barn stall about fifteen by twenty feet. He rigs a come-along with a hook on it to a beam above. After wrapping a rope around Mr. Ed's horns somehow despite all the bull thrashing, Dad hooks on the come-along, then ratchets Mr. Ed up on his back legs. Wow, that's the easy part. Next, as the big bull continues to express his unhappiness, Dad proceeds to dehorn him with a hacksaw. It's bizarre Dad doesn't get injured. He and the bull make it out safe and sound.

ADVICE?

During our senior year, Mr. Roeder allows us to design and build great projects.

Mine is a king-size walnut four-poster bed. That and baseball capture most of my attention during the year.

Now, according to the grownups, it's high time we students consider our future. I'm thinking industrial arts and baseball are sufficient for the time being. It seems they want to give us something called a college placement exam. So, I've checked all the boxes, and we wait for the test results. I'm scheduled to meet with my advisor.

When we meet in the library, he's checking my paperwork, probably trying to figure out what pearl of wisdom to pass along. Now, you have to remember, in the mid-1960s, they have yet to discover anything about the seven intelligences, right? He says, "You should consider this special course they're offering this summer at Centralia College. Boeing is hiring many draftsmen." I told him that sounded good to me. So for now, I'm good to go.

Toledo Indian football captures four league championships in a row. We have balloting in our days, not playoffs. In state, we place second, third, third, and sixth. For almost fifty years, we hold the state record of forty-eight consecutive league wins. It's special being a part of that. Every one of us boys would do anything to stay on that team, which made me think back to the first few weeks of football practice. Coach Hippi comes into the locker room as we suit up for practice with advice for us. "If you want to play football this year, you

Mixed Chorus' First Year Is Success

MIXED CHORUS — Front row, left to right: Jo Anne Nanamkin, Colleen Bowen, Sherrie Holland, Pattie Schroeder, Delly Horton, Judy Schoonover, Sally Johnson and Mr. Ronald James, director. Second row: Dorlene Hinkley, Clara Lowens, Ethel Finney, Jean Hancock, Becky McKinley, Nancy Boggs, Mary Jo Herren and Debby Foster. Third row: Carol Clark, Mary Francy, Leni Thomas, Christine Herren, Alyce Stralee, Linda Henkine, Fran Wooley and Billie Rogen. Fourth row: Barbara Zion, Marilyn Fish, Daniel Smith, Dave Francy, Jerry Cook, Dick Spuin, Jo Ann Jones and Cheryl Homar. Fifth row: Mike Young, Don McEwen, Bill Ludlow, Mark Hile, Gordon Kalich, Mike Wallace, Ken Mahoney and Dennis Davis. Sixth row: Karl Breidenstein, Jerry Ghastain, Randy Cavardell, Ken Norberg, Arne Sippala, Greg Armstrong, Doug Nisbel and Brock Brinson.

Football players had to perform in the mixed chorus

will join Mr. James' new mixed chorus he is putting together." Needless to say, Mr. Ron James had all the male vocal cords he needed.

Mr. James, also our new varsity basketball coach, leads us to state. At the first of the year, the team has ten spots open. He makes it clear to me that I need improvement if I want to fill that last spot. I can't imagine missing that tenth spot. Of all the different sports we play, baseball is the only one I really feel comfortable with, but I want to be a part of all the sports teams. I love the effect of teamwork on me. Working as hard as I could, I fill the last spot. At least I'm pretty sure it was No. 10. During the whole process, I felt like a frog out of water, trying to be a prince.

So here we are, qualified for state and on our way to Spokane. We won our first game 58 to 37 and lost our second by two points. I mostly keep my part of the bench fairly warm, which isn't a problem. Being a part of this is a great experience. Having jumped over to the losers' bracket, we're given free time to explore the immediate area. We're staying in the same hotel as a couple of other teams in our league. With the way things are going, our free time is one bright spot, you might say. I'm walking down the hall from our rooms, wearing my letterman sweater with its four stripes on the left arm, a big T with a tiny football, basketball, and baseball on it, plus three football-shaped patches that read '63 champs, '64 champs, and '65 champs. Here come four

VARSITY BASKETBALL — Front row, left to right: Mike Wallace, Brock Brinson, Gene Cole, Rob Hippi, Danny Wallace, and assistant coach, Mr. Jerry Glaze. Second row: Cliff Spencer, Arne Sippola, Ken Norberg, Dennis Boone, Randy Coverdell, and Mr. Ron James, coach.

cheerleaders from one of the other schools. One of them says, "Would you like to escort us around?" So, with two on one side and two on the other, we spend a portion of the day walking the streets of Spokane. I don't feel so bad about getting off the bench during the final minutes of the last game we lost.

FIRST SET OF WHEELS

I don't remember all the circumstances, but Dad needs a small loan. Mom and Dad are land poor, and the wild animal farm's feed bill isn't a small one. They own six hundred acres of river bottom and small parcels around Toledo. Not wanting to mortgage any of it, Dad asks me what I've saved at this point. He says he just needs it for a short time until he's paid for the job he's working. My response is, "No problem."

So, in December, he pays back the $2,500. He knows I want to buy a car like he did at this age. Dad suggests we take a trip to Ron Tonkin Chevrolet in Portland. On the way down, he says what we need to do is look for a new '64 model that's been there since last year. I'll save a fair amount. They'll want to get rid of it. Dad wrangles a good price of $3,000 for a white '64 Chev Impala with a stick shift on the column. Dad says, "I'm paying the balance for loaning me the $2,500." Unreal. Driving that baby back to Toledo is right up there with peanut butter and jelly.

I go to work on the renovation of that baby. Mag wheels are the first change. Second, I remove the steering column gear shift and install a chrome Hurst floor shift. Third, I paint her a deep royal blue, my all-time favorite color.

SOUTH OF THE BORDER

Months later, a friend tells me about a place in Tijuana that does excellent upholstery work for much less than anywhere in the United States. After figuring out what I want, I schedule an appointment and set a price. By myself, at sixteen years old, I head for Tijuana. They take my car right in and tell me I should check back later in the afternoon when it'll be finished.

You can only do so much browsing in shops. Past lunchtime, I decide to buy something to eat and drink. I go into the closest bar, walk through the main door and to the bar on the right. As soon as I turn, I find myself two feet away from a woman standing naked on the bar. After the shock wears off, I slowly do a one-eighty and head back out the door. Being in a bit of a daze, I find a place that seems focused only on food and drink. The only envelope I push that day is drinking a beer with my tacos.

Later that day, I check back with the shop and find them closed. At this point, I stay close to the shop until they finish their work. When I'm called in to see the finished product, I'm stunned. The job they did is absolutely beautiful with a blue leather interior, all tucked and rolled. I could not be more pleased. I pay them, elated to hit the road so I can show my friends.

A NEW VILLAGE

I have no question in my mind that, for the last six years, a superior village raised me. The following are only a few of the key people who had a positive impact on this season of my life.

❑ Gary Springer, principal and coach—He's patient, caring, and every year around Thanksgiving, he puts together food baskets. He knows the needs from running the grade school. I remember one year buying a turkey and giving it to him for his drive. The smile on his face was worth every penny.

❑ Mel Roeder, industrial arts teacher—My one and only whack with his board of education produced great respect, but more than that, he drew the best out of us.

MEL ROEDER
Industrial Arts
Printing

❑ Luke Asper, geometry teacher—He was a soft-spoken man who, at his worst, still had a genuine smile. He gave sound advice, and I'm not referring to geometry. He asked me to stay after class one day just to find out how things were going. I think he saw things in me that others didn't. I had been going with this girl, but he was advising me to think a little more about my future and where I might be headed and, for example, create a better vision for myself. My advisor told me not to bother with college. I think Luke saw something else in me that my advisor didn't. He created a very positive environment where I was able to thrive.

Geometry class

❑ Coach Hippi—He knew how to draw out of a kid all the mental and physical aspects it took to make champions. I think we had one of the smallest-sized lines on any football team in our league. I remember one game where half of the opposition's line was close to 250 pounds each. Coach quickly figured out they were not very fast with all that weight. They couldn't

MR. HIPPI
Advisor

119

outrun us, so he simply ran plays away from them or to their weak points. Being a Little All-American in college, he was made for coaching. As our principal, he was a balanced disciplinarian.

❑   My entire class of '66—I can't think of one fellow student I had a problem with. We had between forty-five and fifty kids in our class. We knew everyone reasonably well. It was a wonderful environment to grow in.

❑   Ray and Elna—What can I say? For an adopted kid, I continue to be greatly blessed. Mom always offered consistent encouragement and advice and never rammed it down our throats. She always gave it with patience and in a loving manner. I don't know how many times I heard, "If you can't say anything nice, don't say anything at all." She remained consistently strong and steadfast. She had to, being married to a whirlwind. Ray L. was something else, with more irons in the fire than Pittsburgh Steel. To me it was either, "Think big, Son, think big," or "Boy, you're a good worker." Those were confidence builders. Dad had his weak points; he was not perfect. But he had a big heart and knew how to care for others.

❑   Brock Brinson has remained a special friend to this day. We played sports together year-round. Everyone liked Brock, including Dolly, one of our cheerleaders. By our sophomore year in high school, Brock was ready to marry Dolly, not just because she was cute, but because she was wise enough to wait it out until he returned from the service. Later, Brock connected with Dad through their work. Little did he know what endless entertainment would come from their friendship.

❑   Gordon Kalich was a unique individual and friend. His dad, Hugh "Bud" Kalich, the state representative for our district, was reelected many times. Everyone in our class thought Gordon would take his place someday with his gift of gab and command of the language. In English class one day, Gordon stood in front of the class and recited a long poem, Rudyard Kipling's "Gunga Din." No doubt he was good at making speeches and created for politics. We continued crossing paths after high school. Gordon never missed an opportunity to partake of Mom's pies and pastries, which were always available; he loved his food.

❑   Gene Cole was another good friend throughout high school. We also continued to cross paths after graduating. Gene was quite the athlete, our version of Marshawn Lynch on the football field but also a gentle giant liked by all of us.

❑   Kenny McEwen—My Sunday school teacher for about four years, a second father type. What more can you say.

Being raised in several villages over my first seventeen years of life, I look back and think of how fortunate I was to consistently be surrounded by such safe, strong, and steady people. I'm so grateful that Mom and Dad decided it was time to discontinue moving our family from logging camp to logging camp and job to job so I could develop irreplaceable lifelong friendships and experiences. It was a loving and wise decision.

Whatever follows this point in my life, good or bad, leaves me with no excuses. Whether I take a right path or wrong one, it's totally on me and no one else.

TIJUANA 2.0

Dad has a heart for people suffering with cancer. Part of that large pile of magazines and papers by his easy chair contains medical articles. Somewhere in one of those many articles is one that tells of a clinic working on a cure for cancer using Pau d' Arco bark from Tabebuia trees, an old Brazilian herb used by the Inca tribes as one of their most important herbs for healing. Today, it's still used to treat infections and cancer.

Dad asks me if I will go back to Tijuana to pick up a load of what they're using to fight cancer. I tell him sure since I've been down there before. It doesn't seem like any big deal, until he gets to the part about Pau d' Arco not yet being approved by the Food and Drug Administration. He wants me to smuggle it back into the United States. He says, "I've been thinking that when you get to the clinic, what you do is, pull up your rear seat and stash the medicine under it. You shouldn't have any problem." Easy for you to say, I'm thinking.

Friday comes, and I hit the road to our southern border again. The clinic is on the far side of Tijuana up a hill. I admit I'm a little concerned about one area I drive through, but all goes smoothly. At the clinic after I pay for the medicine, they wish me luck crossing back over the border. With the Pau d' Arco hidden, I'm in line at the border, slowly edging forward, growing more nervous each time I move. By the time I make it to the guard, I feel like I'm transporting a ton of illicit something. I think what saves me is not steel nerves but pure ignorance. At this period of my life in Toledo, my friends and I think of "dope" as a glue you sniff, not something called marijuana. Anyhow, the nice officer must think the heat is causing all that perspiration on my forehead.

Dad receives a big load of medicine that he starts giving away to help anyone who takes it.

One of my favorite stories of Dad's medical missions concerns Walt Clark's sister. Walt hasn't lived in the area long. Dad found out doctors gave his sister in Longview, Washington, two months to live because of an aggressive cancer in her cheek. Dad asks Walt if he will take him to see his sister; he agrees. Dad tells her he has something to fight the cancer. She says she has no insurance and certainly can't afford any medicines. She barely has enough to live on as it is. Dad says she should at least try the medicine at no cost to her. She

Demand Quality and Accept No Imitations!

A Cup of Prevention

BRAZILIAN 100% NATURAL
PAU D'ARCO
HERBAL TEA

This ancient HERB has been used for centuries because of its PREVENTIVE PROPERTIES. We import the finest BRAZILIAN PAU D'ARCO HERB to make this wonderful beverage for the whole family to enjoy.

PAU D'ARCO is a famous South American HERB. It is often referred to by its other Spanish names: IPE ROXO, TAHEEBO, LAPACHO, TABEBUIA BOW STICK. PAU D'ARCO is the inner bark of a very large tree that blooms in colors of pink, purple, or yellow depending on the species of TABEBUIA.

Throughout South America, PAU D'ARCO IS USED AS A REMEDY. It was one of the major healing HERBS used by the INCA tribes. People of INDIA also use it for similar problems.

With heart in hand

lived another five years. Many times during that five-year period, she tells Walt that when she took Dad's Pau d' Arco, she felt a difference. Dad continues to check in on her as much as he can, always making sure she has what she needs.

PART TWO

THE GOOD, THE BAD, THE UGLY

CHAPTER 18
LEAVING THE VILLAGE

LOOKING BACK

IN RETROSPECT, THROUGH THE EYES OF AN ELDER, I could not have been given a better start in life. Balance always surrounded me, and I never feel like we lived on the edge. Don't get me wrong; our village wasn't perfect, but we had each other's back when it counted. You always felt safe, cared for, and loved.

In a perfect world, a parent would pass along nothing but good things, but we make mistakes and choices that get in the way.

I have come to look at being adopted as a major plus in life. I hit the jackpot with parents who had a choice whether to have me or not. As soon as I was old enough to understand what being adopted meant, all was revealed to me concerning my adoption. Nothing like being open and honest! Sooner or later, it reaps great rewards.

SEVENTEEN

Seventeen years of age seems to be the magic number for total independence, at least for me. I know just about everything. I'm overqualified for decision-making and have yet to learn that the human male's brain is barely developed enough at age twenty-five to qualify for a lower driver's insurance rate. I am beginning to make life-changing decisions in the last half of my senior year while enjoying my first serious relationship with a girl. She's from a neighboring school. This, of course, has a noticeable effect on me. The first to get hit is wood shop. I had gone three years straight without as much as a scratch.

While I was planing a piece of wood and focusing on my girlfriend instead of what I'm doing, the planer blade nicks the end of my finger. It's bloody but not bad. I ask my teacher to bandage it, so I can still slip on my baseball glove. We have a game in about an hour. He lectures me on paying attention around power equipment, a reminder I need at this time. This isn't the only place I need focus.

My girlfriend not only regularly attends all my games but now also practices. I normally keep tabs on my batting average, but as the end of baseball season approaches, I'm thinking more about her than about batting averages. My average sinks from .500 mid-season to .345. I don't blame it all on her, only partially. Our relationship looks more like a marriage, way too serious at this age. Only after the fact do I wish I had paid more attention to what my teacher, Mr. Asper, was trying to tell me, "Slow down and think a little more about your future."

Earlier in the year, I accidentally stumble across what they call a girlie magazine, which in those days is nothing less than porn and absolutely will not enhance a decent relationship, especially a marriage. What do I know? It's something I carry into this next chapter of my life, and it does nothing positive for my future relationships whatsoever.

HEAD HIM OFF AT THE PASS

It's Friday night, and Dad's late for dinner. We all finish eating when Mom receives a phone call. After hanging up the phone, she says to me, "Get your car ready; I need a ride to Chehalis." We're in the car, heading to this restaurant, when I ask her what's going on.

"You'll find out soon enough" is all she says. We arrive and stride toward the back of the restaurant to the lounge. There, sitting at a small table, is Dad, his new younger buddy, and this woman. Mom wastes no time as she heads straight to their table. She says, "Ray Wallace, you get yourself home where you belong this instant." She turns to me and says, "Get me out of here." We drive home, and Dad isn't far behind us. They don't yell or scream, thank goodness. But Dad gets the point.

All we know is Dad's young friend has taken him places where they shouldn't go. As a firstborn I'm already butting heads with Dad. Now, all of a sudden, I'm thinking it's my job to protect Mom, which didn't enhance my relationship with Dad. It took quite a few years to figure out Mom didn't need my protection. She simply needed a ride to Chehalis.

UNDER ADVISEMENT

Our class of '66 with approximately forty-eight students graduates into the cold cruel world. An advisor earlier told me not to bother with college. Instead, someone suggests that because I do well in drawing and in architecture, I should sign up for a summer course Boeing offers at Centralia College. It sounds interesting, so I sign on the dotted line. Counselors know best, right? There are thirty-one of us in the summer class. Our professor, who was very good and personable, teaches us complicated aerospace drawing techniques. While all this is going on, I'm working afternoon shifts at Yard Birds, a small 1960s mall-type, one-stop shopping business.

Before our high school classes end, all of the males just turning eighteen years of age register for the Selective Service because of the Vietnam War. So, on July 29, 1966, I register and receive No. 240 on my card, which means I could sign up now or wait 'til my number is called. I opt to wait.

Near the end of our Boeing course, I'm still enjoying what we're learning. At the same time, I never really imagine living in a big city. That would be a hundred-and-eighty-degree turn from what I'm used to in my short life. Not giving it much thought, we all show up and take our final exam, which is long and thorough. The following day, we return to see who will head to Boeing. Our professor hands us our grades as we walk through the door. As he gives mine to me, he says, "You received the only 'A' in the class; you might want to consider signing up for college."

Well, that's a bit of game-changer and shifts my thinking. My first thought is that my high school counselor needs to go back to college for a refresher. Nobody taught him all about the seven different intelligences. He has been taught only two, smart and not so smart.

CHAPTER 19
OFF AND RUNNING
WITHOUT A VILLAGE

JUNIOR COLLEGE

IT DOESN'T TAKE ME LONG AFTER SIGNING UP at Centralia College to figure out college is the right move for me. I enjoy every minute. Unsure of what I want to do with my life, I try civil engineering plus basic requirement courses along with baseball, a basic requirement for me. I play baseball my freshman year and also signed up for jujitsu, a defensive form of martial arts. Being a lover and not a fighter suits me just fine.

Toward the end of my first season of jujitsu, my sensei (teacher) asks if I would like to be a student instructor next year—a definite yes on my part. I love jujitsu as much as baseball. Once a week, sensei has us do a session of randori, which is a type of freestyle sparring. Close to the end of each class, he sets mats together to form about a twenty- by twenty-foot square so students can practice moves he taught. Our twenty-some students line the perimeter with me in the middle. Sensei then sends one student after the other at me. The object is to throw your opponent out of the fifteen-foot circle in the middle of the mats.

My toughest competition is a scrappy blonde cheerleader named Kitty, which is kind of weird because Kitty is Dad's nickname for Mom. I'm at a disadvantage in the beginning because she's of the female persuasion. At first I want to back down, but I soon overcome the urge. This girl is scary with the amount of fire she fights with. You would think she spends summers baling hay with her brothers just to make them look bad. She comes close a bunch of times to knocking me out of the circle.

PACKWOOD

Summer arrives, which means I need to find work. Uncle Wilbur and Dad won the bid for a road-building job not far from Packwood. They each need two young guys to buck logs and set chokers behind their TD-25 bulldozers. The timing works out perfect with my school schedule, so I agree to take it. They need one more man, so my classmate Kenny Norberg joins me. Kenny's in good shape from all the sports he played. He's one of our "bigs" in basketball, a tight end for football, and our first baseman with a long reach in baseball.

Uncle Wilbur, above, and Michael bucking in July 1967

Knowing we have the job, we head to Packwood. We decide to rent a tiny cabin in town. I mean tiny, with only enough room for two cots, a sink, a toilet, a little refrigerator, and a small cook stove. It's all we need. Instead of a long drive home, we have time to swim and do other things. It's not long before we discover the manager of the big

lumber mill in town has a big, beautiful, heated pool along with a nice-looking daughter our age. We receive an open invitation.

The job is hard, but I love working behind Dad and Uncle Wilbur. We pair off. I work behind Uncle Wilbur and Kenny behind Dad. Kenny and I feel extremely safe behind those guys for good reason. We know how careful they are. All goes extremely well on the job. It's incredibly beautiful where we work. The smell of the forest and all the different critters provides a wonderful experience with a cornucopia of familiar sights, sounds, and smells. It has been some time since I've been around logging and road-building, and I absolutely love being around Wilbur again. Kenny receives a big bonus in Packwood. I introduce him to my cousin Joan who came up to see her dad, Uncle Wilbur, and it's love at first sight. They marry and are together to this day. Now I have to deal with that girl in the heated pool all by myself.

HARD AT IT!

By now Ray L. Wallace has gone into overdrive with the promotion of Bigfoot. A stream of talk show hosts from the West Coast to the East Coast call for interviews day and night, week after week. Some call at two or three o'clock in the morning, depending on their time zones. Many are repeat offenders. They thoroughly enjoy their time with Dad, exploring many rabbit trails while discussing anything with Ray L. Wallace. You may begin asking him about Bigfoot, but by the time your conversation ends, you may have been drilling for oil, mining a half a dozen different minerals, tracking UFOs, helping someone fight cancer, assisting someone down on their luck, or espousing the evils of smoking.

Speaking of smoking, I can't tell you how many times while driving through some city, Dad would spot someone walking on a sidewalk smoking a cigarette and literally pull the car to the curb, climb out, walk over to the individual to explain the risks of what they were doing. He was a handful for the ever-patient Elna Wallace! What patience I possess comes directly from Mom, the root of all patience, no questions asked. My three brothers could say the same.

Bigfoot researchers continue to stream to our home. They are quite a mixed bag of humanity, to say the least, in strange-looking vehicles with weird antennas, camping gear, and tracking devices. I can never tell if they are tracking Bigfoot or flying saucers. Ray L. Wallace is more than willing to help with either. It's summer when most of this activity occurs.

Fortunately, Mom still runs our restaurant at the wild animal farm and doesn't need to deal with all the weirdness brought by the information-seeking researchers. The hard part comes when she finally gets a day off, but instead of catching up on chores at home, she entertains even more strangers. Within ten minutes, Dad hollers from wherever he is, "Elna, would you get these guys something to eat?" I have little doubt in my mind that word spread about Mom's good cooking, which enlarged the stream of characters who kept showing up.

Roger Patterson continues to glean what information he can from Dad. Patterson is connected with a bunch of Bigfoot sightings east of the Cascades, mostly in the Yakima and White Pass areas.

Tools of the trade, above, and the original footprints, below

I'm shown a picture of a man from Yakima a few years later. In this photo he is over six foot tall. It shows him walking along the backside of a supply shed about twenty-five to thirty feet long. He's walking right to left and at the middle of the shed when the photo is taken. I don't know where or from whom Dad obtained the photo, but if you were to overlay that image on the famous Patterson/Gimlin photo, you would find an uncanny resemblance. Dad and a cousin of

mine make tracks around Mount St. Helens at this time but not around Yakima or White Pass.

Ray's Bigfoot workshop is located in a second kitchen in the basement. He needs an area with a sink to mix plaster of paris for Bigfoot castings. Being a family man, he's hard at work creating the whole Bigfoot family: Dad, Mom, and Baby Bigfoot. The carved versions of the Baby's footprint bears a marked resemblance to Dad's own foot. The more options, the better, right?

Dad also tries his hand at filming Bigfoot. Most of the filming takes place on a hillside, which is a part of Dad's ranch. He orders a gorilla suit made, which Mom and Aunt Bessie wear. Mom is always anxious to escape from the suit for fear of getting shot by a hunter. Ray claims Bigfoot has a liking for Kellogg's Corn Flakes, so he places a box on a low-hanging limb to attract Bigfoot, and sure enough, Bigfoot shows up for breakfast. Dad never spends days or months in one area like every other Bigfoot seeker, hoping to film a shot of Bigfoot. Dad can accomplish it all in a day.

Never having enough on his plate, he brings home an assortment of wild game either wounded or separated from their parents. One fawn (a baby deer), two bear cubs, a baby cougar, and several raccoons that later escaped and were apprehended at the middle school. The school office didn't wonder where they came from; their first call is to our house, which is Toledo's version of the Local State Game Department. The raccoons prove to be ready for the wild once again and are returned to where they were found. Dad rescues these orphans and nurtures them back to a state of good health and strength before returning them to their natural habitat.

BACK TO SCHOOL

Fall quarter is going well. I'm enjoying my classes with no problems other than parting ways with my girlfriend so I can date others.

I hang out with a couple of jocks from Chehalis I had played against in high school. They introduce me to this stuff called marijuana; no big deal, right? Well, not according to Mom. She hears about this old 1936 film, *Reefer Madness*, about the devastating effect of marijuana on teenagers. The film is made for all the right reasons but with best intentions gone sideways. It simply turns out to be a compilation of bizarre scare tactics. Mom tells me smoking pot causes people to go insane, become murderers, rapists, and so on. It's very melodramatic, in other words.

So, being steeped in eighteen-year-old wisdom, I bring a joint home and smoke it in front of her. The worst thing that happens at this point is getting the munchies, and the best place for someone with the munchies is Elna's kitchen, which is filled with cakes, pies, and cookies. But like everything else in this world, marijuana is just one more thing that is easy to abuse, which I do for some time. *Reefer Madness* contains a lot of truth, but the use of scare tactics to the extreme may not have been the best approach for keeping folks from using it.

Marijuana never does drive me insane, but it leads me to experimenting with other drugs later on. The only upside to this is I remain a weekend warrior with the stuff. I never mix it with work, either school or a job. Along with smoking marijuana, I start dating different girls, unsure what I'm seeking. Commitment doesn't seem to be in the cards. I'm pretty positive I'm not ready for marriage, which definitely requires commitment. Like a lot of other guys around me, we just want the benefits without any commitment. Slowly but surely, I head in a wrong direction.

By springtime the only sport I'm interested in is jujitsu; it was going great, but baseball is another story. I don't believe in sitting on a bench. So, when it's time to transfer, baseball is no longer an option, at least hardball, that is. There is always slo-pitch, which I play on the field for another twenty years.

BIGFOOT IS ALIVE

On October 20, 1967, Roger Patterson and Bob Gimlin shoot the infamous sixty seconds of film footage starring none other than Bigfoot in the Bluff Creek area. This is where Ray L. Wallace had been active

The Roger Patterson footage of Bigfoot

building logging roads and making Bigfoot tracks nine years earlier. The Roger Patterson footage shows a female biped, just under seven feet tall, walking near a creek, then disappearing into the timber. All I can really say is "Very well done!" Bigfoot is alive and well, at least in 1967.

SUMMER BREAK

Summer is off to a great start for me, thanks to Erland Aboen of Toledo, Washington, manager at the Darigold plant in Chehalis, Washington. He hires me for a summer job. Erland expects the best out of those working for him, and I respect that. He is a great boss. I'm hired for the 4 p.m. to midnight shift. My job is to first load the ice cream trucks so they're ready for their deliveries the next day. When completed, I'm off to assist the gentleman making butter in enormous vats, a relatively simple yet time-consuming process.

After being the butter boy, I'm halfway through my shift. The toughest part of the day lay ahead of me. With lunch over, I head to the loading docks to meet Big Jim, a six-foot, 220-plus-pound man who is all muscle, even his ears. With Jim, there's no such thing as half speed. Our job is to fully load every trailer at the dock before midnight. With a pair of gloves and a hand truck, we work at it for four hours. Thanks to sports year-round, I have enough in me to keep up with Jim and do my job. He's a good guy but never one for socializing. One thing, though, I earn Teamster union wages and think I've died and gone to heaven. I've never made so much at the ripe young age of nineteen. This sets me to thinking about all kinds of options. Tuition isn't going to be a problem.

UP, UP, AND AWAY

The great part about working swing shift is it gives me a great deal of daylight for play. My good friend, Gary, from Chehalis, owns a ski boat. We spend a fair amount of time skiing Lake Mayfield. I met Gary though playing baseball against him. He has a great family and an adventurous side. I remember a December weekend when Gary asks me if I want to water ski under the Tacoma Narrows Bridge in wet suits. I say yes, without a clue what it entails. I know the reason for the wet suits; the temperature hovers around freezing. But I wasn't aware of the wind and whitecaps on the waves. The Narrows is noted for its rough waters this time of year. Obviously, I never receive that note. Along with another friend, the three of us take turns to see who can stay up on their skis the longest. We end up sharing a lot of laughs.

Earlier in the summer I hear someone is giving parachuting lessons at our Toledo airport, so I sign up. The thing I remember most from my first jump is how quiet it is after my chute deploys. It's absolutely wonderful. The chutes are nothing fancy like today. You better listen to the instructor about how to hit the ground and roll or deal with pain from bad landings.

My favorite part about parachuting is actually showing up early to watch our young instructor arrive all the way from Bellingham, Washington, in his cherry-red World War I Sopwith Camel biplane. Made by the British beginning in 1917, the planes dominated the skies because of their maneuverability and agility in combat. Being there early and the excitement in my eyes buys me a ride fifteen minutes later. I'll never forget that experience. They will never make a carnival ride to match the one I took that day. He performs every maneuver he can think of as I ask for even more. We even fly upside down.

In the process of making a few jumps, I remember sitting in my seat ready to be called and staring at the pilot, thinking that guy is a lot smarter than I am. Here I am getting ready to jump out of a perfectly good airplane when I could be flying one.

Gary has been sharing his flying exploits with Dad on our skiing trips. That, coupled with my last parachuting jump, finds me taking my first flying lesson on August 7th at the Chehalis-Centralia Airport. For the first two weeks, I'm at the airport every day before work practicing touch-and-gos (landings and takeoffs). On August 19th I take my first solo, which is so exciting! My instructor concentrates on mostly dual cross-country navigation until September 10th when it's time to get ready to transfer to Central Washington State College in Ellensburg. Wow, what a summer!

ELLENSBURG

Before I leave for Central Washington State College, I trade my cherry '64 Chevrolet Impala for a new '69 Chevrolet Camaro. I arrive in Ellensburg and sign up for classes. Being curious about the industrial arts department, I take a couple of classes along with some psych classes. The first week there all I hear about is the Ellensburg Rodeo, how cool it is. I enjoy it so much I go out and buy myself a pair of, you guessed it, cowboy boots. People tell me that if I'm planning to spend any time exploring outside the city, they come in handy because of all the rattlesnakes.

Staying in Quigley Hall, I become friends with this tall, thin redheaded dude who was into ornithology (bird watching). I'm ahead of the game only in the fact I already own a pair of cowboy boots. One of the first places we go is a rocky area north of town to check out this special bird apparently adept at surviving around rattlers. I still can't remember the name of the bird. All I can do is concentrate on avoiding snakes.

After my first term, I switch from Quigley Hall to Bardo Hall, which is co-ed. My roommate is from one of the schools we regularly played against in high school sports, which is where I met him. He's great to have for a roommate. I mention him because, on one of my trips with my new redheaded bird-watching buddy, we run into him, sort of, on the south side of town in a large marshy area with many different types of birds and roads and trails all over it.

According to my buddy, the best time for bird watching is about an hour before dusk. So we hide my car and find a good vantage point to observe the area. Before pulling out his binoculars, we roll a joint and start in on it. About thirty minutes later, here come two people in a car I recognize as my roommate's. We're still out of sight at our vantage point when clothes start flying around and windows steam up.

Shortly after this, here comes a police car. More scrambling goes on in my roomie's car as the nice policeman taps on his window. My friend and I do everything we can to keep ourselves from splitting our guts laughing. The birds we end up watching are rare and humanoid. I never do mention anything about the incident to my roommate, although I offer a few vague comments that appear to have him wondering what I mean. You never know what you are going to run into bird-watching.

As far as scholastics go at Central Washington State College, the Industrial Arts Department is a little disappointing for me. The wood shop couldn't compete with the one I left at Toledo High School. Central's was not as well-equipped, which really surprises me, especially coming from such a small school. The metals department was well-equipped, but our professor of German ancestry has a habit of tossing our smaller projects the length of the building if he sees a flaw. It's a little unsettling for some of us. If I'd known ahead of time he was going to fling one of my projects, I would have let him know that my biological mom's side of the family originally came from Bavaria and we might be related. Well, it might have been worth a shot.

My second-term psychology class is interesting. I'm chosen as a group leader. We study dream interpretation. My job is to interview each person in our group. About the only thing I learn is that people dream pretty weird stuff. We are immature and take ourselves way too seriously. The upside is I receive an "A" and meet cute girls.

Physics turns out to be very special, although I have no business signing up for physics. I'm fairly sure if I end up with a C it would be nothing short of a miracle. The only reason I sign up is because a friend who had taken it the term before described this professor, using words like "Star Trek" and "Brings the universe to life." He goes on and on, but he has me at the mention of Star Trek. I waste little time signing up for the class. This professor has me hook, line, and sinker. I find myself fully engaged and amazed at how he brings the universe to life. When all is said and done, I receive an "A," which is even more amazing to me. I think at this point I'm just starting to see a pattern in my educational experiences. Grades never appeal much to me. What I like is the experience, with nothing better than a teacher or professor who brings a subject to life. I simply find that if the subject matter grabs my attention, I'm all in.

As far as extracurricular activities go, I'm strictly a weekend warrior. My work ethic is never a problem, but the sex, drugs, and rock 'n' roll of the '60s starts to have an ill effect. I'm living by a different set of standards than I was raised by—all fun and games, which hurt me down the road.

With the school year coming to a close, I hear that Western Washington State University has one of the best Industrial Arts departments, winning national awards. I'm thinking that's my next stop.

CHAPTER 20
MORE CHANGES

FUEL FOR THE FIRE

WITH SUMMER BEGINNING, I'm back home, working for Mom in the burger bar and keeping the critters fed at our free zoo. On the weekends, Dad fills small paper bags at our zoo with oats for children or adults to feed the animals. They put the oats in their hands and reach through the fence while an elk, buffalo, or one of the many kinds of deer carefully eats out of their hand. It's fun to watch the children brave enough to do it. Most become excited and pleased with their accomplishment.

The best part for Dad, while sitting in his chair by the barn door filling the little bags, is getting the chance to tell a story. Sooner or later, someone would ask a question about the animals and get more than what they bargained for. Most left with smiles on their faces, others shaking their heads. The latter need to be less serious about life.

One particular weekend, a gentleman from Nashville asks Dad a different kind of question. He's a country singer and wants Dad's help to make a "Bigfoot" album. If Dad's day is ho-hum before, it's not now. This fella, Don Jones, gains Dad's full attention. I'm sure that after their conversation, Dad's mind races. The album would add fuel to the Bigfoot fire, since the Patterson film debuted two years earlier, and the Bigfoot scene was cooling down. The album could stoke the fires again.

Don and Ray strike up a partnership. What Don needs from Dad is an original Bigfoot scream, which Dad, by all wonderment and awe, comes up with.

The process ends up taking almost two years before the two sign an agreement and proceed with producing the album, Bigfoot (Northwest's Abominable Snowman), with "authentic Bigfoot screams," courtesy of Ray Wallace.

FUN FLYING

After only a couple of weeks of working at the animal farm, I receive word that a pre-fab home company is hiring and paying good wages. Mom encourages the move. My first week there is memorable as this wily older foreman figures he'll give me a rite of passage in the world of "snoose," a smokeless tobacco made of ground tobacco leaves. It's placed under the lip for nicotine absorption.

I'm quite familiar with it from the logging camps but never tried it before. He gives me this "You're not a man" garbage "until you've tried snoose." After a few days of his nonsense, I'm tired of hearing it. It's lunchtime and I'm sitting there on a pile of two-by-fours minding my own business when here he comes with his snoose can open. "Come on, you wimp, give it a try." So I do. I take a small pinch, which he says isn't nearly enough. After he finishes with me, I'm lying down with my head spinning, watching him with a grin on his face. So much for caving in. Other than that, it's a good job that afforded me more flying and schooling.

After work, on most days, I head for the Chehalis airport to practice with my instructor. We work on touch-and-gos (landings and takeoffs) and a great deal of very high frequency omni-directional range navigation, or VOR NAV, which is a short-range radio navigation giving direction and bearing information to the pilot from a ground-based beacon. These two are a basic must for beginners.

After flying, I head home and study the books and manuals needed to prepare me for my Visual Flight Rules (VFR) test. By the end of June, I'm ready. With my instructor, I fly to the Boeing Field in Seattle to take my test administered by the Federal Aviation Administration (FAA). My instructor picks a beautiful clear day, not a cloud to be seen, which makes the flight to the big city wonderful, uneventful, and calm. Contacting the air traffic controller at an international airport where large jets come and go is exciting my first time. We're in a small Cessna 150 two-seater, dwarfed by all the enormous aircraft around us. We taxi to the FAA building and park.

Now, flying doesn't make me nervous, but testing always does for some reason. Several hours later, we're back in our plane, heading for the Chehalis airport. I feel good about the test. They'll let me know the results several days later. This was exciting because I could fly solo without an instructor and practice what I've learned. I still have much work to do with my instructor.

This guy is meticulous in his teaching, for which I was extremely grateful. Flying an airplane is not like driving a car where you can just pull over to the side of the road if you have a problem. He constantly drills me on emergency and flight procedures.

On one special four-hour cross-country flight, via Olympia, Seattle, Ellensburg, Yakima, and back to Chehalis, we'd either touch-and-go or simply land and take a short break. We enjoy a front-row seat for viewing the beautiful Cascade mountain range, including Mount Rainier and Mount St. Helens. What a spectacular view from a perspective only few experience. During a three-week period after my written exam, we took a total of four cross-country flights, most north to Bellingham and Sea-Tac.

On July 19th, I pass my private pilot flight test and receive my license. A week later, I'm checked out in a Cessna 174 four-seater. I want to take my high school classmate Gordon Kalich and two others to Bayview Farms Airport just south of Bellingham. It's a small airport with a grass runway. The highlight of the trip is flying over Seattle. While over the main part of Seattle north of Sea-Tac, our plane starts shaking like crazy! I look up and all of a sudden I see the tail of an American Airlines jet shooting over us. We're so close the turbulence from its engines tosses us around. Air traffic control gave us a route and speed. I don't know if someone in the tower thought we needed a wake-up call or what. It woke me up.

Another time I take one of the Cessna 150s north toward Rochester to practice figure eights and stalls, which are particularly fun. I'm at 3,000 feet with few clouds in the sky. To perform a stall, you point the nose of the plane straight up until you hear the stall warning buzzer, which means you've lost too much air speed to keep you in the air. You now need to point the plane toward the ground to gain speed or you're in serious trouble.

I've practiced this many times, but this time the buzzer goes off, my engine quits, and I find myself staring at an unmoving propeller. I immediately go through the emergency protocol I learned: nose down, speed up, check for an area to land, get into a pattern for landing, then start going through your checklist. I'm working my way down the list. I go downwind, switch on base with flaps down at twenty degrees, and turn on final approach with flaps now at forty degrees and about seventy-five feet off the ground.

If you're at all familiar with the Rochester area, many fields are inundated with weird mounds. So what looked like a great field for landing at 3,000 feet was pretty scary at seventy-five feet. So, on final approach, I come to "check carburetor heat" on my checklist. I immediately pull the carburetor heat throttle and give it what little time I have left before hitting the ground. I turn the ignition key one last time. The engine starts just in time to pull me out of a disastrous situation. With the engine on full throttle, I couldn't fly back to Chehalis fast enough. After I land and park the plane, my legs feel like rubber; I can barely walk. Who would have thought of a carburetor icing up on a hot summer day? After that I find myself checking for carburetor ice quite often.

MORE DECISIONS

After receiving my pilot's license, I have a month and a half to fly as much as I can before college starts again. By this time I've decided to go to Western Washington State in Bellingham, although arriving at that decision isn't exactly simple. A couple of days before my birthday, being excited about all this flying, I make up my mind to be a commercial airline pilot. The best route to achieve that goal is to join the Navy to obtain jet training. Flying off carriers sounds great. So I go to the Navy recruiter's office to get the lowdown on flying. If I remember correctly, they tell me that with three years of college behind me, I could join officer's training and flight school.

Thinking I've hit the jackpot, I proceed to inform my parents of my decisions to join the Navy. To my total surprise, Dad isn't the least bit happy about my newfound revelation. He goes into great detail over his concerns about the Vietnam War, how it's one of the most unrighteous wars he's ever heard of and it's being fought for all the wrong reasons such as supporting French rubber plantations. He says we have no business there. I remember he's so upset he promises to move the whole family to Canada before letting me join the service.

"Do you really want to go over there and drop bombs out of a plane and kill people?" he asks. "Please, just finish college. I'll help you if you need finances."

This really sets me back. At this point I haven't thought much about the war being righteous or not, but he sounds like he has a good point, especially the part about protecting US Goodyear rubber plantations given up by the French. After ruminating on the whole thing, I decide to go back to my original plan, Western Washington State College.

I continue flying once or twice a week. Instead of using my car for dating, I use a plane. For my first aero-date, I flew to Boeing Field one evening. On the way to Seattle, I ask my date if she wants to see me make a pencil float. After her reluctant answer, I proceed to show her. What you do is go nose up into a stall, then suddenly point the nose of the plane to the ground. As we start down, I put my pencil in front of her face and let go. It appears to float in front of her, when it's simply falling through space at the same rate of speed as the plane. The trip up and back goes without a wrinkle, and it's dark by the time we enter the airspace around Chehalis.

Entering our landing pattern at an altitude of 1,000 feet, we head downwind but just after turning before my final approach, I realize my altitude is way too high. So I tell her to hang on while we go into a slip. To do a slip and make a left turn on final, I point the left wing to the ground, which causes the plane to lose a great deal of altitude in a short amount of time. The only problem is my air speed greatly increased on the final approach. When we hit the runway, I thought the plane would shake apart and we might not have enough runway. Let's put it this way, I use all of the runway, and it's a long taxi back to the hangar. That's the last night landing where my final approach is too high. My date is rather a bit on the quiet side the rest of the night.

A couple of weeks later, with a different date, I fly to the Seattle-Tacoma International Airport. After landing, we catch a cab to the Space Needle for dinner. I experience no stalls, slips, or hard landings with the plane that evening.

At the end of August, Gordon Kalich calls and wants to fly over a rock festival near Tenino. He obtains the shots he wants, and I log more time. I demonstrate the floating pencil to him while we're flying.

My last flight of the summer I take Robin, my current flame. We leave Chehalis and fly toward

Tenino Rock Festival from the air

Castle Rock by way of Dad's ranch and see his extra buffalo. We turn back for Toledo airport and perform a touch-and-go, then head back for Chehalis.

On the way, Robin says she's going to Mexico City in a few weeks before school starts to visit people she knows there and tour the natural history museum. Robin doesn't want to go alone and asks me if I'm interested in going with her. Two weeks later, we take the wildest taxi ride from the airport in Mexico City I've ever had in my life; it's much safer in a plane. I stay for a week because I need to return home and head to Bellingham for school, but she stays an additional week. We visit the natural history museum, which is absolutely incredible.

CHAPTER 21
BELLINGHAM

BEAUTIFUL SURROUNDINGS

BELLINGHAM IS ABSOLUTELY BEAUTIFUL, surrounded by the San Juan Islands on the west and long Lake Whatcom to the east and lush, thick forests. The campus nestles among the trees with Red Square in the middle, which is predominantly a red brick paved area with a huge water fountain as its centerpiece. Red Square is used for student events, activities, and protests.

Adjoining the campus on the east side is the 175-acre Sehome Hill Arboretum. To the south is the Fairhaven District where liberal hippies like me gravitate in the early 1970s. I use the term hippie because by this time I've forgotten barbers exist. My curly afro offers a vast array of upsides and downsides. Tons of little ol' ladies tell me they would give anything for my "do" because they'd no longer need a hair stylist. They love to run their fingers through my hair. The only downside is this older female cousin who makes some comment about a dirty hippie. I'm thinking, "What's up with that? I shower and do my laundry regularly just as I have for years."

SMOOTH SAILING

My psych and industrial education classes and professors are just what I need. I enjoy my twenty-seven-year-old professional psychology prof so much I take him flying over the San Juan Islands and talk about life.

Our amazing industrial arts department wins national awards. They even offer radio and television courses. I'm fortunate to have Professor Southcott for my architectural design classes. He's into Frank Lloyd Wright but leaves plenty of room for my favorites, the old stuff, Tudors and castles. He encourages everyone to go their own way.

For history, my female professor brings history to life for me. I expect little more than credit for the course, but I receive more than my money's worth. She makes history special. She's cute too.

In the early spring, I move my dating to the air again with the weather improving over the San Juan Islands. It's an incredibly beautiful area by boat or by plane.

Unrest over the Vietnam War grows throughout the United States. On May 4, 1970, at Kent State University, the Ohio National Guard opens fire on a group of unarmed anti-war protesters, killing four and wounding nine. This fuels the United States anti-war movement. My classmate Gordon Kalich, whom I am still convinced more than ever will follow in the political footsteps of his father, Hugh "Bud" Kalich, becomes a political activist and leader on campus.

On May 5th, a day after the Kent State shooting, Gordon and campus student leaders organize a protest. About four hundred students gather in Red Square and prepare to march. We all carry as many protest leaflets as

May 5th Red Square protest in Bellingham

possible and head for Interstate 5, which runs right through Bellingham. In no time, we block both northbound and southbound lanes as far as you could see. Once traffic stops, we go car to car, handing out protest leaflets. I work the southbound lane. Maybe they're a bunch of friendly Canadians heading south, but among all the people I talk to, not a single one becomes angry or upset for being waylaid. The protest is about as peaceful as you could want and makes clear to us a growing distaste for the Vietnam War.

I can't describe my Dad as a redneck logger, but what I can say is he's right on the money about the Vietnam War being unrighteous. We need to get out of Vietnam. Unfortunately, it goes on for three more years. By the end of the war, I believe the draft number reaches 189; mine is 240. I can speak only for myself. During all that mess and still today, I feel horrible for the young men who endured that war. I blame only those who got us into that mess in the first place.

SUMMER LEISURE

This summer is the first one since the age of eight when I'm unemployed. While going to Western, I make friends with Mark who has a good friend, also called Mark. I'll call the later Mark (A) and the former Mark (B). Mark (A) has his mom's place, which is a very nice home in Seattle that overlooks Puget Sound and Vashon Island. His mom is hardly ever around.

Mark (A) is talented in electronics and involved in light shows for rock concerts. In his daylight basement, he turns an eight- by ten-foot windowless room into a sound and light show with special soundproofing and an L-shaped cot along two walls. It's like lying down inside of a large speaker box with incredible sound along with a coordinated light show.

The rest of the basement is mostly a large open space with windows overlooking Puget Sound. Mark (A) connects with this psychedelic rock band on tour and in town performing a concert. A baby boomer might remember the band Strawberry Alarm Clock with its hit song "Incense and Peppermint." Mark (A) calls to tell us we will have a big party tonight for some Strawberry Alarm Clock band members who will bring their instruments over after their concert. Mark (A) has a drum set in the basement we tinker on.

So part of the way into the party, and being fairly toasted at this point, they need someone to play the drums, so I step in. The band's drummer is a no-show. At this point in the party, it doesn't matter much what I sound like on the drums. So now I can add to my résumé that I played with professional rock band (for about an hour).

A neighbor of Mark's is a good photographer who watches us come and go. One day she stops by and asks if she can take some shots of the three of

Mike, Mark, and Mark

us and offers to give us copies. Her photos pretty much capture what's happening in and around us.

We spend a fair amount of time that summer in Mark's sound room, which is a very unique setup with unforgettable sound quality. I also spend most of the summer with this nice-looking brunette who lives not far from us.

TOUGH RETURN

I'm back in Bellingham for part of a fifth year after discovering that all my civil engineering courses at Centralia College will not transfer. I need additional credits for a major, which I thought would be psychology until I go to sign up for more of my psych professor friend's classes and learn he committed suicide over the summer. What a shock. I never had the slightest indication of any instability during all our time together. I immediately drop psychology and declare industrial education as my major. I've taken quite a few Industrial Arts classes already, so I'm more than happy to add the few I need from Professor Southcott's design courses.

It's such an eye-opener losing my friend. I've never been around anyone who committed suicide, so I find it a difficult thing to wrap my head around. My first thought is if that's all the good psychology did for my friend, I don't need it. Right or wrong, I'm no longer interested in counseling or giving anyone advice.

I have all my education classes out of the way plus my student teaching, which I did in the Central District in Seattle, a tough area at the time. I still thought I might be a high school counselor, but a couple of notable incidents occurred. First, during a shop class, one of my students has a firearm in his possession. We send word to Mr. Washington, the head counselor. It's amazing to watch him handle this tense situation. After he takes care of the incident, I tell him about my interest in counseling. So, for the last two weeks of my "tour," as it were, I spend each day watching him deal with every kind of situation imaginable.

The second unique situation is having rock star Jimmy Hendrix's brother in my class. (He isn't the guy with the gun.) From what I see of him, he's pretty easygoing. A fair number of pot-smoking students hang around school at the time, but it's not a high-priority problem. I live in an apartment across the street from the school. My students drop by after school and want to smoke pot. I don't know how many times I explain how that's a bad idea. Particularly with the female students.

Flashing back to Bellingham and Cain Lake in particular, Gordon Kalich, Mark (B), Dick B., and I rent this beautiful four-bedroom log cabin on the lake, complete with a dock and a canoe. The log home is nine miles southeast of Bellingham, or about a fifteen-minute drive. What a great place to come after long days of classes. I teach myself fly-fishing, which pays off. Cain Lake has nice trout and is small and peaceful. This place is a far cry from an apartment or dorm in town and makes me feel more at home. We're fortunate to have it.

One of my last classes is a design class. Professor Southcott comes up with a unique final exam. He breaks the class into teams of four. Each team is given a movie camera to make a documentary film. The subject is the same for all six groups: graffiti. The exam begins today and ends by presenting the documentary in class tomorrow. Our team quickly decides the Fairhaven District is the best place to find graffiti. We hit the jackpot at the first tavern. It's now after lunch with very few customers around.

We start with the men's stalls, a copper mine of crude art. But the women's is where we find the gold. We shoot this incredibly intricate dragon that a woman (I assume a woman) drew on the wall of one of the stalls. We gather a decent selection of graffiti in no time, but I think we need more to make our film unique.

After pondering the situation, I ask our cameraman to come back into the men's bathroom. On the counter I lay out four sheets of toilet paper still attached to each other. Taking a marker, I list the credits for our film, listing each team member and their positions: producer (myself), director, cameraman, and so on. I ask the cameraman to focus on the bottom of a toilet and wait for my signal to roll. After placing the credits in the toilet bowl with "The End" at the bottom, I signal him to roll the camera as I flush the toilet. It's a take. The following morning, we turn in our work. After his critique, we receive an "A" from a professor who is stingy with his As. He tells us the finish did it for him.

On March 19th, I receive my teaching certificate and head for Toledo.

CHAPTER 22
LIFE IN THE REAL WORLD

FINDING WORK

LEAVING THE EDUCATIONAL NEST with an Industrial Arts teaching degree in '71 proves challenging, especially at a time when a low percentage of those graduating with teaching certificates find positions in Washington State. Apparently not many teachers wanted to give up their jobs or retire. The only opening is at Forks, Washington, a remote community on the Olympic Peninsula in a beautiful setting between the Pacific Coast and the Olympic National Forest. Having lived in remote areas most of my life, I don't worry about the location. But socially, I want to live in a city.

Instead, I opt to substitute teach in the Olympia School District. With little down payment, I purchase a nice home on Mudd Bay owned by the daughter of a wealthy family in Portland. They don't need the cash but just want out from under their contract. During the process, I meet a guy I'll call Mr. A., the mystery man, from here on out. He's not much older than me at the time but has a knack for dealing with the wealthy and powerful, of which I was neither. We become good friends, and he plays important roles in my life from time to time.

Later in October, I sell my '69 Camaro and buy Mr. A's amazing little British sports car, a 1967 Austin-Healey. I'd been raised in rural areas most of my life, so Mr. A. took it upon himself to do social reformation with me, which I welcomed. In the meantime I meet, through Mr. A., this nice-looking and intelligent lady from a well-off family. Money has never been a draw for me when it comes to dating or friendships. We have fun together. She sews custom clothing and cooks gourmet meals for us. We become engaged, but it's not meant to be. After four months, and don't ask me why, I sell the house, break up with her, and head south toward Toledo. It's one of those headshakers. I have no valid reason for parting ways with her; she has so much going for herself.

THE ROCK GANG

Shortly after leaving Olympia, and before buying my Austin-Healey, I hook up with a local rock band. You might call my position assistant to the manager or founder, who dated Mr. A's sister. The band tours Northwest Washington. Our headquarters is a large home with all the bedrooms fully occupied upon my arrival. I simply pull my waterbed mattress from the trunk of the Camaro, fill it with water in the middle of the large living room, and call it my bedroom. I have expensive stereo equipment next to my bed. Within a short time, it disappears, reportedly sold for drugs by someone playing a guitar. Their music apparently couldn't support their habits.

Someone in our group gets a brilliant idea for putting extra money in our coffers. We head for Nebraska, where we can find marijuana or pot growing wild along the railroad tracks. It's grown there since the late 1800s from seeds blown off the railcars while shipping hemp for making rope. No one in our crew bothers to ask if it's any good. In a short time, without any planning, we head east to Nebraska.

Our fearless leader with two others in one car and me with my Native American female friend in my Camaro. Along our route we stop and check out the Little Big Horn Monument. We later catch up with the rest of the gang before we hit Nebraska. That evening we settle into a motel outside of Lincoln, with plans to rise early in the morning, fill our trunks with pot, and drive back west. Piece of cake, right? Best-laid plans of mice and men. Morning arrives, and we head for ground zero, the railroad tracks, with pot growing all around them. It doesn't take long to fill our trunks. As we're leaving, we suddenly see multiple flashing red lights and sirens. Two police cars pull us over.

"License and registration, please." This officer wears a big grin on his face. Then he asks us to open our trunk.

I'm wanting to say, "How did that get in there?" but I don't bother. Not long after this, being separated from the rest of our gang, for the first and last time, I find myself in the slammer with this stranger. He's an Italian-looking dude who is relaxed and reading a paperback novel. This guy is friendly enough, and I mention I'm from Lewis County in Washington. After several hours of conversing, I discover he's a nephew of Chicago's crime boss. At that point, I no longer have the urge to ask him why he's been arrested. Instead, the conversation turns to the book he's reading about Ken Kesey, an American novelist who traveled the United States during the mid-1960s in a bus with friends while doing a lot of drugs, particularly LSD, or lysergic acid diethylamide. The book mentions Kesey stopping at this Wild Animal Farm to eat and check out the animal attraction. These guys must have been loaded while there because they complained about the food, yet Mom's burger bar is known far and wide for serving only the best food.

I'm thinking this is an extremely bizarre coincidence, or I'm in the Twilight Zone.

Upon my booking, I make my one phone call. Not to Mom or Dad, but to Mr. A. I have no clue if I'll return home soon or not. Clueless is the best choice of words for this whole situation. In retrospect, the last twenty-four hours is kind of funny. Based on the officer's smile, I figure our bust after collecting pot growing along the railroad tracks is a fairly routine situation for the local law enforcement. They probably monitor cameras mounted on corn silos and grin as they prepare to bust would-be potheads. Of course I'm assuming a steady stream of boneheads, or as my Dad would have said "goofy harebrained screwballs," pick the pot to make the oftentimes illusive fast buck.

The following morning, I'm informed I'll be going before the judge. I stand before His Honor, thinking I'm probably headed to the Big House, and remember to say "yes, sir" and "no, sir." I recall little else, other than the judge's last words: "I want you to head for your car, get in it, and I never want to see you in Nebraska again." Not believing what I heard, I say, "Yes, sir." I pick up my possessions and do exactly what the judge ordered me to do.

The two girls with us staying at the motel were never arrested and caught a bus home before any of us were released. I now head for Seattle to meet Mr. A. and this high-powered attorney whose office is full of pre-Columbian art worth a large fortune. I still to this day do not know the details of my quick release. The strangest part is I never pay a dime for the attorney's services. A few weeks later, I reconnect with the band's fearless leader. Something about an upcoming rock festival.

DAD AND THE RECORD

After several attempts, Dad and country singer Don Jones put together their "Bigfoot L.P." Dad provides an original soundtrack of Bigfoot screaming and a storyline for the lyrics of some of the songs. They sign an agreement with Panorama Records in Nashville. On the back of the album, producer John Shriram writes about Dad.

The Bigfoot album featuring singer Don Jones and a soundtrack of Bigfoot screaming, courtesy of Ray Wallace

BIGFOOT
NORTHWEST'S ABOMINABLE SNOWMAN
Featuring DON JONES

There have been many weird and unexplainable happenings throughout the United States and other countries concerning the huge, human-type creature known throughout the Northwest as Bigfoot. Bigfoot is also known as the Sasquatch in Canada, Yeti in Russia, and the Abominable Snowman in the Himalaya Mts. Bigfoot got his name in northern Calif. from a group of loggers, who were working for a logging company in a remote forest area above a little town called Willow Creek, California. The loggers gave him this name because of his huge footprint he left in the soft dirt roads that had been made by the caterpillars.

Many of our leading magazines have photographed these huge footprints and run articles about Bigfoot.

The Indians refer to Bigfoot as the Indian Devil and also the Tee-see-at-co, which means Big Man.

Bigfoot is said to have a covering all over his body of dark brown hair that at times seems lighter in different areas. Bigfoot is known to roam through the forests of the Northwest and Canada eating berries and sometimes meat from animals he or some other animal has killed. There are hundreds of square miles of timberland in this region that man has never set foot on, so this is one of the theories of why Bigfoot is so elusive. It seems he is only seen when he wants to be, which is not very often.

There have been many photos taken of Bigfoot from different parts of the country; some in color and some in black & white. Also, there have been films taken of him; one of these has been shown throughout the United States in auditoriums and theatres, which turned quite a number of the unbelievers into believers.

Ray Wallace also has taken movie film of the Bigfoot, plus he has taped the real scream of Bigfoot during an attempt to capture him. This scream or screams are the ones being used in some of the songs pertaining to Bigfoot.

On the reverse side of the album, Don uses his deep warming voice to sing songs like: "I Believe," "Unchained Melody," and "Love Me Tonight" to name a few. We know you will enjoy his brilliant talent and professional approach to these songs so sit back and enjoy yourselves because you're in for a real treat.

John Shiriam

BIGFOOT
BIGFOOT & LITTLE WILLIE WHITECLOUD
HE WATCH THE MAN
LITTLE BIGFOOT JOURNEY HOME
SHELTER

I BELIEVE
LOVE ME TONIGHT
MANKIND
GUESS WHO
UNCHAINED MELODY

Produced by John Shiriam
Arranged by Cliff Forman
Engineered by Tommy Streng
Cover Photograph and Bigfoot's scream and all other information furnished by Ray Wallace, of Toledo, Wash.
Recorded in Nashville.

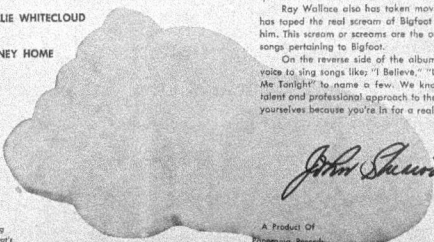

A Product Of
Panorama Records,
Division of Pano and Binako Music
1819 Broadway
Nashville, Tennessee

Stereo
PRS 204

Panorama

Collectors Item

A PRODUCT OF PANORAMA RECORDS / 1819 BROADWAY / NASHVILLE, TENNESSEE • 37203

The phone at our house continues ringing as Dad keeps up a constant stream of communication with disc jockeys and Bigfoot researchers. By this time, Mom and the rest of us learn to sleep through the night with the phone ringing at all hours. Dad's having a ball. For the rest of us, it is what it is.

THE FESTIVAL

Things come to a close with my band gig. It's interesting, needless to say, but definitely time to move on from that experiment.

Our band's fearless leader and I receive a call from Mr. A., who says a friend of his and others are organizing what will be the first legal outdoor rock festival in the state of Washington, a four-day festival starting September 3, 1971. They need hundreds of volunteers to help with all the logistical problems.

The Satsop River Fair and Tin Cup Races, as it is called, has several promoters, including Gary Howard Friedman. *The Seattle Post-Intelligencer*, in a later article, described Friedman, who was nicknamed The Wizard, as an "ex-black marketeer, ex-convict, ex-narcotic agent, ex-computer operator and self-proclaimed promoter." The first and often the most insurmountable problem for most outdoor festivals at this time is obtaining a festival permit. By midsummer, Friedman raises enough money to start planning what would later be referred to as Washington's Woodstock. This is where Bill O'Neill comes in as partner. By July 7th, a site has been secured in Grays Harbor County called the Reality Farm, a seventy-seven-acre hippie commune with sixteen residents, chickens, ducks, and a pig.

The legal battle for a permit begins July 9th in King County Superior Court and ends on August 19th, when the permit is issued, just two weeks before the festival is to start.

The largest investor, a woman from Portland, Oregon, is a good friend of Mr. A.'s. She initially put up $70,000, along with other investments, for a total of $210,000 to launch the event.

With rain, the seventy-seven acres quickly turns into a quagmire. Eight hundred volunteers try to set up ninety-five concessions, 104 Sani-Cans, a state-of-the-art 500-watt sound system, and two helipads, one for medical and one for entertainers. Workers also run power poles and water lines to support the concessions and stage.

Then we experience every problem imaginable. Broken bottles everywhere send many feet to the onsite open-door clinic, where medical personnel spend most of their time dealing with overdoses from bad drugs; two with gunshot wounds; eight people seriously injured when their bus from the parking lot ten miles away tumbles over a thirty-foot cliff. Fights fueled by alcohol and bad drugs bring others to the clinic. Pot smokers cause little if any trouble.

On September 5th, a truck full of watermelons traveling slowly along the muddy road onto the festival site becomes blocked by attendees who decide to liberate the melons, saying they belong to "the people." The driver doesn't share their opinion. He steps on the gas and runs over several campers. Without the mud, the liberators would have suffered much more than broken ankles and contusions.

On this day, I'm thirty-five miles away at festival headquarters in Olympia inside the Evergreen Motor Inn. I'm eating brunch with Mr. A. and one of the Beach Boys (although not all the Beach Boys attended the festival). I'm given a cushy job as liaison to the entertainers and told to have as much fun as I can.

The initial lineup of entertainers lists Ike & Tina Turner; Derek and the Dominos (with Eric Clapton); Quicksilver Messenger Service; War; Earth, Wind & Fire; Leo Kottke; The Everly Brothers; and Captain Beefheart. However, the entertainers either demand their money up front or find other reasons not to show up.

The problem, after the first two days, is the gate proceeds fail to total what they should have. With at least 100,000 festival-goers each paying sixteen dollars, we should have brought in more than enough money to cover all the bands. We are being ripped off and do not know by whom. Allegations are swirling about counterfeit tickets; it's a mess and getting tense.

About this time I find myself in a four-door sedan with shotguns and a trunk full of gate proceeds, heading for a safe depository. Much of the money isn't showing up where it's supposed to, so we take it upon ourselves to see that it does. Other than that, I have a great time mingling with the stars by day and the evening receptionist by night. We are enjoying just as much entertainment at the Evergreen Motel Inn headquarters as those at the Rock Festival, if not more.

Then the ticket takers, cleanup crew, and the man with the sound system threaten to leave at 9 p.m. on Saturday if they are not paid. An emergency meeting is held right before the deadline. The head of security overseeing forty personnel tells the sound man that if he pulls his equipment, they'll no longer have a crowd but instead a large mob. Friedman sits by, unusually quiet, during the meeting, which is interesting for him.

At the last minute, the female investor from Portland steps in and pulls the festival back from the edge of disaster. She pays all the bills, which amounted to a large sum, to keep the festival afloat. It's a gutsy move as she has no idea whether she'll see any of her money again. From this point on, the money is more carefully watched.

The brave entertainers who hang in there and perform are Delaney & Bonnie (they liked arguing and whiskey); John Hammond Jr.; Wishbone Ash; Jimmy Witherspoon; Charles Lloyd; Spencer Davis and Peter Jameson; The Youngbloods; Albert Collins; Steve Miller; and last but not least, Eric Burdon. Eric is a quiet and mellow dude. Some of these performers play much longer sets than scheduled because of bands that opted out. Despite all of the chaos, things actually end well.

Our financial hero is the first person paid back in full for every dollar she put into the festival.

Two undercover Washington State Patrol officers, posing as concession workers, wrote in their post-festival report in regard to the deteriorating health standards: "We feel that if the promoters had at least two weeks to prepare the site and better governmental control, most of these problems could have been eliminated." You can thank Grays Harbor County commissioners for all of the delays. But for the rest of the problems, with drugs and alcohol being mixed with humanity, no amount of preparation would suffice.

One last note concerning Gary Howard Friedman. In December 1971, it's revealed that from March to June, he worked for the Washington State Patrol's drug control unit for $150 a week setting up undercover drug buys to bust dealers. This is when the ticket counterfeiting came to light, but nothing was ever proven. This guy is not the New York cardiologist Gary Howard Friedman.

A ROCK TOUR

Shortly after the rock festival, four of us—Mr. A., the female investor, me, and a gentleman claiming to have Rolling Stones connections in England—decide to promote a United States tour with either the Rolling Stones or another well-known group in England. So the investor buys this guy a ticket to London, and he's off. It's my job to contact all the venues between the Kingdome in Seattle and Madison Square Garden in New York to set up a schedule based on availability.

My office is the female investor's poolroom in her thirty-two-room mansion on the east hillside of Portland. Her husband had passed away. For many years, she owned and ran a successful furniture store in downtown Portland. After several months of dead-ends in England, I start feeling like a kept man, which doesn't work for me. I inform all those involved with this endeavor that I'm heading north, and that if any of them hear positive news from England, let me know.

CHAPTER 23
KEEPING BUSY

WATERBEDS

I'M A LONG WAY FROM FINDING MY NICHE in life while bouncing from one thing to another. Returning to Toledo, I run into my former classmate Gene Cole, our class's version of Marshawn Lynch. I say I'm thinking about making waterbed frames but don't have space or the machinery to make it happen. Gene tells me his dad happens to have the perfect setup. Larry, Gene's dad, a builder with a well-equipped shop, has plenty of room to set up an assembly line and all the right machines. I contact the Portland investor who says she can take what we produce after I show her our light, but strong, model made from cedar.

In our off hours, we hang out in his dad's basement. Having built his home, Larry constructed a chess room with a floor made of twelve- by twelve-inch black and white tiles arranged to look like a large chessboard. The room has a fireplace on one side with a raised sitting area opposite it, allowing people to look down on the board. All the pieces are handmade with the king and queen about eighteen inches tall. It's a unique way to play the game.

My 1967 Austin-Healey is heavy for its size with a wide wheelbase, which enables it to corner well at high speeds.

A 1967 Austin-Healey

The Healey has a pop-off hardtop and a tucked-away rag top for Washington weather. She also has a British name, Arabella. A little rough on the freeways, she doesn't smooth out until I hit ninety miles an hour, and then she goes almost completely quiet. Arabella is one of the most amazing cars I've ever owned. I never had the money for a Lamborghini, and if I'd had the money, I wouldn't have invested it all into a car at this point in my life.

Gene and I ship out the frames until after Christmas when things slow down.

In early January, I get a call from Dad, asking me a strange question: "Would you be interested in buying a small convenience store? A man by the name of Myron Linder wants to trade it for one of my small pieces of property. It would come with a house behind this old store with gas pumps." I tell Dad I'll meet with them and take a look. Neither Gene nor I were particularly hot on making bed frames anymore. I figured, being fresh out of any good ideas, I might give it a whirl. So on January 19th, 1972, Myron and I sign papers and close the deal for Hillcrest Grocery & Gas.

ANOTHER EXPERIMENT

Hillcrest is named appropriately. Built in 1927, the store sits on the crest of a small hill (a bump in the road). The trick to turning into the store is to stay on the road until reaching the crest of the hill. If someone speeds from the opposite direction, and a driver turns too early, it's easy to get T-boned. Best not to drink until after leaving with the six-pack and arriving home.

The old store literally leans ten degrees toward Highway 505. The walls grow more tired with each passing year. The floor consists of rough-cut two- by twelve-foot boards that alternately sag, which gives the illusion of walking on ocean waves.

Mike with brother Larry fixing up the old store

156

It's quite rustic. The fancy part is the covered portico customers drive through to reach the two old and tired gas pumps. At least it keeps them dry while pumping their petrol.

The difficult part about having a liquor license isn't particularly the licensing process; it's dealing with Shiny Shoes, the liquor inspector, an ex-Marine who hid out near the store with his binoculars in hand, trying to catch me selling booze to underage customers. I never knew when he lurked about, not that it mattered.

Mike with brother Larry

I purchase an old '36 Dodge pickup to use once a week to pick up my groceries from West Coast Grocery, a wholesaler in Chehalis. On nice sunny days, I crank out the front windshield for a cool breeze and pick bugs out of my teeth. It's a nice break from the store, where a couple of wonderful older ladies work part time, which enables me to pick up supplies or take a day off, once in a blue moon. During a normal work week, I open the store at eight in the morning and close at ten at night, seven days a week. I don't earn enough profit to spend much time away.

On a typical day, after the lunch crowd, I might have twenty minutes between customers, which gives me time to scurry back to the house and make a sandwich. For dinner, at 9:30 p.m., I pop a Swanson's TV dinner in the oven and start closing up shop. For a culinary pre-function, I occasionally grab a pickled sausage and a Budweiser on my way out of the store. I know, it's amazing I'm still as healthy as I am.

Quite often, Gene Cole comes over after 1 p.m. and we play chess between customers. That's how busy I'm not. I sell enough gas and groceries to stay afloat, but that's about all I'm doing.

HERE WE GO

By the time fall rolls around I'm restless again. Mr. A. is in Portland or headed there. In a phone conversation with him, I say I'm somewhat dismayed with my situation. He mentions a bridge engineer who needs a draftsman in Portland. So, I lease out my store in a hurried fashion and go to work for a structural engineer with an office in northeast Portland.

My daily commute across town after work averages about five to ten miles per hour. Eventually, Arabella, my Austin-Healey, starts overheating. She absolutely does not like being driven at slow speeds. After six months of city driving, I've had enough. I need to get Arabella back to the wide-open spaces. My brother Rick, who looks more like country artist Charlie Daniels every day, tells me he's interested in logging with me. Next thing I know, I'm heading north to Toledo.

One log load for Christmas

BACK TO THE WOODS

In late spring of '73, Rick and I put together what resembles a logging company. Dad lets us use an old mountain logger skidder, which is an articulating machine with a large motor and cab where the operator sits in the front half of the machine. The back half consists of a drum with a heavy wire cable that runs through a small heavy-duty arch to pull logs. We buy chainsaws and miscellaneous equipment and go to work. We do the falling and skidding and hire self-loader log trucks to do the hauling.

To increase production, we lease a brand-new Timberjack skidder that Rick operates. It runs circles around the old mountain logger skidder, which I'm pretty sure Lewis and Clark brought with them to the Great Northwest. I think we spend as much time repairing it as we do logging with it.

When the machines perform as they should, we make a good living. It's great to be back in the woods again.

One day I'm operating the mountain logger in a small draw. To reach the landing where the logs would be loaded on trucks, I go up and down the small but steep one-hundred-yard hill. While pulling a turn of logs up the hill with a steep bank on my right, my brakes fail. I slam my foot through the floorboards but discover no brakes. I find myself going backward down the hill.

At this moment I clearly remember my father telling me when I was much younger that in a situation like this, never jump from a piece of equipment. Instead, grab the safety bar and hang on for life, which is exactly what I do. By this time the skidder is rolling down over the hill, tumbling three or four times, and comes to rest upside down at the bottom of the ravine. Brother Rick happens to be at the top of the hill, while I'm dangling with a death grip on the upside-down skidder's emergency bar. Once Rick sees I'm okay, he starts laughing. He tells me later I looked like a monkey swaying on a limb.

After climbing out of the skidder, I work my way up the hill, but something seems all too familiar. My legs feel weak and rubbery, similar to what I experienced upon returning to the airport after temporarily losing my engine while practicing stalls a few years earlier. It's all I can do to reach the top of the hill.

I hand the skidder keys, which I grabbed out of the ignition, to brother Rick and tell him, "It's all yours, big fella." I couldn't wish for a better guy to work with than brother Rick, but even though I'd grown up around logging and respected it, I decide I've not yet found what I'm meant to do. Some people know from an early age. I'm not one of them. The only upside to all of my experimenting with jobs is, being the MacGyver type, I file away in my brain everything I've learned.

THE FREE ZOO

Meanwhile, back at our free zoo, all is as well as it can be. It serves its original purpose. Many children who lack an opportunity to visit a zoo stream by daily during the summer to feed unique critters for free. Income from the burger bar helps to feed the animals and adds to the winter coffers when work is slow for Dad. Mom cooks great burgers at our small restaurant, and Dad occasionally gives out free burgers to anyone looking like they can't afford one, mostly hippie-looking characters in cars that make it look like they're desperate from lack of funds.

It's a small world, and during this summer, a family stops by to check out our free zoo and feed the deer, elk, and buffalo. They simply grab a small bag of oats and put some in an open hand through the fence. Not knowing these folks at this time, the little fella with a binky in his mouth, Wayne, becomes my son-in-law some fifty years later.

Fortunately, we end up with a few good photos of the Wild Animal Farm, although I wish I had one of Mom's burger bar. I'm pleased to have the photos we do have. They provide great memories.

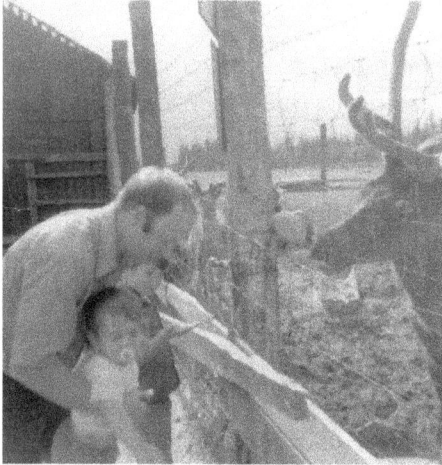

Wayne with a binky, above, and an article in The Daily Chronicle *about Ray and his wild animal farm*

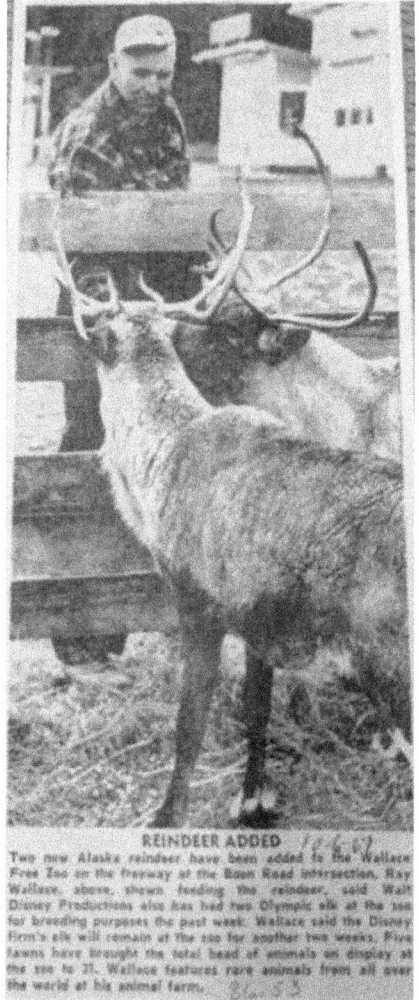

REINDEER ADDED

Two new Alaska reindeer have been added to the Wallace Free Zoo on the freeway at the Boon Road intersection. Ray Wallace, above, shown feeding the reindeer, said Walt Disney Productions also has had two Olympic elk at the zoo for breeding purposes the past week. Wallace said the Disney firm's elk will remain at the zoo for another two weeks. Five fawns have brought the total head of animals on display at the zoo to 31. Wallace features rare animals from all over the world at his animal farm.

CHAPTER 24
GOING FOR IT

I RETURN EARLY IN 1974 to take Hillcrest back from the couple who leased it. On a handshake and our word, unfortunately, I lost the $5,000 of inventory I left unsecured. Yes, we signed no legal documents, simply gave a handshake and our word. Although my morals drifted by this point, my ethics remain intact. This, of course, left me with no way of recovering any of the inventory. They simply packed their bags and left without even a goodbye. Firmly believing a man is only as good as his word, I still do the majority of my business with a handshake and my word. I find this philosophy a bit more difficult the older I get. I must temper it with a great deal of discretion.

Despite the setback, I'm determined to make a go of it. After building up the inventory, I'm back to playing chess with my good friend, Gene Cole. At the same time, I've formulated a plan. With just under two acres, I have plenty of space to build a new store, one much larger and up-to-date with more to offer. First, I need to meet with a certified public accountant. Gordon Kalich has a cousin, Roy, who is an excellent accountant. I ask him to put together a financial proposal for Security State Bank.

Fortunately, at this time, the bank offers small business loans with great rates. I begin my design work drawing up plans for a new convenience store. I'm also contacting vendors to secure more competitive prices. One of the more important is a fuel supplier. Mobil supplied fuel for Hillcrest for a long time, so I begin talks with them. The local supplier promises they will supply, for free, two large underground fuel tanks if I stay with Mobil. Such tanks are quite costly, so that seems like a fairly decent plan. With all of this underway, I figure I'll be ready for the bank by late winter or early spring of next year.

ALL WORK AND NO PLAY

In the meantime, I acquire a couple of cool dudes for roommates, Paul and John. This turns out to be great timing for me. They take turns cooking and occasionally help in the store when I need it, all for free room and shared expenses for food, which I get at wholesale prices. Paul introduces us to a great deal of soft rock and, best of all, "The Ocean Set" at ten every evening on radio station KINK in Portland. At bedtime, the soothing sound of ocean waves drifts from room to room as we fall asleep.

John always has a smile on his face or a giggle. He's never reluctant to help wherever needed. Paul is contemplative, offering good ideas from time to time and a decent cook. He loves throwing spaghetti noodles on the ceiling; if they stick, they're ready to eat.

With this new situation, I take more opportunities for fishing. One particular adventure I'll never forget with my friend Ralph Olson from Toledo. He's close to Dad's age and formerly ran the Mobil distributorship for many years with his brother, both reputable men. Ralph and I hear the spring salmon run is in, so we head for one of the better spots, the mouth of the Green River where it converges with the north fork of the Toutle River. The fishing hole isn't simple to reach, which normally means few fishermen are there. We hike in, go over an old, abandoned railroad trestle, and then ford the mouth of the Green River to a great fishing hole on the other side.

This particular time, we wade the mouth of the Green River in about twelve inches of water in rapids that aren't real strong but still require care because of slippery rocks. As we cross the mouth of the river, the water looks like it's churning. In no time we discover why. Ralph and I stand in the middle of an enormous salmon run. Fish swarm all around us, even swim between our legs while heading upstream. It's difficult to believe what we are seeing. By the time we near the opposite side of the river, I tell Ralph, "I can't take it! I'm using my hands, not my pole."

I toss my fishing gear to the bank, turn around with my bare hands, and grab one salmon after another. I manage to throw four of those beauties onto the bank. We punch our salmon cards, grab the fish and our gear, and head back across the river. Unlike my father, I didn't even need a trojan lure. The apple doesn't fall too far from the tree when it comes to hunting and gathering.

1996
TOLEDO CHEESE DAYS
1996 Big Cheeses

Ray & Elna Wallace

The picture on this cover is one example of Ray and Elna Wallace's support of the community. The Wallaces donated 10 acres of land as part of the new high school site.

CRITERIA FOR SELECTION OF BIG CHEESES—

1. Must be at least 75 years of age.
2. Must have lived in the area most of their lives.
3. Must have dedicated many hours to community service.

July 12th, 13th and 14th
Toledo, Washington

Speaking of parents, in September of 1975, the Toledo School District plans to build a new high school up the hill on the north side of town Where Dad over time had purchased several smaller pieces of property. Dad and Mom decide to donate ten acres for the new campus. Generosity is never an issue for those two.

BACK TO BUSINESS

It's the spring of 1975, and all our preparations for the new store are complete. I'm ready to apply for a Small Business Administration (SBA) loan at Security State Bank in Chehalis. Roy, my accountant, helped me put together everything I need. I meet with one of the vice presidents at Security State, Bob Hendricks, my loan officer. We end up developing a good friendship and a smooth working relationship. Ten days later, Bob calls to say I've been approved. The SBA is a government-sponsored agency that makes money more readily available to small businesses. Bob mentions this is the fastest loan he's seen go through. I owe most of that to Roy's professional help with my proposal. We're ready to break ground and begin

Preparing to build the new store

construction. I enlist a local builder, Lee Wheeler, to guide me. With Lee's guidance and good subcontractors, all goes relatively smoothly.

SHANE AND ANNE

My brother Gary built his new home on ten acres that Dad gave him adjoining the new high school. He also constructed a small one-room cabin with a woodstove in the forest below his house for a getaway space. Gary informs me a blonde about my age with a cute little two-year-old lives in the cabin and says Dad's been taking food to them, including Hershey bars for the little one. I end up inviting them over. I fall in love, right off, with the little guy and think the blonde is cool and adventurous, living in a small cabin in the woods heated by a woodstove. Something about her reminds me of women I grew up around in the logging camp, which I think attracted me to her. They end up moving in with me, while Paul and John slowly move out, but John stays around a lot, helping me with the finishing touches of the new Mike's Hillcrest.

Anne, her son, Shane, who is a year and a half, and their border collie, Norbert, are now part of the scene.

With fish still running in the Toutle River, I think Shane and Anne might like to go with me. We find a good spot with no one else fishing around us, and I bait the hook, looking to entice a salmon. After a few nibbles, we know fish are around. I'm using a thirty-pound test line, which should do the job, and finally hook one. Realizing I've caught a big one, I'm careful not to overplay the fish and lose it. This salmon fights me longer than any other in my lifetime.

The battle lasts more than an hour with the fish continually swimming upstream and then down again. As I draw him close to shore, I realize why the battle takes so long. This salmon weighs fifty-five pounds. Now, this isn't just another big fish story. What's unusual is how long it takes to knock that monster in the head. I don't want to lose him to the river. I hit the fish with a big rock repeatedly until it died, but I didn't realize at the time that little Shane is a sensitive child. All this time he observes me trying to kill the fish. He tells me years later he never had a desire to eat fish until he was much older. Oops!

THE WORK CONTINUES

In September I contact the Mobil distributor who promised me two large underground fuel tanks at no cost if I buy my fuel only from Mobil Oil. He now says he can't remember making the agreement. I waste no time moving on from him, determined to turn lemons into lemonade. After many inquiries, I finally reach a company in Seattle, Time Oil, with a ridiculously low price for fuel. The only hitch is I need to finance my own tanks. After penciling things out, it's a no-brainer. I sell gas, not a little cheaper, but a lot

The crew

Ready to open

cheaper than anyone else for miles around.

Our grand opening in December is definitely grand. The gas tank debacle is the best thing that could have happened. We had gas lines and people coming in I'd never seen before. Our first day was four times the best day I'd ever had in the old store.

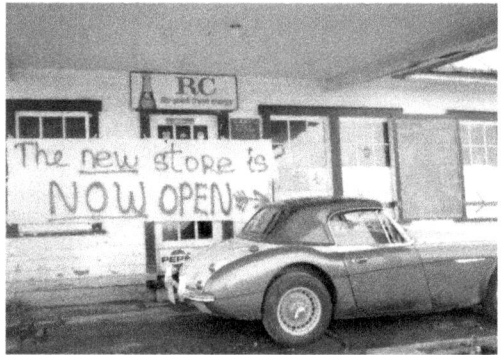

Goodbye to the old store

Three months later, I tore down the old store and put work into the house. Unfortunately, little of the store is worth saving.

SOUTHWEST WASHINGTON FAIR

The summer of '76 brings a memorable event for our family to the Southwest Washington Fair, held midway between Chehalis and Centralia. Bigfoot will be featured in this year's Destruction Derby at the fairgrounds. Ray Wallace gave Jim Cook, a local, his old 1957 Cadillac. This car, I'm positive, holds the record for an auto surviving the most abusive uses ever. Among them: 1) Hauling a carload of loggers in calk boots to work; 2) Hauling barrels of oil and diesel to logging sites in the trunk; 3) Hauling large heavy chokers for pulling logs; 4) Hauling a jackass (animal version) in the back seat; 5) Taking the family for occasional rides, long and short; 6) Hauling bullfrog polliwogs to parts unknown; 7) Finally, participating in the Destruction Derby.

Here is where we insert a General Motors commercial.

Jim Cook prepares the '57 Caddy for war by beefing up the grill and side panels, adding a roll bar, and installing safety gear. As a finishing touch, to honor Dad, he paints BIGFOOT in big bold letters the length of the car on both sides. Jim, with his crash helmet, is ready to roll. We watch maybe a dozen entries one at a time get knocked out of competition and dragged off the course. Eventually, it's a battle between Bigfoot and one other car with a nasty-looking front bumper. Bigfoot gets the last lick and comes out a champion. It's fun watching the battle while rolling years full of special memories through my mind. The most special memory for me is lying in that big rear window as a kid watching the stars at night while rolling down the highway.

Speaking of Ray L. Wallace, I have another Cadillac story that Walt Clark tells best, since it concerns him.

Walt, new around Toledo, is looking for a radiator for his TD-24 bulldozer. He's heard this guy by the name of Ray Wallace might have one. Ray shows up at his place, tells Walt he has a radiator that will fit his needs, and orders him to follow him to his ranch. Dad drives his new Fleetwood Cadillac he purchased after giving Jim Cook his old '57 Cadillac. Down along the river nearing the ranch, they're driving along this fenced field. Walt's following Dad in his pickup. All of a sudden, Walt sees Ray's brake lights flash on, and Ray takes a sharp left through a gate into a pasture, driving like crazy.

The Fleetwood bounces up and down over the bumpy field as he heads toward this farmer trying to herd cows into a makeshift loading pen. One cow escapes and Ray, seeing this, speeds across the field with cow manure flying off his tires, going like a madman.

Mom with her newish Fleetwood

He looks like he's been herding cattle all his life. Quickly he has that critter rounded up and heading toward the loading pen. Seeing this, the farmer hops on his motorbike and helps Dad herd the last one into the pen. Not stopping to talk to the guy, Ray gives him a quick wave with his index finger and tears off back toward the gate where Walt watches in disbelief, trying to piece together what he's just witnessed. Walt's only problem is he simply hasn't known Ray L. Wallace long.

FIRST TIME IN BOULDER

Anne left Boulder for several reasons, in part to get away from where she grew up and her ex-husband, a psychiatrist. Her parents are financially well off, which is a bit of a surprise after finding Anne living in a cabin in the woods. Discovering her roots is, at first, a case of cognitive dissonance for me. Her parents live in a beautiful home bordering a greenbelt up against the Flatirons near the Rocky Mountains in Boulder, Colorado. Two things I remember most about their home: first, a large tapestry made for a princess from one of the Chinese dynasties woven partially with gold thread and amazingly beautiful, and second and most interesting is her father's library. It's fascinating to pore over all the old history books in Pete's library. He grew up on a family estate on Long Island with a rich history.

During our first visit, being the hippie-looking type, I felt a bit more comfortable with Peter than with Anne's mother, Jeanne, who had been a high-fashion model in England, modeling with future movie stars. Jeanne is still somewhat cordial. The entire trip is an eye-opener.

Having returned to Hillcrest, Anne continues to work with Shane's reading skills. We discover

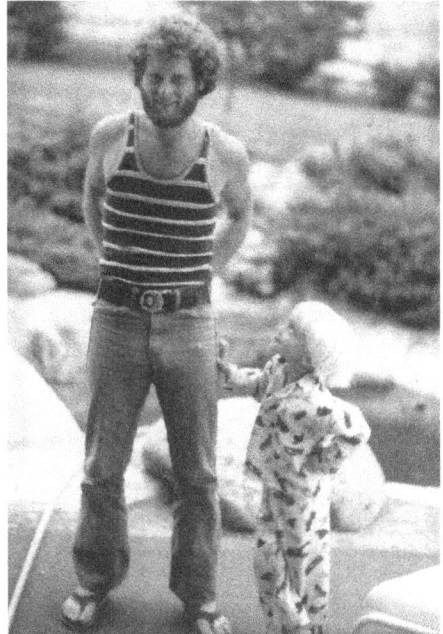

Mike with his cute little towhead

this little guy picks things up quickly. At age three, he's reading comic strips to me out of *The Sunday Oregonian*. I truly remember only one time getting upset with him for some silly reason. Outside of that, Shane always has better things to do than get into trouble. He's an easy and wonderful child to raise. Even though I have yet to adopt Shane, he's already mine in my mind.

CHAPTER 25
A MIXED BAG

MIKE'S HILLCREST II

W E RUN SUCH A THRIVING BUSINESS at our Winlock location that I begin researching a second location, which ends up being an easy process. I go to the Department of Transportation in Olympia and locate records on traffic counts for Lewis County. I discover an intersection about two miles west of Chehalis and find a piece of property available at the location where the old Claquato Ballroom once stood. By now most of the former ballroom lies on the ground. I recognize the property as an ideal location for my second store. With a speedy loan from my friend Bob at Security State, in no time, we hold our grand opening in March of 1978. I hire Linda Armstrong, a fabulous people-person and very trustworthy, to manage our new store while I remain at the Winlock store. Hillcrest II is an instant success with higher sales volume than Hillcrest I after only a few months.

BOULDER AGAIN

We head for Boulder again, this time to get married at Pete and Jeanne's place. Ray and Elna are a day behind us on our drive out. Pete arranges for his Episcopalian minister to perform the ceremony in Pete's beautiful backyard with the Rocky Mountains as a backdrop. We spend about a week there before heading back to Washington. When we aren't exploring Boulder

Canyon and the Rockies, I'm exploring more of Pete's library. Anne's sister, Susie, who lives in the area, joins our small wedding party.

The wedding party and a thirteen-foot marlin

KONA

Some months later, we head to Kailua-Kona on the Big Island of Hawaii with Pete and Jeanne. This is my first trip to Hawaii. Our first excursion is a snorkel boat to the Captain James Cook Monument, where the British explorer first landed in Hawaii in a small cove teeming with tropical fish. The conditions are perfect for snorkeling.

Several days later, Peter charters a fishing boat called The Rebel operated by a couple of young gentlemen barely out of their twenties. It's a thirty- or forty-five-minute run to one of their favorite

spots for catching marlin. Twenty minutes later, we have our lines in the water and not long afterward, one of the reels goes crazy! "Fish on!" the captain barks.

Pretty soon what looks to be a small submarine comes out of the water with its long pointed nose pointing to the sky while shaking wildly. The marlin repeats this action, running fifty yards beyond the bow, then fifty yards past the stern, back and forth. The captain tells us these fish are fairly intelligent in their efforts to shake hooks snaring them. He says if their efforts fail, they dive to incredible depths, hoping to lose the line. Often fisherman simply cut the line if the marlin dives too deep.

Another half hour goes by and the fish dives. Our captain looks at the reel and estimates this marlin has gone down approximately 2,700 feet, which is more than half a mile. Our captain says, "Now you have a choice. We cut the line, or you three guys put on these gloves and, for probably the next forty-five to sixty minutes, you hand-line this fish up to the surface, one pull at a time." Everyone is unanimous to pull the marlin up by hand. No way are we letting a fish of that size go anywhere.

The interesting thing is that when the marlin surfaces, it will die from surfacing from such a depth too quickly. One hour later, up it comes. What a sight at thirteen feet in length. Next to our boat it does look like a small submarine. It weighs 625 pounds at the dock. The fishing trip turns out to be much more exciting than anyone expected, including our captain.

AARON

Anne is now pregnant with Aaron. We have an experienced midwife checking her regularly, and we're comfortable with her abilities. The plan is to have our baby at home. Anne has come to full term and is having contractions. We contact the midwife in the afternoon, and she wastes no time showing up. The labor drags and toward evening the midwife isn't saying much. When the baby finally comes, things are strangely quiet. Finally, our midwife emerges from the bedroom and informs me our baby is dead, and it has been a hard labor. Aaron was born anencephalic, creating a great amount of cerebral damage. She said it's a blessing he didn't survive; the situation was severe. I'll say one thing, it doesn't feel like much of a blessing.

The following day, still feeling like we were in some kind of a B-grade horror movie, Anne informs me something strange happened while she delivered the baby. She's describing how she watched the delivery from the upper corner of the ceiling as she points to the spot she's referring to. "I left my body and observed the birth while it was happening from up in the corner of the room," she says. Neither of us ever mention the incident again. For days it's like living in the Twilight Zone. We're both numb. If they had offered a class in school called "How to lose a baby 101," we both missed it. I definitely could have used it. My drug use and partying increases as a way to ignore the pain. I pour myself back into work instead of dealing with the trauma. At the time, I didn't know what else to do.

HAY FEVER

During the summer of '79, with both stores running smoothly, I feel the need to get outside more, or maybe I simply want to escape the loss of our baby and our personal lives.

Myron Linder, the gentleman I purchased Hillcrest from, and I start a small hay-baling company on the side. Myron, a gifted MacGyver type of person, isn't afraid to take on anything. Myron encourages that in me, teaching me plumbing, electrical, and many other things that come in handy later in life. He also encourages persistence, saying, "Don't let anyone tell you something can't be done, without exhausting every possible avenue." This, coupled with Dad constantly telling me how good a worker I am when I was younger, starts turning me into a workaholic.

GOING DEEP

In July, I decide scuba diving is my new sport of choice. Seeing a class offered in Centralia, I sign up and can't wait to start. Not really knowing what to expect from the instructor, I soon find out. Sitting in our first class, waiting for the instructor to arrive, I'm envisioning this Adonis-looking dude with bulging muscles who can swim for hours without a rest. Wrong. In walks this guy who is probably thirty or forty pounds overweight with a non-filtered Camel cigarette dangling from his mouth, and I'm thinking, "You've got to be kidding."

As the classes progress, he explains how the best divers are not necessarily the best swimmers. Not being a strong swimmer, I'm relieved now that I know I don't need to swim like Mark Spitz as I had earlier envisioned. We swim a certain amount of laps in a large pool to qualify. By the time I finish, I'm certain I qualify for a heart attack if not much else. As it turns out, those of us who finish the course are hauled up to Potlatch, Washington, on the south end of the Hood Canal for our first dive outside of a swimming pool. This is to weed out anyone who might be claustrophobic. To my surprise, the visibility is poor in this part of the Puget Sound, but it's still fascinating to check out the sea life there.

Not long after this, Anne's dad calls and invites us to go with them to Guaymas, Mexico, on the mainland side of the Sea of Cortez, now called the

Gulf of California. Pete's place is next door to singer/actor Burl Ives' vacation home. We never meet Mr. Ives, which would have been fun. He's an interesting character. What a beautiful spot though. We look out over the Sea of Cortez to the Baja California Peninsula. Jacques Cousteau called the Sea of Cortez "the aquarium of the world" because of the variety of species and abundance of marine life. I soon discover this for myself. Before we leave for Mexico, we purchase and study a book about the Sea of Cortez. I couldn't have wanted a more amazing place to dive with so much beauty to enjoy. Finally, the day arrived. Pete arranges a dive for me with a man he called The Pescador, which is Spanish for fisherman. This man knows all the good spots to catch fresh fish, snorkel, or scuba dive.

The Pescador

After a half-mile boat ride, we reach our dive location. The Pescador puts on his fins and a snorkel while I'm in my scuba gear. We anchor in an area with about forty feet of water and go overboard. Knowing I'm a rookie, The Pescador swims circles around me, collecting sea fans and anything else that might make a good souvenir. I'm mesmerized at thirty to forty feet of depth, swimming in large circles, taking it all in. I didn't need to go far to see underwater beauty. My dive ends abruptly when, all of a sudden, the light is blocked overhead. After swirling around several times and finally looking up, there is no mistaking what I saw only a few yards from me—the tail of a stingray. Feeling somewhat fearful, I immediately head in the opposite direction of that tail. I do not want to get stung by this fella. Few people die from their sting, but the results are extreme pain that persists for hours. People can suffer nausea, vomiting, seizures, heart irregularities, and in rare cases, death. Knowing all of this, I can't return to the boat fast enough. The Pescador simply flashes me a smile. The dive, in more than one way, does not lack intensity.

After returning home, I'm actually able to use my scuba diving skills for something useful for someone else. Bob, my friend at the bank, knows I take diving lessons. He calls to let me know about a problem with one of his commercial fish ponds. The dammed-up end has sprung a leak. To patch it, someone needed to use an inch and a half hose with a shut-off on the end to spray bentonite where the water was escaping. The trick is to find where the water flowed out, despite visibility of about three feet. Snorkeling won't do it because I had to move slowly and not stir up impurities, which worsened visibility. Yet I needed impurities to track the leak. It's a challenge but a fun one. We succeed in locating and plugging the leak. I'm able to return some kindness to Bob who looked past my afro hairdo and my beard. Not bad for a guy wearing a suit and tie every day in the '70s.

A CHRISTMAS PRESENT

December 1979 turns out to be a special month. Anne and I had worked for months on adopting Shane. Finally, after pulling the "back child support" card on her ex, the adoption is final. I cannot be happier. He is now, officially, my son.

Shane pays a little bit of a price for technically not being my son. After arriving home from daycare, Shane mentions that the lady working the day care called him what he thought was a "custard" child. Mrs. What's Her Name actually called him a "ba-----" child. We prefer to call him a cute little custard, which, of course, is Shane's preference also. Hopefully, Mrs. What's Her Name will mend her ways. It's mind-boggling how someone working a day care, of all places, can be so insensitive to a child. She apparently has issues and one less child to watch.

Shane spends more time at the store with me, which he's done for the last several years anyhow. When he was smaller, he sat on the checkout counter and entertained the customers, especially those guys buying any other beer than Budweiser. My old roomie, John Huffman, unbeknownst to me, had coached or encouraged Shane to give his opinion on choices of alcoholic beverages. At the age of four, perched on the counter next to me, Shane spouts off when one of our regular customers sets down a six-pack of

Schlitz. All of a sudden, Shane looks straight at this guy and this commercial spews from his mouth with a slight German accent. "Don't drink Schlitz, Schlitz gives you the sh---, drink Budveiser" with a v instead of a w. Needless to say, these words catch my customer, who now has a smile on his face, and me both off guard. Shane and I might have to discuss altering his advertisements for Bud slightly.

CHAPTER 26
THE CURE

WHAT TAKES PLACE BETWEEN 1977 AND 1981 would easily fill a book, but I'll simply give a general overview about how my life evolves over that four-year period.

In June 1977, a grassroots citizens' group forms in Lewis County in response to the Washington Public Power Supply System (WPPSS.). WPPSS, a municipal organization formed in 1957, proposed placing two nuclear power plants near Toledo, Washington, on the Cowlitz River.

Citizens from Toledo, Winlock, Vader, Onalaska, Napavine, and adjoining communities form Communities United for Responsible Energy (CURE) to combat the proposal. As word spreads quickly of the WPPSS plans, volunteers quickly join. In no time we form a twelve-person board and acquire a long list of eager volunteers. Among those involved are Dr. Dan Dugaw, a family physician and CURE president; Mike Owen, CURE vice president; Beverly Meister, secretary; Paul Dugaw, CURE attorney and legal advisor; teachers Mike and Diane Morgan, who publish the CURE newsletter, attend WPPS meetings, and explore nuclear waste and decommissioning issues; Jo Gefre, who coordinates information for CURE; Dr. Rick Shepard, dentist and CURE treasurer; Ron Carmichael, businessman, fundraiser who speaks before the House of Representatives; Dan Godat, banker and financial advisor; me, a businessman, director of alternative energy sources, and fundraiser who speaks before community Grange gatherings; and George Murdock, superintendent of the Toledo School District. I apologize for those I fail to mention. So many people become involved.

Our group forms not solely to fight off two nuclear plants but also to educate the public about alternate energy sources such as solar, wind, and wave power to help meet energy demands. At the same time, we try to convince governmental leadership to pull away from use of nuclear fission and invest research dollars toward nuclear fusion. In a nutshell, nuclear fission splits heavy nuclei into smaller fragments while using most commonly uranium-235. While this generates energy, it also creates extremely toxic nuclear waste with a half-life of 703.8 million years. Nuclear fusion, on the other hand, involves light nuclei (hydrogen) fused to heavier nuclei (helium) under extreme heat and pressure, which releases large amounts of energy without producing long-lived radioactive waste. It's a cleaner and more abundant source of energy.

OUR FIRST YEAR

During our first year, CURE becomes a well-oiled machine. Through donations and fundraising, we begin a CURE newsletter, thanks to the diligent work of Mike and Diane Morgan along with Jo Gefre. We also run radio and newspaper ads to raise more awareness of what our county faces.

We quickly become a thorn in the side of WPPSS (we pronounced it Whoops) for good reason. In our minds, these nuclear power plants would be a huge mistake for our area. We raise concerns over the downsides of nuclear power, which no one else seems to do at the time. We point out shortcomings, ask questions, and offer alternatives.

By October 1978, we even capture the attention of our nuclear-minded governor, Dixy Lee Ray, who in one of her tirades against the anti-nuclear citizens of Washington uses words like "Pap" and "Flap" to describe our doubts over methods of storing nuclear waste, nuclear power plant cost overruns, and, of all things, "the value of conservation." With regard to CURE, she says, "It is fear

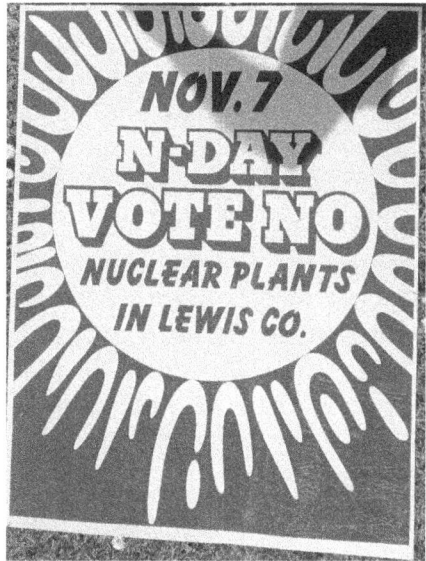

Sign urging voters to oppose nuclear plants

which causes our ignorance." Governor Dixy Lee Ray clearly supported the proposal. Appointed by none other than President Richard Milhous Nixon in 1973, she chaired the Atomic Energy Commission until 1975. Then President Gerald Ford appointed her as Assistant Secretary of State for Oceans and International Environmental and Scientific Affairs, but she resigned after only five months, complaining about a lack of input into decision-making.

Then in 1977, Washington State voters elected her governor, a role she held until 1981. Guess what she wanted? At least five nuclear plants as soon as possible in the state. Among her peers, she was an intellectual whiz kid, but wisdom does not always follow intellect. I see a tremendous lack of wisdom in creating more nuclear waste on this planet.

Our case grows stronger. In the midst of our research, we discover a geological fault line running through our area, either overlooked or ignored by those hired by WPPSS to find appropriate nuclear plant sites. On top of that, the sites were relatively close to a potentially active volcano (Mount St. Helens). Whoops!

THE VOTE

By October 1978, we collect more than enough signatures to put an advisory question on the upcoming November ballot for Lewis County.

On November 7, 1978, 64.6% vote "no" on the construction of thermonuclear plants in Lewis County. We generate a great deal of support, but the fight is far from over. WPPSS spokesperson Richard Romanelli, quoted in *The Aberdeen Daily World* two days later, says, "This does not mean we will automatically eliminate Lewis County as a potential site. This means for us we double down. The fight is nowhere close to being over."

In response to the advisory vote in November, Lewis County commissioners pass a resolution in the first week of December asking WPPSS and the Lewis County Public Utility District to abandon the nuclear plant sitings in Lewis County and, as CURE advised, focus on conservation and alternate energy sources. Despite the advisory vote, PUD commissioners, having invested heavily in proposed plants Nos. 4 and 5, remain reluctant to abide by the advisory vote. They simply decline to make a statement for or against nuclear power while admitting that nuclear waste is a problem. Really?

THE MESSAGE

In his first State of the CURE address from his Camp Winlock retreat, as recorded in the February 1979 newsletter, President Dr. Dan Dugaw says,

"We've made some major accomplishments from scratch to boot. We have: 1) organized a viable and reputable organization; 2) made a major contribution to assuring that Lewis County remains a desirable place to live; 3) become recognized by members of local and federal government; 4) become a thorn in the side of WPPSS; 5) made people aware of the shortcomings of nuclear power; 6) made people conscious of the different aspects of the energy problem; 7) introduced the public to viable and alternative solutions to the energy problem; 8) gotten to know some top-notch people—you!" He goes on to thank the many people who put in countless hours to achieve this outcome and reminds us many more hours may be needed to ensure our communities have responsible energy.

In March the Bonneville Power Administration announces that WPPSS overruns are at 152 percent, which is bad news for the Lewis County PUD. Before CURE organized, the PUD purchased a 2 percent interest in the proposed Nos. 4 and 5 plants in our area. By November it's clear the PUD would not recover its losses. (Whoops.) By this time, it's clear our citizens won't back down from their opposition.

WHAT A MESS

On March 28, 1979, a reactor at the Three Mile Island nuclear plant has a partial meltdown, releasing radioactive material, supposedly mostly contained. Nuclear plant safety features help prevent catastrophic consequences like the global nuclear disaster seen when a reactor at the Chernobyl plant in the Soviet Union exploded on April 26, 1986.

During this same time, 43rd District Senator Jim McDermott opposes the idea of Washington State becoming the nuclear dumping site (Hanford) for the rest of the world. "We are destroying a beautiful state," he says. "We, as voters and citizens, and in groups like CURE, can turn it around if we participate and reclaim local control." This is the exact opposite approach President Jimmy Carter takes at this time as he says nuclear energy should go where the government sees fit! Hmmm!

CHAPTER 27
UP, UP, AND AWAY

THE RED ZONE

A FEW MONTHS LATER, ON MARCH 16, 1980, a series of small earthquakes rumble on Mount St. Helens. Four days later, equipment records a 4.2 magnitude earthquake on the mountain.

On March 27th, an eruption of steam and ash opens a new crater on Mount St. Helens. For about a month afterward, the volcano shakes with many tremors. Two days earlier, on March 25th, equipment registered twenty-two earthquakes in an eight-hour period.

Shortly after this, the U.S. Forest Service begins evacuating personnel and creating closure zones. One of those closures, The Red Zone, created a no-fly zone in the air space around St. Helens.

Not long after this Gordon Kalich calls me. He wants up close and personal photos of what's occurring on the mountain. I inform him I would risk losing my license for this grand tour. He gives me this once-in-a-

Mount St. Helens in 1980

Up close

lifetime speech, and he's top-of-the-line when it comes to giving speeches, I relent. Being a bit of a rebel in the first place, I probably don't need much of a push or a speech. We take a small Cessna out of Chehalis and head east to St. Helens.

The plan is to turn off the radio to ignore any warnings and let ignorance be bliss. Not really a good plan, but fortunately no one comes after us. It's a beautiful day with only a few broken clouds. We shoot the photos we want and head back, feeling good as we put distance between our plane and the mountain, not knowing if today would be the day it decides to blow. Needless to say, I never list that flight in my log book.

THE FINAL BLOW

On Sunday morning, May 18, 1980, at 8:22 a.m., I awaken and prop myself up in bed. I'm sitting there, trying to gain full consciousness from a good night's sleep, staring out the large second-floor picture window, which faces east toward the Cascade Range, framing Mount St. Helens. After only ten minutes of consciousness that Sunday morning, all of a sudden, I find myself watching a huge white column ascending into the sky from the direction of Mount St. Helens. The column rises at an eerie pace to eventually reach a height of 80,000 feet. The word "awesome" would be a weak descriptive term for what it felt like watching the eruption. It only took about fifteen minutes to reach that height.

The aftermath is very strange. Over the next

Mount St. Helens erupts on May 18, 1980

ten days, people wear masks, and we take special care of anything that consumes oxygen. We also take care in exposing our equipment until the ash settles.

I'm concerned for our stores, wondering if their flat roofs will support the weight of the ash. We go to work immediately, clearing not only the roofs but the parking lots also, thanks to Dad who owned several large water tanks with pumps and fire hoses. The mess is mostly taken care of in a couple of days. But all around us, it looks like a gray colorless planet, like what the moon might look like up close. We're fortunate on the west side of the Cascades because we don't get nearly as much ash as those east of the mountains. Of course, historically, volcanic ash is why Yakima and other Eastern Washington areas

Cleaning up on May 28, 1980

grow such rich crops, along with the sunshine they get.

Many people in the mudflow area down the Toutle River are fortunate to escape with their lives, let alone save their homes. We're indeed fortunate in only having to deal with a little ash. It took months for most of the ash to

Toutle River mudflow

be absorbed by nature. A huge pile of ash dredgings remains at the end of the Toutle River.

BOOM AND JUSTIFICATION!

The eruption of Mount St. Helens justifies all the work we put into CURE and preventing construction of nuclear plants. The seismic activity alone could have damaged any plants and possibly leaked radiation into our communities.

With the fault lines, the earthquakes, and the eruption of Mount St. Helens, residents of Lewis County are exuberant that WPPSS did not get its wishes.

By 1981, the battle is pretty much won against WPPSS. With enough roadblocks and opposition, WPPSS officials decide to abandon the projects. Talk about nuclear plants anywhere near Lewis County ends.

CURE stays on guard for some time, eventually disbanding in 1987.

Just a couple of footnotes: As I write this chapter, news pours in from all over the world concerning major breakthroughs in nuclear fusion research. This is thanks, partially, to today's faster and more powerful computers coupled with new and different approaches to fusion energy issues. When fully developed, fusion will be good news for our world, offering a clean energy source to add to solar, wind, and wave power.

The second news flash a week later says Spain will shut down seven nuclear plants within the next decade and fill the energy gap with solar and wind power. Now we are talking wisdom with intellect. Go Spain.

THE FINAL STRAW

Unknown to me, my good friend and flying buddy, Gordon, reaches the end of his proverbial rope with drugs and alcohol. I find out later from him that he consumes enough of those to see demons. One evening while driving his car, he thinks he's running down a demon with it. The only problem is, he actually tries to chase down a woman walking along the street. He fortunately misses her. When he later comes to his senses, Gordon reaches out to a friend who tried to get him to change his life. Soon after this, he decides to give God a shot at helping him change things going sideways in his life. I didn't see Gordon until the following year.

The drug scene for me isn't much better. Cocaine is a constant. The one thing that saved me from diving as deep as Gordon did is another habit, work. I abuse myself mostly on weekends or days off, which is still pretty lame. Drugs and alcohol certainly don't enhance our marriage by any stretch of the imagination. They only hurt it. We continue to avoid the heart of the problem, which we never take the time to identify.

HIS NICKNAME WAS TAY-TAY

On January 7, 1981, Michael Taylor Wallace enters the world. His big brother always helps him. From what I remember, things go pretty smooth with no trauma this time.

It's not long before it's apparent this little fella has an affinity for the culinary arts, which only grows the older he becomes. Actually going forward to his senior year in high school, he wants to skip college and attend a culinary school in Seattle. With coaxing from his parents, he goes to college, which I know he is still glad he did. He later becomes an amazing cook at home.

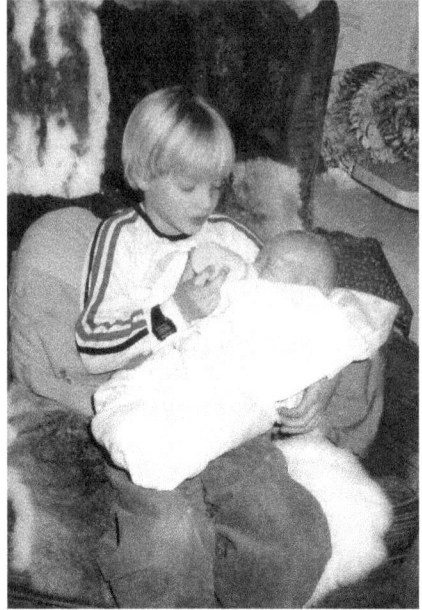

Shane holds baby Michael Taylor, while below he's asking, "What do you mean you want to cook?"

I'm a little surprised about his culinary decision, especially after all the carpentry training Joe Bear, our pet otter hound, gives him. I thought for sure he would end up taking after his old man, but hey, what can you say? The kid becomes an awesome cook.

The cook

CHAPTER 28
A NEW PATH

STRUGGLING

I CAN ONLY PARTIALLY SPEAK FOR ANNE as to what she experiences after losing Aaron. One thing becomes clear; she does not want to live in Lewis County any longer. I think it's become one bad memory for her. As far as I know, our two boys are doing as well as anyone could expect at their young ages. I couldn't have been happier with those two. Business goes so well that a third store would be the next logical step for us.

But with a storm of dissatisfaction brewing inside of Anne, the next thing I know she's pushing to move away. It's taken me many years to finally learn to read the room. If I had been equipped to do so at this time, we might have attacked the heart of the problem or problems. Instead, we run. Guess what? The problems run with us, which becomes a pattern eventually.

By the first of July 1981, I sell Hillcrest II to an interested buyer, Time Oil, our fuel supplier, which was apparently branching out and did not hesitate to purchase Hillcrest II. By the time '82 rolls around, I make plans to sell Hillcrest I. We break the two acres in half, keep the house as a rental, and prepare to move, thinking this might solve our problems.

Through friends who had moved from Seattle to Winlock, I make a connection for employment with Jonathan Loop Inc. in Seattle. My friend describes the business in a positive light. So, I put together my first résumé and apply.

We scout around for a safe area to live and, before leaving Winlock, purchase a house on Queen Anne Hill just north of the Space Needle. I go to work for Loop, which produces high-end office furniture in a plant across from the Kingdome. Loop builds and installs furniture

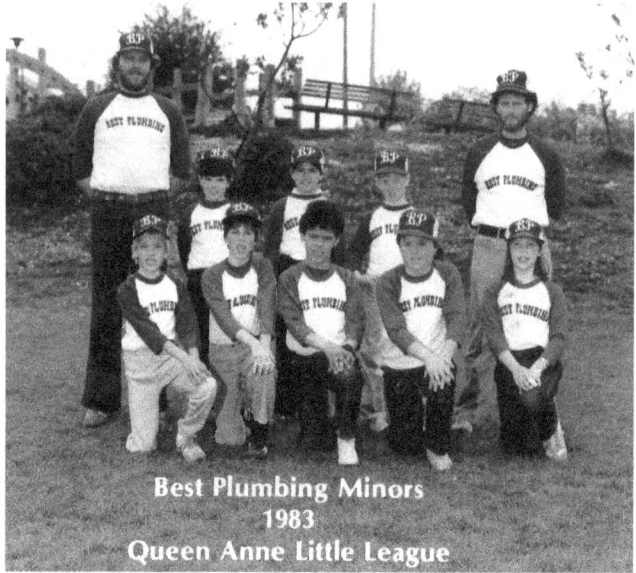

Best Plumbing Minors
1983
Queen Anne Little League

Coaching Little Tigers

for many corporate offices in the Seattle area and ships to buyers all along the West Coast. Loop's business is growing to the point he needs to create a new position, plant supervisor. The following year I'm being groomed for the new position.

While the work situation is positive, things are not well on the home front. Our wonderful sons, both easygoing, thankfully are seldom ever difficult. We are so fortunate to have them. Taylor is too young to comprehend what Anne and I are going through. He knows he is loved, fed, and taken care of. What little Shane knows of his parents' issues he takes in stride. Shane makes friends easily, does well in school, and enjoys baseball and soccer. But after more than a year in Seattle, Anne wants to move to San Rafael, California, just north of the Golden Gate Bridge in San Francisco, to be near her sister, Susie. I won't delve into details, because it's not all my story to tell. But here we go again, from the frying pan to the fire for me as I move farther and farther from what I love most—nature and wide-open spaces. Not facing our problems, we are off again in search of I know not what.

ON A RANT

On the lighter side of life—well, maybe not according to Rant Mullens— things grow a bit overheated concerning who did what and where. Rant is upset that Ray L. Wallace gets so much "Bigfoot" attention. No one in our

Ray paid Rant Mullens to carve the original set of large feet used for the Bigfoot hoax

family, and I'm probably repeating myself, ever denied Rant crafted the original "Big Feet" for Dad and received payment in the form of a fifty dollar check. Dad mailed the check with a letter stating if that's not enough money, send the check back and he'd pay him more.

Rant later claims the feet he holds up perpetuated the Bigfoot hoax. Rant's big square block-shaped carvings are nothing similar to the castings made by Jerry Crew in Bluff Creek in 1958. No one tried to take anything away from Rant who had carved Big Feet since the early 1920s and made prints with them. Up until 1958, the big hairy mysterious creature in the woods was known as Sasquatch and by a dozen other names. Bigfoot was born in 1958, and Dad and his crew of merry hoaxers deserve credit for that one.

Just after the article in which Rant claims he's the father of all big-footed hairy monsters, Dad must have felt he needed to respond. I came across a notarized affidavit that Ray and Edward von Schillinger cooked up. I'm not exactly sure how they intended to use it, but here they are twenty-five years later still hard at it, promoting Bigfoot. The affidavit reads:

> *To whom it may concern:*
> *I have been with Ray Wallace when he was taking 16mm movies of*

Bigfoot eating frogs in Onion Lake in northern California and around Mt. St. Helens in the state of Washington. I have taken movies of Bigfoot for Ray Wallace in California as I have worked for him for five years as an engineer.
Signed — Edward von Schillinger

Now, every word of that is true. Ray was Bigfoot, and I have in my possession some of those sixteen-millimeter movies, so this affidavit appears to be quite factual. Bigfoot was born April 21, 1918, and did not make his first appearance until August 27, 1958.

OFF AGAIN

Before leaving Seattle, I need to deal with a couple of tough things. The first was Norbert, our highly intelligent border collie and wonderful family pet. Norbert, having a severe case of cancer, needs to be put down. I'm not about to have anyone else touch her. Knowing my brother Rick is on a road job close to Mount Rainier, I call to ask if he would cover her with twenty feet of soil if I drove her up to the mountain to put her down. I don't want any wild critter digging her up. "No problem," he says. That's a long hard teary drive, but in the end, I feel good about where she's buried. She had amazing mothering instincts, taking in and protecting any baby critter that lost its mom.

Norbert with Joe Bear

Selling my Austin-Healey

Joe Bear, our otter hound, became Norbert's buddy ever since he wandered onto our porch and refused to go back home. Joe Bear is noticeably different with Norbert gone.

The second hard thing is having to sell my beloved Austin-Healey. That's tough. I think the Healey is the last car I ever polished.

Gary

The last, and by far the ugliest thing to occur this year, is the death of my brother Gary. On the afternoon of July 30, 1984, I receive a call at work. I can't even remember who called because their words hit me like a ton of bricks. "Gary has been in an accident at work and didn't make it." Wow, this is hard to wrap my head around. I'm numb with disbelief.

Jonathan, my boss, can tell I'm not doing well. He comes up to me and says, "Don't worry about anything. I've called the airport and have a plane waiting to take you to Toledo. You call Anne and the kids and let them know what's happening." About an hour later, I find myself on a private plane heading for Toledo. As if things aren't already weird enough, all around us for as far as I can see, the sky is extremely dark. Then lightning flashes. I remember looking out the plane's window, expecting to see Rod Serling sitting on the wing, turning to me and saying, "You've now entered the Twilight Zone."

It takes a couple of days to obtain solid information from Weyerhaeuser Co. as to what actually occurred. Gary had teamed up with another man logging blowdown timber in the Mount St. Helens area. Both alternated between operating the bulldozer and setting chokers on the logs. That day Gary had been the choker setter while his partner ran the dozer. After setting the chokers on the logs, workers usually walk to the side of the dozer where the logs would be dragged, generally to a landing site.

The Twilight Zone

Gary had hooked up the logs and felt tired, so he hopped on the dozer, sitting next to the dozer operator on the downhill side. As they traveled laterally along a steep hillside, the dozer hit a solid ash-covered stump that turned out to be rotten. It gave way, causing the dozer to roll over sideways on Gary, killing him instantly.

It's a quiet ride toward Mount St. Helens with Dad that day. When we arrive, we find the only thing not damaged is the bulldozer. His partner is okay physically but mentally shaken to the core. It's not his fault, but at the time he didn't feel that way.

Gary died at thirty-two and left his wife, Sherry, and two little ones, Eric and Lee Ann. I don't think Sherry ever experienced much joy again after Gary's death, a life-changing loss for her.

Mom and I, for a good solid year, think we've mentally lost Dad. Things go gray and somber for him. He takes it extremely hard. I think of the four of us boys, Gary seemed to have all his ducks in a row. I certainly did not.

I vividly remember Gary's funeral. What sticks with me is seeing my friend Gordon Kalich, who has dramatically changed his life over the past twelve years. He fills me in as to what he's been doing since I took him on the photo shoot over Mount St. Helens. After his drug-induced encounter with his demons and turning his life over to Christ, he served as a missionary in the Philippines. "It would not be a bad idea for you to consider," he says. I just smile.

Anne and the boys come down. After a few days with all the family, we head back to Seattle. Mom is badly shaken but stable, but Dad is nothing like himself, totally introverted, almost lost. I don't blame Dad. Gary had so much going for himself and his young family. His death is an enormous loss for all of us.

SAN RAFAEL

With Anne's mind made up that she needs to live near her sister Susie, we find ourselves heading for California's Marin County. With most of our money gone, we find a rental in San Rafael. I need work, so I immediately begin cleaning houses during an apparent shortage of dependable house cleaners. I figure it's a quick avenue to pick up home repair work. In no time, I have all the repair work I need and no longer clean homes.

I don't remember exactly how long we live in San Rafael, but by the first part of 1985, the idea of moving is the topic of choice again. I never wanted to move in the first place. The only difference this time is I inform those around me that I'm making the choice this time. My decision is to head for Boulder, Colorado, where Anne's parents live. So, we pack up what little we own and leave San Rafael behind.

CHAPTER 29
WELCOME TO COLORADO

OUR NEW HOME

PETE, ANNE'S DAD, finds a nice two-story home for sale. He agrees to put the down payment on the place if we pay the mortgage, taxes, repairs, and all other expenses. If it's ever sold, we promise to give him the amount of the down payment. It's a solid deal for us and an opportunity to start over.

A new home

Boulder, nestled at the base of the Rocky Mountains in a portion called the Flatirons, a fascinating rock formation, is quite an impressive sight. The city is home to the University of Colorado campus, which makes the area somewhat eclectic.

In no time I'm employed with Square One Construction, which is involved in both commercial and residential construction. The owner, a Buddhist in his theology, is great to work for. I couldn't ask for a better person to work for than Roger Folsom, my foreman. He is solid as rock. We soon become close friends and create a great work environment.

Our family settles into our new home and starts making new friends among neighbors in the laid-back community. Being a college town, downtown Boulder is a fascinating place to people-watch.

I enjoy getting to know Peter better. Living in Boulder, I have more opportunities to spend time in the family

Mike with Roger

library and at Pete's backgammon board. He's an excellent backgammon teacher. With his skills, it's no problem for him to make good money, which he didn't particularly need, at his club. Backgammon is still one of my favorite board games.

Pete with Taylor ten years later

Peter provides opportunities to meet fascinating people. Yearly, Peter generously supports the athletic department at the University of Colorado. The huge upside is we enjoy box seats and an incredible banquet before each game. It gets even better. Peter takes me to the university where Hall of Fame football coach Bill McCartney lets us sit in on his locker room chats with the team. Bill, a well-liked man, held the record for the most wins of any coach in the history of U of C football. Bill often comes to Peter's home for meetings or just to chat. After transforming Colorado's football team, Bill founded The Promise Keepers, a Christian men's group. He passed away on January 10, 2025, in Boulder Colorado, well-loved by many.

SQUARE ONE

Concerning my work at Square One Construction, I become what you might call a utility player. My bosses send me on all the weird jobs no one else wants, which eventually turns out to be beneficial to me. I'm constantly learning new things in the trade. I especially enjoy the problem-solving aspect of my position. One of those jobs, at the University of Colorado, requires a major upgrade to one of the kitchens, and I'm called to the century-old library in the finishing stages of a small walnut addition resembling the old portion. The new walnut needs to match the hundred-year-old walnut perfectly, not just close. I thought, "Awesome, interesting challenge." I sit on the library floor by myself for two days, mixing stains to find the right match, and finally come up with something they approve. That's the kind of job I enjoy most, the unique ones.

POLAR OPPOSITES

Two large remodels on which I work could not have been more polar opposites.

The first job is for a powerful couple. Name withheld to protect the guilty. A portion of this job is going to be photographed for a national trade magazine. After months of interior and exterior work, we inform the lady of the house to draft a punch list of any problems, and we would return in the morning to deal with them.

The next morning, two of us show up to find, throughout the house, somewhere between a hundred and two hundred small pink Post-it notes scattered in every area we had worked except the one to be photographed. The majority are on the walls with an orange peel texture. Apparently, in her mind, each little splatter should be exactly like the one next to it, which is a physical impossibility. Looking at the rest of the Post-it notes, we only shake our heads in wonder.

One issue did need to be addressed. We poured a concrete patio of exposed aggregate, and the temperature dropped so low overnight that cracking occurred. We informed our boss and left. Fortunately, he dealt with her. We requested not to come back. We'd had about all we could take from this difficult lady.

Our next project is a block off campus in a home built by one of Colorado's premiere masons for himself many years earlier. I believe he lived there until he passed away. James Cargill III later purchased the home when he attended the University of Colorado. Cargill hired us to make a few interior changes, but mostly to repair the home to its original state. Repairing locksets that are more than seventy years old and required skeleton keys proves tricky, but we pull it off with two of us working full time for about six months.

Before and after

We find out in the meantime that James Cargill III is a billionaire whose father adopted him. Eventually, he takes over part of the family's business. The Cargills are the wealthiest family in the United States. Their name is on many boxcars that haul grain, mainly in the Midwest. The family with a 158-year history in the United States has fourteen billionaires.

Reaching the completion of the project, Herschel, my supervisor, wants me to meet Jim and his wife, Susan, to go over what might be on their punch list. The following morning, Jim and Susan arrive. I'm a little surprised to see Jim in a plaid shirt and jeans, very casual-looking, climb out of what looked like an older Mercury. I'm not sure what I expect, probably something a little fancier. My first thought is, "This is good." With smiles on their faces, they view our work. I stay in the living room, leaving them to go over all we've done. It's not unusual to have a few concerns on the list, but not usually more than a hundred.

After about a twenty-minute tour, they hand me their punch list and, to my shock, I see one item on it. A nailhead isn't set on a windowsill. I run to my truck, grab the nails set and hammer, and, with a small dab of putty, repair the oversight. "Since you were here every day doing the majority of the work, follow me," Jim says. He takes me down to the basement where he has a new table saw waiting for me. I can't believe it. "Thank you for taking such good care of us," he says. I've recently received a diverse education on how the human race handles wealth. For the next ten years, Susan always sent me a Christmas card. She passed away unfortunately.

The last philanthropic adventure I remember the Cargills being involved in is setting up ways to send food into remote areas of Mexico. Being wealthy has its drawbacks like anything else, but it's so important to examine how we use the things we have and how we treat the people around us. Later, independently of Square One, Jim Cargill hires Shane, who is now thirteen, and me to build a nice fence around the large lot where his house sat. I always

Cargill fence

enjoy working for Jim, and allowing Shane to help makes it even more special. I have fun working with Shane that summer.

THE FAR EAST

The following year is filled with one oriental experience after another. We host a Japanese exchange student, Wakako, a delightful young lady who speaks good English. With such good communication, it makes our experience even richer. Exposing her to the Rocky Mountains and taking her fishing is fun for all of us. Wakako, Shane, and Taylor make the best of their time together. We missed her when she finally left.

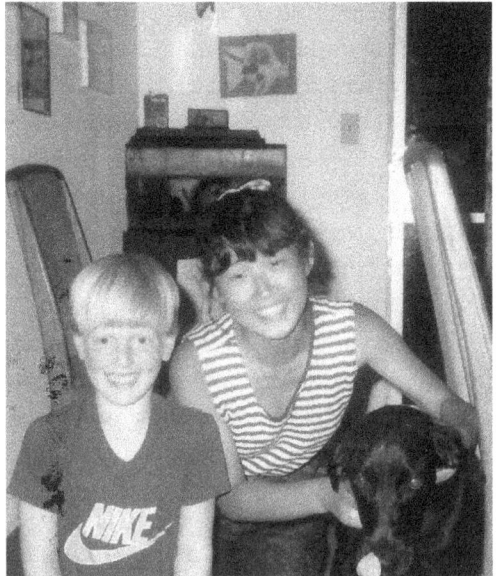

Wakako

196

Shane and I end up taking Japanese classes together. They're difficult for me, but I enjoy the time spent learning Japanese. It's not as much of a struggle for Shane who goes on to the next level.

Anne and I experience a Japanese tea ceremony, a meticulously orchestrated ceremony of preparing and drinking green tea. It is also a cultural experience where the focus is on harmony, respect, purity, and tranquility. I need a heavy dose of all four. These ceremonies can last an hour or more. This is one of several experiences offered at the Buddhist center, funded by my employer, but certainly not required for employment. My boss is quiet about his faith and never mentions much about it.

UNDER A LOOKING GLASS

It starts to seem like every Square One job I work has a strange twist to it. One particular job is for the owner of The Falafel King, which has a Middle Eastern menu. This couple owns franchises in Boulder and Denver. We are hired to remodel their home in Boulder. The work is going well and on schedule until midway through, when two police officers stop by the worksite. They start questioning the three of us about a ring with a large diamond in it. We feel like deer in the headlights as they take us separately for questioning. Then we return to our work. About a week later, we discover what occurred. Apparently, our plumber hired his brother who has a prison record. This guy, for some brain-dead reason, thinks he can make a quick buck by grabbing a ring while one of us takes the fall. It's no wonder he served time in prison; getting captured is apparently his forte.

SUMMER FUN

Shane is still being patient with my fanaticism over the sport of baseball. Here we are again; me coaching and him playing. I'll bet plenty of times he wished it was the other way around. Shane hangs in there playing for the Mighty Thunderbirds Little League baseball team. In the evenings I play slo-pitch for Juanita's restaurant where the only required uniform is a hat. Juanita, being a lady, decides hot pink hats with her name on them are the way to go. The bizarre thing is, she's dead-on. Everybody wants one of those hats. Unfortunately, Juanita ordered only a limited edition of baseball caps. Spectators and other team players love our flashy ball caps and offer to buy them for a decent price. One big problem is, if you sell your hat, there goes your uniform.

CHAPTER 30
INDEPENDENT

THE BRONCOS

HAVING NO SHORTAGE OF SIDE JOBS, I decide to break away from Square One Construction. I connect with a retired National Football League player who is trying to figure out what to do with his life after football. After serving as a backup Denver Broncos quarterback and playing on several other teams, he ends up back home in Boulder. He has a lovely wife and is a terrific guy to work with. The only problem is he's doing fire and water restoration. After a few months, I decide it's not what I want for a career as it lacked a creative side. As much as I enjoy working with him, I pass on that type of work. He tired of it later and ended up working with major league sports venues.

GREENBELT

Late in 1987 I receive a call from Roger Folsom, my foreman at Square One, informing me he's leaving the company. He wants to know if I'm interested in being his partner. I do not hesitate! I know I can trust Roger as a partner and will definitely enjoy working with him. Roger knows the mechanics of construction, and I possess the business acumen from running my convenience stores. Roger is well-known and liked in Boulder. He has a long list of connections that goes well with our new company. Folsom Stadium at the university is named after his family. Roger is indeed connected.

TURNING POINT

During this time, things come to a head at home. As much as Anne and I try, something needs to give. We certainly both take full credit for problems in our marriage. Things rattle me months before we decided to part. I think it comes to a head when we want to buy Shane a keyboard for his birthday. We put off repairing the dishwasher and buy the keyboard instead, figuring the following month we will fix it. I have no problem washing dishes by hand, so we buy the keyboard. Shane loves it, and I feel good about the decision. But when Peter finds out, he's upset that we're not keeping up with repairs of the house. Of course, that was the deal, right?

That's the straw that broke the camel's back for me. Peter isn't necessarily wrong, but that's how I feel. I have absolutely zero solutions for our marriage, so I ask for a divorce. We don't argue; we simply experience a great deal of sadness. By April 1988, the divorce is final after ten years of marriage. Anne later moves to Seattle, and I keep the boys. I drop the keys to our house with Peter and call it good. With Peter, sometimes business is business. I respect that. No hard feelings on my part. He did many good things for us, which I appreciate.

With nowhere to go, I grow acquainted with a neighbor lady. Our kids go to school together, and my boys spend time at their place. We had no prior emotional connection, but knowing my situation, she offers Taylor, Shane, and me a place to stay. This didn't come with any strings attached for either of us. It's simply a convenience for both of us. We support each other. Since we both recently divorced, I take her up on her offer. Her two sons hit it off with Shane and Taylor as well as anyone could under the circumstances. The house has a huge backyard that the boys mow. Also in the back is an old small building that Roger and I remodel and use for our office.

The toughest part of all this is how the divorce affects Taylor, who is seven years old. Not having his mom anywhere near is rough, mostly at bedtime. The only thing I can do or say is to promise him I'll never leave him.

Shane is introspective about the whole thing. I don't remember if I voice the same promise to him as I do to Taylor, but I hope he felt it.

Caretakers

Roger and I hit the ground running. After some remodeling, our first new home comes quickly, a beautiful multi-level custom home. The only unfortunate aspect is one of our men nails his foot to the floor while decking it. Big ouch! Fortunately, he suffers no permanent damage to his heel. Not long afterward, he decides carpentry isn't his bag.

MY DREAM

In January of '89, I'm called out on a small job concerning a leaking six-by six-foot skylight. Several tradesmen looked at it, but nothing they tried worked. So I tell the owner we'll check it out. While I'm there and having conversations with him, I find out he's a jet pilot who flies governmental department heads wherever they need to go. I mention my long-ago dream of flying jets. I tell him his job sounds ideal, and I'd

Roger

New job

New job

give it another try if I were not so old. He says he started his jet engine training when he was two years younger than me. He also mentions I may not end up flying for a commercial airline, but plenty of companies like UPS and others hire pilots. "It's worth a shot if that's what you really want to do," he says.

I'm excited over the possibility of recapturing that dream. And yes, I figure out where his skylight leaks. He says Jefco Airport between Boulder and Denver has one of the best flight schools around. Part of what makes Jefco such a good place to learn is the winds pilots deal with flying close to the Rocky Mountains. He says some small planes flip over trying to land in the crosswinds.

Three weeks later, on February the 18th, I'm up in the air. I begin studying during every spare minute I have, and by May, I'm ready to take my instrument rating test. So on May 25th, I go in for the instrument rating exam. I'm the first one to finish and out of my seat. My instructor says, "Hang on a minute while I check your test." I'm not sure what's going on. Maybe he thinks I gave up early and quit. He comes back from his office and says, "I want you to take the instrument instructors test now. It follows the one you just took." I tell him I don't feel ready, but he says by the looks of my first test, he thinks I'm ready. It's too good to be true, because I don't feel confident, but he obviously is. I don't do as well on the second one, a B instead of an A, but hey, this was awesome! I'm one step closer to my dream. My next step is jet engines classes. I'm pretty excited about the possibility of flying for a living.

Roger is good with all this. He has a "Go with your dream" attitude. He's supportive, and I appreciate it by not letting my flying time cut into our work. I had no guarantee for what I attempted to accomplish, and I'm not about to burn any bridges.

One thing bothers me about my resurrected dream. It involves the boys. The struggle is not knowing where flying would take me in regard to a work schedule. Would I be away from the boys for extended periods of time? That's the biggest issue. I'm not comfortable being very far from them at any time, in light of what we've all just experienced. It's a mixed bag though. I'm having an absolute ball flying again, but that nagging concern of whether I could be home every night stays with me. I have no desire to give up being close to my boys. I've made plenty of mistakes as a parent and don't want to add more, although it's foolish to think mistakes will end. I just want to keep them down to a dull roar.

DOING AND BEING

Self-examination, up to this point, has never been one of my strong points. Twenty years ago, it might have kept me from walking down slippery paths that created unhealthy habits. I've become a much better "Human Do-er" than a "Human-Being." When it comes to "doing" I'm at the head of the class. I do a great deal of exciting things and meet quite a few interesting people. But more important is my "being." Am I just a human-doer or am I also the human-being I'm meant to be? A human-doer can be self-absorbed with tunnel vision and worry more about getting things done than who is around them.

A certain emptiness goes along with the human-doer. It's like having a hole in the middle of yourself that you don't know what to do with. My life up to this point has been so much more about experiences and much less about my state of being. When it comes to the things of value in life, I've bypassed a great number of opportunities. I feel adrift without the right village. At this point I don't have a good idea how to deal with my current state.

THE CALL

After arriving home from work one evening, I find a voice message from Dad on the recorder. He wants me to call him as soon as I return home. This is rather unusual considering Mom is the one who periodically checks in on us. The first question to come to mind is, "What does he have going?"

PART THREE

THE FINAL VILLAGE

CHAPTER 31
A DIFFERENT COURSE

THE DEAL

ARRIVING HOME FROM WORK, I find Dad left a message to call him, so I do. What he says, getting right to the point, is indeed a surprise. "I'm going to start selling portions of the ranch and want to give you the first opportunity for a part of it." This catches me off guard. It's been many years since we last talked about this possibility, at which point he only wanted to buy land, not sell it. Dad says he's retiring and selling land for money that he and Mom can live off of. The deal is to start with a small piece, build a house, and sell it at the going price per acre with a good interest rate.

Knowing we are starting over, Mom and Dad want Shane, Taylor, and me to move in with them for a year and pay only a small amount for food. In a year's time I can save enough to start a new home, a small one I can add to as needed.

This is not a tough decision for me. I know where I want to be—back in the middle of a great deal of evergreens. When I talk to the boys, Taylor doesn't seem to mind, and Shane remains rather quiet. Right or wrong, I take this as the time to move. All of a sudden, everything changes. All my friends support the move. Within a month, I put all of our personal and business affairs in order. We load up a medium-sized U-Haul and head for Toledo.

THE DUNGEON

It doesn't take long to settle in. Shane and Taylor each have a bedroom on the main floor. I plant myself in the two-room dungeon-esque space in the basement. It looks as dingy as I feel at first. I spend many evenings reflecting

Unpacking

on my last twenty years away from this home. I've come full circle, returning to the same starting point only twenty years older with two good sons and not much else.

Having Mom's support with the boys is wonderful. Her endless array of cookies, pies, and cakes are just a bonus. Aside from the dungeon, I am basking in the midst of nothing but good memories from this place I am now at again.

With the help of a good builder, Art Merzoian, who advises me on who to use as local subs, I am almost ready to resurrect Greenbelt Construction. First, I need my license and liability insurance. The following morning, I leave early for Olympia to obtain my license, wanting to give myself plenty of time for testing. Arriving at the Department of Licensing, I ask at the desk where I can take my test for a contractor's license. She says, "There is no test. You just pay us a hundred dollars, and you are a licensed contractor." While not complaining, I think in my head, "You've got to be kidding; no test." I pay it and leave.

In Colorado, if you want to call yourself a contractor, you take a four-hour test for residential licensing and a much longer one for commercial. This seems like a joke. You need little knowledge about construction in this state; you simply need the correct amount of money. Running the clock forward to the 2007 and 2009 recession, caused by subprime interest rates and the bursting of the housing bubble, so-called contractors ripped people off left and right. If they had tested contractors, I believe fewer people would have been ripped off. To this day I advise people to be cautious when giving money upfront unless confident of who you're dealing with.

As the months pass, I feel like socializing again. I figure it is time to crawl out of the basement and do something more than work. Mom and Dad take the boys to Sunday school each week, which is part of the package of living with them. I stay in the basement, which is a good place to feel sorry for myself. Then I receive a call from an old friend who heard I was back and divorced. He asks if I might be interested in going to dinner with a certain lady friend of his and his wife. It will be a semi-formal dinner at a fancy restaurant in Olympia. Good, bad, or indifferent, it is time to do something, so I accept the invitation. By the time dinner ends, he is right. She is nice-looking, intelligent, and wealthy, but something tells me the situation isn't right. For some unexplained reason a second date does not occur.

MORE CHANGES

The first thing I know, Shane wants to return to his friends and school in Boulder. This is a tough decision. I love and respect Shane. He never raises a fit or asks for much. I don't know if his high IQ makes me think he knows what he is doing or what causes me to give him the okay. My thinking is still skewed. He is only sixteen years old. It doesn't occur to me that IQ is not directly related to wisdom. Had I asked Taylor's opinion, I don't think Shane would have left us. Taylor is still dealing with Anne being gone. It isn't until later in my life that I realize the depth of despair Shane's absence causes Taylor.

All I can say is, this isn't the "Leave it to Beaver" show.

I let Shane return to Boulder. Having made arrangements with friends in Boulder, he quickly returns. The rest is in Shane's hands now.

Before Shane left

CHAPTER 32
NEW LIFE

THE NEXT DATE

FOR THE LIFE OF ME, I'm still unsure what all transpired, but here goes. A lady friend calls and asks if I'm interested in dating her friend whom I'll refer to here as Kathy. I know who she is. She married a friend of a friend and is now divorced. I know little about her other than she is an attractive blonde woman. We have no problem with each other's company right from the start. Kathy has a son about the same age as Taylor. At first Taylor stays with Mom while I go up north to see her on the weekends until things grow more serious. Before long we are engaged, and Taylor isn't given a choice. He comes with me.

IT'S TIME

On February 28, 1990, I stay with Kathy for the weekend. We wake up early that Sunday morning. The first thing Kathy says is, "Do you want to go to my brother's church this morning?" This catches me completely by surprise, but I'm so taken by her that I remember thinking if she wants me to go with her to the landfill in a three-piece tux, I'm all in. So, with little more thought, Kathy and I head to church. Her brother's church is in a rented space in a local school with about a hundred metal chairs set up and an aisle down the middle leading to a small podium. I have an aisle seat with Kathy next to me. To this day, I cannot remember one word the pastor said or what he even looked like.

But I will never forget one thing that happens at the end of his sermon. He makes an altar call. For those of you who do not know what that's about, the pastor asks if anyone feels led to come forward and commit his or her life to Jesus. I'm sitting there in my little metal chair when, all of a sudden, I feel something or someone grabbing me by my shirt collar, and it's not the guy sitting behind me. Flooding through my brain at the same time is a voice inside, not audible to anyone but me, saying, "You've wasted enough time." It's about as loud and clear as you can get.

I find myself standing up and heading toward the pastor. It's like walking in a thick fog. I remember repeating something he wants me to say, and I head back to my metal chair. I sit there for a short time, trying to assimilate what just happened. Shortly afterward, we are all excused.

If I remember, Kathy's brother shakes my hand before we leave. That is my first time meeting him. We proceed back to Kathy's house. Not a word is spoken about what occurred on the way back or that evening before I leave. After dinner, I return to Toledo. The first thing I do is to search my belongings for that old King James Bible Mom gave me in high school, the dust-covered one with all the "Thee" and "Thou" references in it that had not been touched for a quarter of a century.

For the next three years, after Taylor goes to bed at nine, I read the Bible from nine at night until midnight or sometimes one or two in the morning. I take seriously those words from Sunday, saying, "You've wasted enough time."

I go back and forth to Seattle for three weeks. On the third week, Kathy meets me at the door with an engagement ring in her hand, saying something to the effect that I'm changed or different and she wants to break off our relationship. This is a serious case of cognitive dissonance for me. I didn't feel like debating at that moment. I hop into my Toyota pickup and drive back down I-5 with tears in my eyes and anger my voice, telling God how swell it is being a Christian. I don't waste time blaming God for what happened. I remember saying I'm giving Him six months to prove He's real, or I'm out of here. Now remember, I'm a three-week-old baby Christian with little knowledge of what that entails.

I do know I promised God six months of 100 percent open and honest seeking. I continue reading my Bible and take extra classes offered by Pastor Tom Colby at the Toledo Assembly of God church. By the end of three months, I'm never turning back. God reveals enough through His Word to capture my full attention. Now, reading His Word is different than when I was in my teens. I'm honestly seeking. All the hard work is just starting!

I launch into a journey that will turn my world upside down. All of a sudden left becomes right, down becomes up. I'm learning God's economy is the polar opposite of most of the world; give instead of take; be humble instead of proud; love your enemy instead of hating him; be a peacemaker, not a peace breaker. The list goes on.

Many times I remember those words that flood through my mind before I walked the aisle and committed myself to something other than myself: "You've wasted enough time." During that first year, I start to feel like I'm wearing an astronaut's suit, strapped into a spaceship with thrusters ignited for take-off. I feel an urgency I don't understand. My promise to commit 100 percent to God rolls through my brain. I'm okay with diving into God's Word, hanging out with His people, listening to His music. Like with most things in my life, I'm all in or all out—no half-heartedness.

Those first 2½ years are a "rebirth," providing an entirely different direction for my life. Christians use the term "born again" for good reason. I start as a baby Christian. Some cry more than others. We need milk, not meat, and fill our spiritual diapers with, let's call it, our S-T-U-F-F. I, for one, have plenty of S-T-U-F-F built up over the past twenty-some years, enough to create my own large landfill. My S-T-U-F-F flies in the face of everything I find in the Bible, which is so much better for my life, an entirely different set of values and standards. What was once normal now has no place in my life. The process is similar to peeling a strong onion. I need to rid myself of one layer after another of things that do not belong in my life. Some layers make my eyes water. I don't want to let go but know I must.

At this stage I'm not aware it will be a lifelong process. Spiritual progress varies widely among all of us because of our different life experiences and personalities. This is one of the hardest challenges I ever face, living the way Christ wants me to versus the way I want to.

Surrounding myself with good spiritual leadership and sound biblical doctrine is critical. But first and most important, I need to familiarize myself with God's manual (Bible). At the same time, I ask God to reveal what He knows I need to read in it. If I avoid that part, how will I know if those around me are leading me down the right path? I don' want to end up drinking some bad Kool-Aid like Jim Jones' followers.

GOOD SENSE

After living in the basement (dungeon) at Mom and Dad's for just under a year, I've saved enough money from building Uncle Wilbur's new home and a few smaller jobs to start on a small place of my own. With a contract on a five-acre portion of Dad's ranch, I can draw up plans for a new home that I'll pay for out of pocket—with no loans, if possible.

One of the great aspects about being a builder at this time is I can draw up a set of plans, submit them to the county, and have a permit in hand in a couple of weeks (which is totally unheard of nowadays). Cowlitz PUD and

Cowlitz Building and Planning work together in a program called "Good Sense Homes," which is ironic as I'm starting to use good sense in more than one way. This program is all about energy efficiency. Having been involved with CURE in the not-so-recent past, I find

Good Sense Home

this appealing. My project will be one of the first in the county. If successful, the state may adopt new energy codes. It involves less wood, more insulation, better quality windows, and so on. The program is a success and new codes follow, which improves the quality of homes I build.

I design my new home so that I can easily add on when the need arises. It is a simple three-bedroom and two-bath box. Phase two actually adds a nice brick porch and a garage with a master suite that overlooks the valley. This will come three years later, built out of pocket also.

DAD'S ADVICE

About this time, Dad offers advice in a letter to the leader of Oregon, Gov. Neil Goldschmidt. The letter concerns contemplation of the government advancing offshore oil drilling. Dad feels it is a bad idea that will mess up the beaches. He was right about the Vietnam War; he might be right now. He and his brothers have tried to drill for oil on their ranches. I guess they don't want any competition. Dad's last letter is to the president of the United States on a different political issue. His next letter, a couple of years later, is to David Rockefeller. Dad tries to get Standard Oil interested in his oil pursuits. I'll say this about him, he is not shy about going right to the top. I think all these gentlemen have secretaries who never advance all the letters they receive. Dad is always at it; he always put a smile on our faces.

THE ADVENTURES OF BROCK AND RAY

Over the years Brock Brinson has shared with me his many adventures with Ray L. Wallace. Everything is an adventure when you spend time with Bigfoot. His intensity level generally lingers around the high-water mark.

Ray came to know Brock, my high school buddy, and his family when we returned to Toledo in the early 1960s. It's now the late 1980s, and Brock and Dad attend the same church. Dad wants to build logging roads again with his bulldozer and needs someone to haul rock for the roads. He calls Brock to see if he's interested. Brock owns the trucks and will do the job. I would now like to share some of those with you.

At this time Plum Creek Lumber, a notable player in the Pacific Northwest timber industry, is letting out contracts for the construction of logging roads. Submitting a bid requires an interview with one of two supervisors. Fortunately, they receive an interview with the supervisor who is best to work for. They begin the interview and, instead of talking about road-building, Dad has this guy in a conversation describing all the advantages of taking bee pollen.

Within five or ten minutes, this poor guy has a confused look on his face. But Dad, with his gift of gab, can capture and hold people's attention. He goes down a long list of all the reasons to take bee pollen. At last he says, "One more thing, bee pollen will be good for your sex life." Brock, while looking at the ceiling, is thinking, "He's not even going to let us bid the job, let alone get it."

To Brock's surprise, the supervisor looks at him and says, "Well, I guess you know, we should be thinking about stuff like that." Brock cracks up inside and thinks, "Well, whatever you say." They actually end up getting the bid for a five-mile logging road. Before they move their equipment to the job near Morton, Washington, the supervisor calls and asks if they would trade the Morton job with another company that already has their equipment in the area. Brock and Dad say, "No problem."

So they take the other job. Come to find out, the Morton job includes dynamiting rock, which is not a problem in itself but, unknown to the company doing the dynamiting, a short distance from the rock, hidden behind a dense stand of timber, is someone's home. Due to the blast, that home is shifted off its foundation. Needless to say, the road builder lost his shirt on that one. Someone is watching over Brock and Dad.

On another Plum Creek road job north of Centralia, Washington, they build roads and reach a place where the engineer designing the road mistakenly placed a culvert in his drawings at a high spot that will never see water. So Ray tells Brock, "We're not putting in that culvert; it's a ridiculous waste." Brock says, "They call for a culvert, so we probably need to put it in, or they won't approve it." Dad says, "We are not putting in the culvert! That's stupid!" Brock says, "Whatever you say." So later the inspector comes out and tells them they missed putting in that culvert. Dad tells the inspector it's stupid to put a culvert there. The inspector tells him, "Well, I'm not going to approve the road." He leaves and, after a lengthy debate between Brock and Dad, they reluctantly install the culvert.

Soon after, the main supervisor inspects the road to approve their work. The first thing the supervisor says to Ray is, "Why did you put a culvert there? There's never going to be any water there." Ray just goes into an absolute tizzy fit. He tells the supervisor, "They made us put the culvert in there, and I'm not taking it out!" The supervisor responds by saying, "Well, I'm not going to approve this until you take it out." Ray comes uncorked at this point. After a much longer debate than their first one, Brock finally says, "Do you want to get paid or not?"

They finally remove it, and common sense does not necessarily win the day. While growing up in logging camps, the rule was common sense. Dad grew up during the Great Depression, which for most people developed a waste-not-want-not mentality where common sense is a must, not a luxury.

MUNDANE NEVER

Brock speaks of working with Ray, and I quote, "I never had so much fun working with anybody as I did with Ray Wallace. You knew every day was going to be a different adventure. The mundane was never mundane because Ray would always change it around."

Not being busy enough with road building and keeping Bigfoot alive, Ray decides to throw mining for rhodium into the mix. For those of us unfamiliar with that mineral, rhodium is a valuable silver-white corrosion-resistant metal.

He invites Brock into his latest venture. He tells him he has talked to a man in Denio, Nevada, just over the Oregon border, who is looking for rhodium to mine. He wants Ray to help him. Brock, always up for a new experience, knows with Ray it won't be boring. So Brock, his wife, Dolly, Elna, and Ray head in the car to the middle of nowhere. Denio, Nevada, which has a post office and a burger bar/store, is this dusty spot in the desert occupied by a few dozen people. It's a five-hundred-mile journey. They leave early and arrive in Denio around noon. They meet Jim, the man looking for rhodium.

The plan is to leave Elna and Dolly at the store with the car. Brock and Dad pile into Jim's little Datsun pickup and take off, having told the girls they will probably be gone a couple of hours. So they drive down to the mining site, and Jim shows them the situation. He then takes the guys over to the rancher who owns access to the mining area. The rancher is an Oregon state representative, which hit some cords (vocal cords, not musical chords) with Ray. Dad starts talking politics with the rancher, which goes on for some time, so long it's getting close to dinnertime. Brock, being the rational one, says to Ray, "You know we should get back. The girls probably think we're dead." Ray replies, "There's no problem; everything is fine. They will be all right." If Mom had heard that and could reach him with her black frying pan, he would have been in poor shape. They ate dinner with the rancher. After three more long hours of Dad shooting the breeze with the rancher, they arrive back at Denio.

Needless to say, Mom and Dolly are furious. Mom says, "How could you leave us so long?" Dad's standard reply is, "Well, the time just got away from us." It is so late they drive for a couple of hours to the nearest hotel. The women are hot in more ways than one. All Brock can say later, while cracking up with laughter, is, "It was a funny trip. Every time you went on a trip with Ray, it was entertaining." Despite all the stories Dad comes up with, it isn't entertaining for Mom. She's heard most of them a thousand times already.

ROUND TWO

Later, definitely without Dolly and Elna, Ray and Brock work the mine near Denio and hit what they think is rhodium. Their next step is to take ore samples to the nearest assay office in Fallon, Nevada, a three-hour drive. Two others, a gentleman from Cypress who wants to invest in the mine and Jim, who originally brought Dad into the mining venture, go with Brock and Dad. In Fallon they meet this assayer. Brock has always thought, like the rest of us, that when the Lord made Ray, he broke the mold. But it appears that might not be the case. The Lord used a similar mold on this assayer character. Sitting in this guy's trailer, where he assays the ore, he and Ray start talking about aliens.

Dad, with that twinkle in his eye, asks the assayer if he has ever seen a spaceship. The assayer says, "Seen one! How'd you like to take a ride in one?"

At that point, Brock goes outside and leans over the hood of the pickup, laughing. The assayer explains to Dad how, with his quick thinking, he used a fire extinguisher to revive an alien who had a difficult time breathing our atmosphere. Dad and the assayer talk in there for another hour and a half, filling each other with sunshine, if that's what you call it. They finally leave the trailer and start to head back to Denio.

Not far down the road, Dad says, "You know, I forgot to ask him where they took him for a ride in that spaceship." Brock says, "I know. They took him to Mars and cloned him because that's not a human being back there." With a smile on his face and that frequent twinkle in his eye, Dad says, "Well, yeah, you're probably right." I think Brock is in it for the entertainment.

On one trip to the Denio mine, they start late. They are supposed to leave in the morning, but Brock has problems on his job, so he doesn't show up at Dad's until five in the evening. Dad is upset, expecting Brock at nine in in the morning. Brock says Ray finally finishes chewing him out by the time they drive past Portland. Heading for Bend, Oregon, Brock says Ray has talked nonstop, without taking a breath for four hours.

They finally stop to get a motel in Bend around midnight. In their room, Ray is still talking. They lie down in their separate beds, and Ray is still talking. Brock tries to sleep, thinking that if he shuts off the lights, Ray will sleep. Brock finally passes out while Ray continues his stories. In the morning, they wake up, and the first thing Dad says to Brock is, "I had to get up in the middle of the night to go to the bathroom. I hope I didn't wake you." Brock rolls his eyes, saying, "No, we're good." Brock is one patient individual; but to him, Dad is an endless stream of entertainment.

Speaking of entertainment, back home, Brock and Dad sit at the kitchen table while Mom does dishes. Ray says to Brock, "I have two tickets here to the Johnny Carson Show." He shows them to Brock. They are legit. Dad says, "Carson wants me to come down and talk about Bigfoot." Brock says, "Oh," thinking Mom is going with him. Dad says "Elna does not want to go. Do you want to go with me?" Brock says, "Well, yes; I'd like to go." Mom immediately turns to Dad while pointing her finger at him and says, "Ray Wallace, you're not going down there on national television and telling any more lies." Dad says, "Well, I guess we're not going."

TRUSTING

While I'm trying to shake all the bad habits that need to disappear, to my surprise, God clearly wants me to be faithful in tithing, giving a tenth of what I make back to Him. This takes time to digest. Nothing makes sense about tithing, especially just having lost everything and starting over from scratch, until I come across a verse in the Old Testament. The subheading in Malachi, "Robbing God," grabs my attention. This is the way God works in Scripture. When the timing is right, and I'm ready to listen, He gives me what I need. The English Standard Version of the Bible says, "Bring the full tithe into the storehouse [temple/church], that there may be food in my house. And thereby put me to the test, says the Lord of hosts, if I will not open the windows of heaven for you and pour down for you a blessing until there is no more need."

This is the only place in Scripture where God prompts you to test him. Starting the following Sunday, I take Him at His word. I begin tithing regularly. I'm not much of a believer in coincidences. As the months turn into a year, my business supersedes all my expectations. It soon becomes clear I can never outgive the Lord. Clearly, He is only wanting me to put Him first, not my money.

CHAPTER 33
A BETTER LIFE

TRUSTING

PUTTING MY TRUST IN GOD'S WORD is the second best thing I've done to this point in my life. The first is taking that step of faith and finding God does exist. To reach this point, I first need an encounter with Christ/God, something to turn my head and heart. Within three months, I no longer question whether God is real. He has given me the will, the strength, and the desire to change so many thoughts and deeds that no longer have any place in my life. For me, not following God is like speeding the wrong direction on a one-way road. Now I'm in the correct lane.

I absolutely love reading history. The Bible will continue to be the most-read book in history, both nonfiction and fiction. I'll never completely understand all of it, but I do trust the One who inspired it and what it means to me. Reading the Bible without first taking that "step of faith" is like reading any other book. The Bible says its words will appear only as foolishness or folly to those who refuse to give God a chance to reveal Himself. To those who give Him the opportunity, it offers the power of God to transform lives. I'm now in that process.

My value system changes, doing a complete one-hundred-eighty-degree turn. Don't get me wrong here. Some habits go kicking and screaming. We, God and I, tackle them one at a time, for however long it takes.

LEAVING THE DUNGEON

With our new home finished, it's time to rise from the dungeon and deal with life anew. I'm so thankful for the year at Mom and Dad's. The three of us, now two, because Shane returned to Boulder, Colorado, start over in a safe and healthy environment. It is hard letting Shane go, for both Taylor and me. I still don't see letting Shane move as one of my brighter decisions.

Taylor is easy to raise. He doesn't create challenges until he is fifteen or sixteen, like every other teen. This is about the age when I left the rails for the road, seeking my own path, right or wrong.

I'm an advocate of just about all team sports as an opportunity to learn to work and play with others while keeping your body in good condition. I like a balance of mental and physical.

I encourage both of my boys to get involved in sports. Coaching becomes an avenue to commit my time together with them instead of just dropping them off. I coached in the past for Shane and now do so for Taylor.

He has given baseball his best shot, but baseball ends after some years. During one of our practices, it's Taylor's turn at bat.

Taylor's squad

I put my top pitcher on the mound since he has one of the best fastballs in our league. That fastball occasionally runs amok. His second or third pitch nails Taylor, who is catching, in the ribs with one of his fastballs, knocks him down, and sucks the wind right out of him. After Taylor recovers, I tell him to hang out in the outfield and take it easy. This sounds like a good idea to Taylor, so he's picking flowers when he hears the crack of the bat. A fly ball heads his way. He raises his glove to shade his eyes from the sun and positions his glove for the catch. The ball grazes his mitt and clobbers him in the forehead. He lies in the grass, out cold.

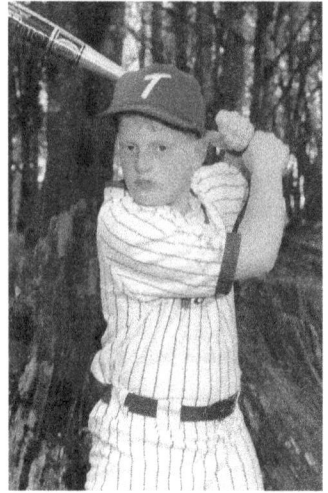

Taylor

When he wakes up, the first thought that comes to him is, "Do I really want to keep doing this to myself? It's cool; it's something to do, but I'm not really that good at it. Am I terribly motivated to keep taking this? Not really?" To make matters worse, at an earlier game, when two of our pitchers were injured and our relief pitcher never showed up, I told Taylor, "You've been to the pitchers' meeting; get in there and pitch." Although uncomfortable with the idea, he went in to pitch. Before he finished, he hit at least four batters. He just kept nailing those poor batters and apologizing to them as they mean-mugged him.

YOUTH FOOTBALL

For Taylor, youth football is even worse. I decided we should give fourth- and fifth-grade football a shot. As much as I love sports, Taylor reassures me he is not there because he has to be, which I appreciate. It is, again, an opportunity to join in an activity together.

We have thirty-eight boys who turn out in our small town. We divide them into two Toledo squads, the Indians and the Lions. Mark Jarvis and I coach the Indians for the next four years.

Football isn't Taylor's passion, either, but he hangs in there for two years and discovers he lacks the killer instinct of the better players. Some of the better players bully him in school, so he is happy to abandon that sport.

Later in high school, Taylor finds and falls in love with soccer. He's a decent player and even coaches the sport years later.

Mark Jarvis moves to Toledo about the same time I return from Boulder. My initial reason for coaching is to be with Taylor. Mark has a different

Toledo Indians Youth Football in 1991

reason. These young boys joining youth football will be the same age as his daughter. Mark wants to make an impression on these boys to squash any wrong ideas they may later acquire concerning his daughter.

In a short time, Mark and I love coaching the boys. We work great together and form a good friendship that has lasted to this day.

The first year is rough. The boys are not the only ones on a learning curve. Overconfidence bites us in the backside during our first game, which we lose by six points to one of the other small towns, Oakville. We put our loss behind us and make adjustments that put us in a victorious mode, you might say. We still face Centralia, the only team likely to pose a big problem, with a running back who, in track, is the fourth fastest boy in the state. Not one team has come close to beating Centralia. Its entire offense is letting that running back go left, right, or up the middle. Mark receives the lowdown on this kid. By the way we're acting, you might think the Super Bowl is approaching. Our kids, pumped and positive, possess attitudes that are every coach's dream. This, to some degree, reflects their parents. Positive support from parents is a deal-maker or deal-breaker. Ask any educator. It can be heaven, hell, or anything in between.

The night before the game, I stay up until one in the morning looking at my offensive plays. I run the offense, and Mark is great with the defense. Most of my time is spent thinking about Centralia's running back; he is the key. We must somehow contain him. The following day, Mark and I share a plan with our players before the game. Because none of the other teams contain him, we feel like it is worth the risk for our front four to focus strictly on that running back who is lined up behind the quarterback. We tell our defensive line to keep that runner in the center of the field.

Our front four are pretty fast, so all our defensive ends need to do is slow down the runner, giving one of our linemen enough time to tackle him. Our linebackers protect the middle. Centralia, on the kickoff, receives the ball first. Play number one and play number two end in negative yards for them. On the third play, one of our front four on defense tackles their speed demon in the end zone for two points.

Before the first half ends, our defense, after holding Centralia to little or no yardage, reports to Mark that Centralia's running back is swearing out of frustration every time he is contained. By the time the game ends, each team has scored one touchdown. Centralia's speed ball manages to score one touchdown but ends up with plus six yards for the game. The final score is Toledo nine and Centralia seven with the clock running out. At the final second, our boys go wild! Mark and I did the same. It is so much fun watching them enjoy the fruits of their labor.

CHAPTER 34
GROWING PAINS

HEART CHANGES

GROWING MENTALLY, PHYSICALLY, OR SPIRITUALLY can be a slow and painful process. When it comes to sharing my newfound relationship with Christ, I do not always come across the way I should. My overzealous state probably chases people away from the Lord rather than draws them to Him. I'm so excited I must learn to temper my excitement. Despite setbacks, good changes happen. I'm heading in the right direction.

Unknown to me, my good friend Mark has done a good job of concealing his anger issues. I am always comfortable around him. His anger helped destroy his first marriage. Now he is about to ruin his second marriage to Janie, a lovely lady, who he's been married to a short time.

I stay close to Mark after youth football, sharing my faith with him, never knowing what goes on inside. Mark is a whiz at diesel mechanics. He works with Gordon, his father, at their truck repair shop. Occasionally I stop and talk to Mark on my way home or to a job. Visiting him on one momentous occasion, Mark describes how he and two of his buddies, who are all well over two hundred pounds, dressed as women and performed on a float in the Napavine parade the previous weekend. On "The Napawino Float," a toilet represented a well-used throne due to overindulging. Mark tells me later they are three of the worst-looking women ever seen. Being in a relatively conservative area, they take heat for it after the parade but think it is pretty funny. Without thinking first, I say something to the effect that I didn't see anything funny about a man dressing up like a woman. He knows me well enough. Mark says, "What do you mean? I'm a good guy." Like someone who does not think before he speaks, I shoot back, "There's going to be good guys in hell." After hearing my heavy-handed opinion, he responds with no kindness in his voice. "What do you mean by that?" If looks could kill, I would be dead.

Wasting no time, I head for my pickup and hightail it home. Ten minutes later, after re-examining my comments, I arrive home. The first thing I do is grab the phone and call Mark. After a short apology, I say, "Let me make it up to you. I'll buy you breakfast first thing in the morning." I spend the entire evening trying to figure out what to say to him. What keeps coming to my mind is, "Share the Romans Road with him." For those of you who are not aware of what that is, it is a set of small verses from the book of Romans in the Bible offering the biblical path to Christ. I'll give a brief version that I prepared for Mark. First (Rom. 3:23) All have sinned and fall short of the glory of God. The second verse (Rom. 5:8) God showed His love for us by Christ dying on the cross for our sins, paying the price for all. The third (Rom. 6:23) The wages of sin are death, but the gift of God is eternal life through Christ. The fourth (Rom. 10:9–10) If you confess Jesus with your mouth and believe with your heart God raised Him from the dead, you will be saved.

So I figure it all out. Early the next morning, we sit in the restaurant, waiting for our order. I set my little pocket Bible on the table, ready for my big presentation. For the first ten minutes, we share small talk. Before I start my great presentation, Mark says, "I want to commit my life to Christ like you have." I go into shock. This is not the way it is supposed to go. I'm supposed to talk him into heaven, right? Wrong! It doesn't take me long to figure out that, despite my haphazard comments the day before, God can use anybody. Jesus has obviously been working on Mark for some time. He didn't need a well-timed speech from me, just an "encounter" with Jesus, similar to the one I had when I committed to Christ, only under different circumstances.

Mark does a big one hundred eighty after that. You can ask Janie. It saves their marriage and then some.

BIG CELEBRATION

It is Ray and Elna's fiftieth wedding anniversary. We pack the Cowlitz Prairie Grange with friends and relatives who love Mom and Dad. Boy, if anybody needs to celebrate, it is those two. They have earned it, especially Mom, riding trail herd on Ray L. Wallace most of her life. Now when it comes to Ray, that's a different story. He is a constant source of entertainment or at times cognitive dissonance. Take your pick. When it comes down to it, I believe he has figured out how to make the best of life while he's here.

Elna and Ray celebrate fifty years together

During the celebration, Ray says about Elna, "She has one special little smile that causes me to catch a glimpse of her in her youth." She's still his "Kitty Cat."

About a half an hour into the celebration, in comes a family friend, six-foot Scott Thompson, dressed in a Bigfoot costume. If the crowd wasn't telling Bigfoot stories before, they are now. We all have a great deal to talk about. I'm fairly positive a good time is had by all.

HILLCREST 1 1993

In the past ten years, Dad never stops telling me what a mistake I made by selling my Hillcrest stores. On February 26, 1993, early in the morning, a nineteen-year-old entered Hillcrest 1 near Winlock to purchase a six-pack of beer. According to state law at the time, clerks couldn't sell liquor that early. Being high on meth, the enraged teenager pulls out a 9mm pistol and shoots and kills Joyce Robertson, the forty-two-year-old owner, who has just opened up. Two years later, the murderer from Port Angeles, Washington, is finally caught and convicted and sentenced to sixty years in prison.

After that, Dad never mentions my selling the stores again.

CHAPTER 35
A THREE-YEAR-OLD

NEARLY THREE YEARS AFTER MY "ENCOUNTER" with Christ, I discover God is not a helicopter parent who swoops in and fixes all my bad decisions. He requires me to clean up my messes and walk the right path with Him. He even hands out tests and quizzes. If I don't pass them the first time, I can take them over and over until I do. Some tests involve walking away from wayward friends and bad situations. To them I appear a hypocrite. For me, I risk falling back into a lifestyle I no longer desire. My choices from here on always focus on God's way, not man's way. I love my relationship with God and don't want to go backward.

WORK

My construction business thrives in a good place. Through our lifelong friend, Anor Buswell, I am introduced to a local couple that needs a contractor for construction of a 5,300-square-foot estate. Through the job, I develop a good working relationship with him and his wife. The subcontractors I chose meet our expectations. One is a young man who ends up working for me. In sharing with him what I've experienced the past three years, I triggered something that grabbed his attention. He occasionally comes to church and confides in me about his life. Raised in an extremely abusive household, he struggles with suicidal thoughts. I invite him to stay with Taylor and me. The three of us hit it off. This guy, despite his struggles, adds much-needed levity that Taylor

Beautiful estate

appreciates. Losing everything and starting over robs much of the levity from my life. With God's help, someday levity will find its way back to me.

CRAZY WONDERFUL

My friend Brock expresses concern for me at church. Here I am in a small town where my only consistent social event is going to this small church. I'm thinking how on earth am I going to meet the woman I need and not just want. Brock suggests that we go forward together in church, kneel down, and ask specifically for God to bring His version of a mate for me, a wise woman who loves God above all else.

After returning home, I fall to my knees at my bedside, clearly confessing to God. I have not relinquished everything from my past. I have drug paraphernalia, even though I haven't done any drugs for quite some time. I'm not sure why I've got these things, but I throw them out. In my words to God, I say, "If You never give me a woman, I'm going to serve you the way I should."

Two months later, my second cousin, Lisa (Hoffman) Collins, visits her tax man in Toledo. Lisa sees a folder on his desk. She asks if by chance this is the same Michael Wallace, son of Ray and Elna. "Isn't he still in Colorado?" The tax man says, no, Mike is back and plans to build churches overseas. Lisa responds, "That can't be my cousin Michael Wallace. No way!" She leaves the tax office and goes straight to my mom's house four blocks away. To her shock and awe, Mom confirms that I am a committed follower of Christ. My mom, Elna, gives Lisa my phone number.

On the 20th of February, I arrive home from work to find a message from cousin Lisa that catches me off guard. First, we have not seen each other for quite some time. Second, it sounds rather urgent that I return her call, so I do.

After getting reacquainted, Lisa raves about this lady she's teaching with in Kelso, Washington. She urges me to call this lady and arrange a date. At first I think, "Great, a blind date; just what I want." Before Lisa finishes, I think, "If her friend is half of what Lisa says she is, I at least need to give it a shot." I jot down her phone number.

Lisa has already told her friend, Rose, about me, describing me as a "wild guy" in the past. Lisa babysat for Shane when he was little and found a marijuana plant drying in the oven. Lisa stated later, "I would have never encouraged Michael and Rose to meet had I not had a prompting from God. Rose was too dear a friend, and I knew Michael's sordid past."

Lisa describes me to Rose, but she isn't interested in another blind date. Lisa adds something to the effect that I'm the kind of guy she might want if times get tough, an intelligent problem-solver (their words, not mine). We felt something unusual going on here.

After thinking about the blind date, I work up enough nerve to call Rose a couple of days later. All I remember of that conversation is feeling I stepped all over my tongue, like being back in the seventh grade again. I have not dated in some time. The only words I remember from our conversation is Rose saying, "Yes, I'll go out."

On February 27th, four days later, I nervously walk up the sidewalk to her house and knock on the door. When Rose opens it, the first thought that rushes into my head is, "Thank you, Lord. I'm going to marry her." Rose suggests a small Thai restaurant called Hart-C's. Our conversation is wonderful. We lose track of time. The waiter informs us they are locking up.

We go back to Rose's home and talk until three in the morning. I give her a hug, which she later described as melting her heart and scaring her half to death at the same time. She hasn't been hugged like that in a long time. After the hug, all I want to do is kiss her goodnight and leave. She quickly turns her head, informing me she is not ready for that. That's fair. It is only the first date.

During the following week, knowing I have a retreat in Yakima, I send nine red roses and three white ones to Barnes Elementary, where she teaches. There is no further communication until the following week. Her principal, an intuitive Christian, looks at the flowers and then at her, and says, "What makes this guy different than the rest?" Before receiving the flowers, Rose feels reluctant to pursue a relationship, frightened by the look on my face after our hug. She wants to back away. But the flowers and then not hearing from me for a week and a half gives her time to think without feeling pressure. She tells me later she thought, "Maybe I don't want to lose this guy."

After returning from Yakima, sometime during the following week, I call Rose for a second date. After work, I have been building a two-story addition onto my house with a double car garage/workshop and a new master suite with an awesome view into the valley. The plan is to make dinner for us and show her my project.

So, after a pork chop dinner, I give Rose the grand tour. We are in the master suite for less than twenty minutes, talking and enjoying the view, when I turn and ask if she will marry me. After a long pause. with a stunned look on her face, she says, "I will, but first, if you can, with all honesty, tell me that you will always love Jesus more than me, anybody, or anything else. Second thing, we take counseling from our present and former pastors. The third and last thing we do is, for the next two months, go through this counseling manual designed to show any relational red flags that may exist. If it does, we call off the marriage."

All I can focus on at the moment is her first condition, putting Jesus first. That is the point when I realize I have exactly and precisely the woman I need. I know my prayers are answered. Because of this moment I am reminded of the Sunday when Brock and I prayed for a woman who loves Jesus.

Two months later, here I am, engaged to an amazing lady.

GAINS AND LOSSES

Now, being engaged, counseling with pastors, sharing with Rose, finishing the addition, and building the pilot's dream home, I realize I'm in over my head. Mike the pilot informs me I am not focused enough to build his home, and he is comfortable taking over. We settle up financially, but it doesn't sit well with me because I always finish what I start, and now I haven't. But it's nobody's fault but mine. Everything else feels like I'm on top of the world. I am excited for our wedding. Although I lost a job, I am about to gain a beautiful wife.

After Rose and I are engaged, Lisa has an intense talk with God, saying she did what He wanted her to do, by introducing the two of us. Now, with her fists clenched, she demands that God send her a good Christian man to marry. In less than a year's time, she is married to a handsome young Christian man. God loves to give good gifts to those who love Him.

A counselor friend of Rose's comments to her after our engagement that Michael probably thinks he's rescuing you when, in fact, he's going to find a strong woman who knows who she is and what she believes. I don't know about the rescue part, but the rest is a fact.

The last couple of months are a picture of how God weaves His will and blessing into our lives if we let Him. At the same time, it is like living in a whirlwind.

CHAPTER 36
MY NEW FAMILY

NO RED FLAGS

HAVING SUCCESSFULLY SWEPT THE MINEFIELD of much love and counseling, we find no red flags to stand in the way of Rose and I marrying. After an intense couple of months, to make matters more challenging, I insist we get married as soon as possible. Rose wants to wait for a time later in June. If common sense prevails, we will wait. But we don't always use common sense, at times putting our emotions in the driver's seat. Rose is exhausted from teaching third-graders at their Title 1 school, where at least 40 percent of students qualify as low income. Along with the wedding plans, our evening counseling session at least three times a week and meeting with two different pastors, we are both exhausted. Waiting is still not an option in my mind. We stick with the original date. Rosie and I determine from day one that we will be celibate until after our wedding, to honor the Lord. This was nothing new for Rosie, but it was a complete one-eighty for me, although I had done fairly well during the three years before we met.

OUR WEDDING

I don't know if anything, up to this point in my life, ever feels so right as marrying Rose. When it comes to matchmaking, God always takes first seat, no offense to those dating sites. God has the upper hand when it comes to what people need versus what they want.

Under God

Our commitment is to God first, then to each other, our families, and then the rest of the world, in that order. When Rose responds to my proposal on our second date with a yes as long as I always love Jesus more than anything, I know with everything in me that she is precisely the woman I need as my wife. How true this still is. Rose always balances me.

Here I am marrying a lady that first encounters Jesus near a forest not far from her home at the age of five. Rose discovers something exhilarating in the wind that swirls around her. She senses a presence that is wonderful and good. As a child, she finds herself sharing fear and delight with this entity. She

Together, with Rose balancing me

cannot put a name to this until a neighbor lady invites Rose to her church, Beacon Hill Baptist. She hears talk about this special someone named Jesus. From that moment forward, her faith focuses on Jesus.

I don't know much else about the situation, but I do know Rose will have my back, front, sides, bottom, and top. She matches all the good aspects of what a wife is biblically. I know because I have pored over the Bible for the last three years, daily.

We have so many friends and family to invite that we move our wedding to the larger Baptist church just north of us. The wedding is simple yet beautiful. We will now be a family of six. Rose's lovely daughters—Molly, the oldest, and Christina—will now be attached to me and my handsome sons, Shane and Taylor. Our sons and daughters express skepticism for good reason as everything

Merging into a blended family

is occurring at Mach speed. However, they display no signs of resistance to our marriage.

The wedding on May 29, 1993, is everything we hope. In just three short months here we are with two pastors officiating our wedding—Tom Colby, my first pastor, who helped me get off to a good spiritual start three years ago, and my current pastor, Gerry Goitt. My cousin Lisa, who the Lord used to introduce me to Rose, with her lovely voice, sings before us. With our four wonderful children, we tie the knot that binds.

Our reception is five miles north at the Cowlitz Prairie Grange. We even splurge for a long white limo to drive us there. After a wonderful reception with friends and family, we leave in Rose's car on a four-hour journey to the Starfish Inn in Newport, Oregon. We have only three days. Something is added to our journey. I have become good friends with a retired nuclear engineer whose home I remodeled. Saul and his wife, Alice, are talented folks, with Saul's passion for gourmet cooking and Alice's artistic bent. To our great surprise, before we leave on our honeymoon, they load three coolers into our car and give us a beautiful custom menu that looks like it comes from a fancy French restaurant. As we unfold each page, we read on the left side a wonderful sonnet by Elizabeth Barret Browning and on the right side the menu for breakfast, lunch, and dinner.

In each cooler we find simple prep instructions. We have a kitchen, which makes this wonderfully easy. We don't need to leave the place. Saul takes care of even the smallest of details. We could not have been more blessed. As busy as we were, it is wonderful not to go anywhere for anything. With so little prep required of us for our meals, all we do is enjoy each other's company while gazing at the old lighthouse on the point with the ocean behind it. By choosing to remain celibate and putting God's wisdom first, our marriage is off to an amazing start, unlike anything I've ever experienced with a closeness like no other. Wow, three delightful days and nights we'll never forget! We did occasionally walk the trail down to the beach.

ADJUSTING

At first she was Rose. Now, she is Rosie. It's Mike and Rose when trouble brews, and Michael and Rosie when all is well, with some variation. I'm her diamond in the rough (her words). I've spent the last three years undoing a mess I made of my life twenty years prior. We have a three-year-old Christian now married to a thirty-six-year-old Christian. To put it simply, patience is required by both. In all marriages, couples sort out the imbalances and deal with them appropriately. It's committed love to Christ and each other that binds the strongest.

In the midst of making adjustments with my new family, Dad and I butt heads, which has been going on for some time. Despite my changes over the past three years, he has a habit of verbally criticizing me. Rosie asks me why I just take the verbal abuse without confronting him over it. The only answer I have is, "No big deal; I'm kind of used to it." She says, "You need to bring an end to it. Talk to him." So, like a coward, I make her come with me for backup. Mom meets us with her warm smile and asks Rosie and me what we are up to.

I tell her I just want to see Dad for a minute. I know exactly where he will be, on his green recliner in the corner of the living room, chatting with a talk show host or a Bigfoot researcher. This time, he's reading about some natural cure. I get right to the point and ask him about the verbal abuse. His response was such a surprise. His eyes widen, and in a soft voice, he says, "Oh, really?" Like Rosie says later, he just needs information. Spiritually, Dad and I are both growing and need to show grace to one another as Christ does to us daily.

By the end of our first year, the young man working for me moves out. Shane lives in Boulder, Colorado, where he attends the university. Molly is away at college in Oregon. When she returns home on the weekends, we spend some of that time butting heads. No one ever explained to me what a controller is. Apparently, I am one. Molly is not ready to trust. We spend more time going head-to-head than we should. Rose is thinking, "Oh, Lord, what are you doing here?" It takes time and the right tools for us to make the necessary changes that draw us close together.

Christina is in her senior year. I'll never forget her red Subaru BRAT, short for "Bi-Drive Recreational All-Terrain Transporter." Unique is the word. It is great in bad weather, a half-car, half-pickup with two seats mounted in the open back. Watching her drive off with two friends strapped in the back is an experience. That car always brings a smile to our faces. Christina is heading off to college soon on a basketball scholarship.

Once Christina leaves, it will mostly be Taylor, Rosie, and me. Taylor, being the passive-aggressive type, is pretty easygoing. Yet we know a lot goes on inside.

MORE ADJUSTMENTS

Rosie and I regularly attend the Toledo Assembly of God. She is used to a large community church in Longview. Together, we decide to find a church to fit us as one. First and foremost, the church doctrine must match Scripture. We start by simply having fun with the process. Both of us listen to the Christian radio station KPDQ out of Portland, which features many different pastors. We decide to check them out, one at a time. For months Rosie and I enjoy close-up encounters with these different denominational leaders. Good leadership is critical in any church. Great leadership is even better. Does their walk and talk match Scripture? The same goes for all those coming through the church doors. Following Christ is all about keeping it simple, but at the same time, it's the greatest challenge I've ever undertaken.

After months of exploring other churches and their leaders, we know that finding, joining, and supporting a local church is the next step. The following Sunday is spent attending that Baptist church on the hill where we were married. After walking through those double doors, I sense we are home. By the time the service ends, God has spoken to both of us in different ways but drawing us to the same conclusion. Toledo First Baptist Church becomes our new church home.

Summer approaches with my crew in the finishing stages of a new home I designed for John Mitchell, north of Toledo. He is great to work for. It helps having my focus back.

After our wedding, I promise Rosie a delayed, month-long honeymoon in Europe. Germany is our first stop, and then we head to Italy.

Three weeks before our flight to Germany, I finish John's home, and now I'm working on a small project for a retired couple, longtime friends of my parents. I'm working on a cabinet in their kitchen when the lady of the house says to me, "You know you have relatives in Switzerland, don't you?" I answer, "No, not really." She informs me of Fluckinger relatives in Switzerland and recommends I contact them. I am familiar with the Fluckingers around Toledo but not those in Switzerland. This sounds like a great idea. We send a letter to the Swiss address explaining our pending journey. In two short weeks we leave.

CHAPTER 37
DELAYED HONEYMOON

GERMANY FIRST

OUR INITIAL PLANS MORPH as they are not set in stone on purpose. Our plan is to stay flexible as much as possible. We have four priorities. First, we want to spend the better part of a week in Germany, most of it with Rose's Aunt Anneliese in Wiesbaden near Frankfurt. Second, we want to visit the Neuschwanstein Castle in the southern portion of Germany. Third, we hope to visit my Fluckinger relatives in Auswil, Switzerland. Finally, we want to spend time in San Margherita, Italy. All this will happen over four weeks. Those four destinations are the only ones we plan. From there, we pretty much play it by ear.

After an uneventful flight we land in Frankfurt, rent a Volvo wagon, and head for Wiesbaden to stay with Anneliese, a very elegant lady. When her husband, Carl, was alive, they owned a graphite factory that provided well for them. They had no children, which left her with little family. Fortunately, Anneliese befriended a wonderful couple who lived next to

Rose and Anneliese

her—Michael, pronounced (Mish-E-Ale) in German, and his lovely wife, Carla. Michael is a lawyer and an amazing artist. Carla is a Mercedes-Benz executive. They watch over Anneliese. After a day's rest, we are given a wonderful tour of the Rhine that includes dancing. We visit grand cathedrals and enjoy all the sights of Wiesbaden, a beautiful city.

After seven wonderful days with Anneliese, Michael, and Carla, we prepare to start our next adventure. I mention to Michael our plans to visit Italy before returning to Germany. He says his father was the German ambassador to Italy and would take him to Montefalco, a medieval hill town in the region of Umbria, Italy, and to a special place called "The Falisco Ristorante." He says, "If you are anywhere close to Montefalco, you will receive a meal you will never forget." What can you say to that?

We bid our farewells and drive down to the Autobahn. Traveling the high-speed freeway was exhilarating. With no speed limit, I find myself averaging ninety miles per hour. Even then, what we came to call Rockets shoot past us at incredible speeds. You put your life in your hands changing lanes.

Our next stop was the castle, Neuschwanstein, built by King Ludwig II of Bavaria. Construction started in 1869 and ended in 1884. He lived in it only 172 days. If there was ever a fairy-tale castle, this is it. Rosie always had a huge poster of Neuschwanstein hanging in her classroom and longed to visit the castle. After a half day's drive, we arrive and tour the castle. The artwork and craftsmanship are incredible, well worth the effort driving there.

Neuschwanstein

AUSWIL

We find our way to Auswil, Switzerland, a small country town with a population of four hundred. My relatives instructed us to rendezvous in a small restaurant at the edge of town as it's easier to find than the family estate. We arrive and find a table. Fifteen minutes later, the matriarch of the family walks straight to our table without hesitation. She says to me, "As soon as I saw you, it was obvious you're part of the family." I could not have wanted a nicer welcome. We drive on rolling hills, past green pastures and forests, to the family estate, where a large family of friendly faces greets us. Samuel, the family patriarch, recently built a new home next to their old classic Swiss abode.

Our view

A typical much older home is a large barn with living quarters on the top floor. I mention this because the master suite looking over the valley is now ours to enjoy. The woodwork in that place was something to behold. Outside of each window are beautiful flower boxes with plants in full bloom. We are instructed to settle in, and in a couple of hours, a party will take place in our honor. Their hospitality goes above and beyond anything expected. Ursula is one of many bright spots that night. She keeps whispering to family members and looking at me. Hannes, the oldest son seated to my right, says, "Follow me to Ursula's room and you will see."

Ursula and the Baywatch Dude

Entering her room, I see a life-size poster of David Hasselhoff, with his name and Baywatch written on it. Hannes says, "Ursula told me you remind her of him." What do you say to that, other than, "Give me a hug." It's difficult to find someone as sweet as Ursula.

After the party, it grows late and time to retire for the evening. With a view through two large windows past the beautiful flowers in each window box, Rosie and I snuggle under a goose down feather coverlet. As we enjoy a gorgeous view with the sun setting, we hear the tinkling of cow bells in the distance. It's quiet and peaceful as we turn to each other with smiles on our faces. I say to her, "Are you thinking what I'm thinking? Are we in a movie? Is this *The Sound of Music*?"

The next morning we join everyone for a scrumptious breakfast. Then Hannes says, "Come with me. I want to show you something." As we head to Auswil, Hannes explains to Rosie and me that the family owns a car dealership. This at first seems odd, being so far from any metropolis. We later discover the family owns a "Class A" Lexus dealership, one of the bigger ones in Switzerland. Customers come from great distances for the deals they receive.

Alps tour guide

A tram in the Alps

The shop is closed because it's Sunday, but Hannes opens up and invites us in. On the showroom floor in front of us is a new Lexus. Hannes walks over to it, opens the doors, and says, "Hop in; we are going to spend the day touring the Alps." Surprised is not a sufficient description of the moment. The rest of the day is even harder to describe. High in the Alps, we walk through fields of beautiful wildflowers. Wow! We are in an area of the Alps reached only by tram, which feels like it's going straight up. Breathtaking is an appropriate word.

Later that day, we descend into the valley to visit Emmenthal. Hannes wants us to visit the Emmenthaler cheese factory that began in 1293. It's one of my favorite cheeses. It must be genetic. After an impressive tour of the old and new factory, we head for Auswil. The following day we visit the city of Bern, experience the beautiful Gothic Bern Minster, a Swiss Reformed cathedral, and window-shop. I can't resist purchasing an engraved Swiss army knife, which I still possess.

Of all the amazing experiences we witness, the Fluckinger family tops the list. They are warm, welcoming, and loving. Rosie and I feel blessed.

When it's time to leave for Italy, Hannes suggests we go by way of St. Moritz and stay at their place there. He wants to spend a few days there and figures now is the right time. St. Moritz is a three-and-a-half-hour drive. It's midmorning when all the good-bye hugs are completed.

ST. MORITZ

St. Moritz

St. Moritz is a luxury resort on Lake Moritz nestled near the Alps. This gem is famous for skiing, skating, snowboarding, and bobsledding. The 1948 winter Olympics took place at St. Moritz the year I was born.

After settling in, Hannes suggests a tour of the town. As we stroll, it's evident we can't afford to shop in any of the stores. That evening, Hannes and his delightful lady friend prepare a wonderful meal. We spend the rest of

St. Moritz as seen in an iStock photo by Siyue Steuber

the evening enjoying each other's company. After breakfast, we cannot express enough appreciation for all that Hannes has done for us. We bid farewell and point the Volvo toward Italy.

SAN MARGHERITA

Rosie is an absolute lover of just about any beach. San Margherita just happens to have a beautiful one. Not having booked ahead, and sticking to the original plan, we find a pay phone with a phone book and start calling hotels. The second or third call, we find one that might fit us. Not far up the hill sits the Villa San Giorgio.

We meet the owner of this small two-story villa who just happens to have one vacant room. After signing in, our kind hostess informs us that dinner will be served at five o'clock. All her guests eat at the same time and table. I'm thinking, "How different." We have no idea what we've stumbled into. At dinner, a gentleman next to us informs us that our hostess has entertained generals and dignitaries consistently for many years. He says, "I don't know if you realize how fortunate your timing was to get a room here." The meal is exquisite. We soon understood why people come so far to stay at this lady's quaint hotel.

Our second day is memorable for several reasons. First, we enjoy a delightful boat tour to Cinque Terre and back. Then, after dinner as we drink tea and eat cakes on our balcony overlooking the ocean, we hear gunshots firing all over the city and what sounded like people cheering or yelling.

This happened to be July 13th, 1994. We thought it prudent to leave the balcony until we soon discover that Italy's soccer team just beat Bulgaria in the World Cup semifinals. What a relief to find out we aren't spending our honeymoon in the middle of a coup d'etat.

The following day I get the big idea to visit the St. Francis Basilica when all Rosie wants to do is hang out on the beach. Part of my reasoning includes

San Giorgio

the fact that Montefalco and its restaurants are thirty minutes from Assisi. Maybe yes, maybe no?

ASSISI

Rosie, being gracious, lets go of the idea of a few extra days at the beach. We are off for a four-hour trip to the Basilica of St. Francis. On the outskirts of Assisi we find a small yet uncomfortable hotel. Being overly hot outside, we spend most of our time exploring the basilica. We enter a large room filled with paintings for sale. In the middle of the room, a gentleman sits at a large table. We notice him bent over reading a book through his wire-rim glasses. As he sets his book on the table, it becomes clear he's reading a small Bible. He acknowledges us and identifies himself as the artist. After examining all of his work. we continue to be drawn to one specific, rather spendy piece. After leaving and debating with Rosie for the third time,

San Margherita Villa Giorgio, July 13, 1994

Assisi

we decide to return and purchase Marcello Silvestri's painting, an original. That particular painting speaks volumes to what Rosie and I believe. Tremendous power comes from the cross by what Jesus did there and especially when He rose three days later.

MONTEFALCO

Taking our lawyer friend's (Mish-e-ale) advice, we leave Assisi for the ancient city on a hill, Montefalco (Hawk Mountain). As we approach, the medieval walled city appears ominous

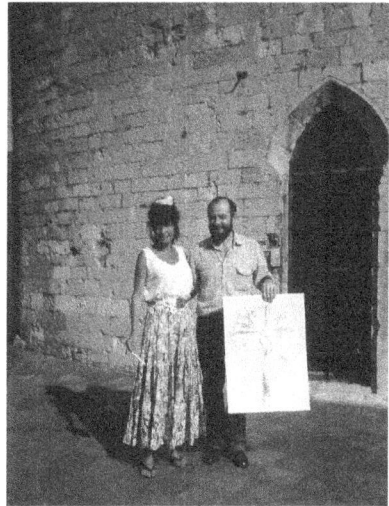

Marcello

from a distance. As the sun sets, a sprinkling of soft lights shimmers from the city. Winding uphill and closer, we feel like someone, at any second, will yell from the wall, "Who goes there?" Following our instructions, we wind our way through several narrow alleys and finally find the old green door with "Il Falisco Ristorante" written over it. Upon entering, to our left and standing in front of his open flame brick oven, the owner and chef Lunedi Chiuso greets us.

Beyond us eight gentlemen sit at a long table. At the far end is a single table on a raised platform, which is ours. Watching Lunedi prepare our meal is special. He produces a phenomenal five-course meal. Near the end of our dinner, we are invited to join the eight men at their table. We learn they have driven an hour from their BMW dealership. Having finished our banquet, we need no explanation for why the BMW boys make their long drive to eat here.

Chef Lunedi, above, and eating with the Beamer Boys, below

David in Firenze

Spending time with the Beamer Boys tops off a wonderful evening. For an ancient city, Montefalco is pristine and well-kept. It is hard to leave my favorite style of architecture, Gothic, which is so strong and lasting and beautifully preserved.

FIRENZE

The following day we drive north. Rosie suggests we spend a day in Florence. The most sought after venue in Florence (Firenze) is the Accademia Gallery that holds Michelangelo's iconic statue of David. David is one of my favorite flawed individuals, as we all can be, so I'm all in.

Without tickets, we quickly discover the waiting lines are hours long. That being our goal for the day, waiting and patience become an art form. Many hours later, we reach a fifty-foot hallway that opens into a beautiful domed room. In the center stands the iconic seventeen-foot statue, excluding the base, of David.

It was first unveiled to those of Firenze in the year 1504. Up close, the statue is one of the most impressive works of art I've ever seen. I understand why the lines are so long, day after day. I've seen the Mona Lisa, the King Tut display, the crown jewels of England, and more. But nothing compares to standing in front of Michelangelo's work.

AUSTRIA

It's time to make our way back to Anneliese in Wiesbaden. The drive back through Austria is enchanting.

Most of the small towns we travel through display shops and homes covered with amazing murals

Nassereith, Austria

and craftsmanship. Seeing the classic architecture always captivates me. I have some difficulty keeping my eyes on the road while driving. Crossing the Austrian/German border takes us past the Castle Neuschwanstein again. Tempted to visit the castle, I decide to continue driving a little farther. Passing by a small German town, we spot a bed and breakfast. What happens next is typical of our trip and no small deal for us. Our hosts, the accommodations, and the food are delightful and very German. The following morning we leave on our final four-hour leg to Wiesbaden.

WIESBADEN

Arriving at Anneliese's, I'm ready to be a passenger again. The following days before our return home we spend exploring. Michael and Carla take time from work each day to graciously serve as the best tour guides we could ever want. Between the cathedrals, museums, and countrysides, we enjoy a break with music, food, dancing, and smiling faces.

We are so grateful for the care and experiences that Anneliese, Michael, and Carla give us. It's now time for farewells and a flight home.

CHAPTER 38
BACK HOME

THE GOOD WITH THE NOT SO GOOD

THE "NOT SO GOOD" HAPPENS ON DECEMBER 10, 1994, when one of my cherished uncles, Wilbur, passes away. The part he played in my first eighteen years of life is special. I love and appreciate his calm soul. Knowing where he is now provides comfort in our loss.

The "good" occurs during Christina's Christmas break from college. She tells Rose she has been wrong about me, and Michael MAY be okay, after all! I can't tell you how good that feels.

PROMISE KEEPERS

I first attend Promise Keepers on July 7, 1995, when I join 65,000 others in Seattle's Kingdome to worship God. The theme is "Raise the Standard" for men who want to follow Christ. The themes address faith, integrity, and community. I met Bill McCartney, who founded Promise Keepers, years earlier in Boulder, Colorado, while he was coaching the CU Buffaloes football team.

It feels strange at the gate entrance. Looking across the street, I see Jonathan Loops Furniture Factory where I worked fourteen years earlier. This brings back interesting emotions. My life has taken such a turn.

The most eventful moment for me is when Jack Hayford describes Moses's "encounter" with God on the mountain. Jack explains that we need to do what Moses did: one, turn to God; two, listen up; three, strip yourself of worldly care; and four, allow His spirit to fill you with all the good things God has to offer.

Jack continues by asking all 65,000 of us to be completely silent. What happens next completely catches me off guard. Three weeks prior to this event, I pray for God to speak to me. I feel like I am doing all the talking. I should be listening. With all of us silent, all of a sudden in my head I hear these words: "Michael, I love you." That's the last message I ever expect to hear God say to me, although, being a Type A personality, I wait for marching orders from headquarters. Those words capture my attention and hold it!

WHAT'S RAY UP TO?

Busy boy, above, and the aftermath of a flood

Dad still waits for a response to a letter he wrote to David Rockefeller of Standard Oil in New York. Dad wants to know if Mr. Rockefeller has interest in buying the only oil-producing well in the state of Washington. I don't think it has produced anything other than bills. I figure by now someone at Standard Oil has discovered that Bigfoot is behind all this oil stuff in the state of Washington, and they think Ray is pulling another one of his pranks.

Dad is always busy with talk show hosts from St. Louis to San Diego, but I'm sure he can fit Rockefeller in if he has to, even if it's Christmas.

Just a month earlier we experience the official version of a 500-year flood in the Cowlitz Valley. In front of our home, which, thankfully, is twenty feet above the valley floor, we watch a ten-foot-tall road sign below us be slowly covered by water. We leave for Mom and Dad's with almost a foot still showing on the road sign.

We just make it out on Imboden Road to the south in my pickup. We cross a small section of the road where the water reaches to the floorboards but make it through without stalling the engine.

We stay at my parents, and the next day we hear waters are receding, so we safely return home that evening.

For more than a month, fourteen families in an area east of Toledo lose access to their homes after a dike along the Cowlitz gave way. Half of the Cowlitz River cut a new channel around homes on Collins Way, which are essentially now on an inaccessible island. After those affected receive no governmental assistance, on January 2, 1996, the Wallace Brothers Construction Company with fifteen Toledo volunteers repair the breach in three days. That area is named "Fantasy Island" by the locals. After being forced from their homes for so long, the locals begin to feel like ever returning home is a fantasy.

Later in the summer, Mr. and Mrs. Bigfoot are named grand marshals of the annual Toledo Cheese Days festival and parade. Notice the garlic necklace hanging from the antenna.

According to Ray L. Wallace, garlic cures many things, but not bad breath. Ray is in his element. He

Path cleared to 'Fantasy Island'

Supervising, above, and Big Cheeses at Toledo parade in 1996

has the attention of many. It's a good thing they never hand him the microphone, or the parade never would have finished that day.

TFBC

Months after our return from Europe, we make the change from the Toledo Assembly to Toledo First Baptist Church, where Rose and I feel very much at home. The three pastors complement each other well. The senior pastor is Joe Martin, who has been at the church for fourteen years along with Pastor Mike Stavig, music and children's ministry leader, and Pastor Danny Brown, youth pastor. We attend TFBC a short time when Pastor Joe asks if I'm interested in a one-on-one once a week for twelve weeks. He's interested in vetting potential workers or leaders. He wants to know where I'm coming from spiritually, what I believe, and how I interpret Scripture. We waste no time.

The first four weeks he seeks evidence of my salvation. Have I encountered Jesus? Do I have a new supernatural sensitivity to sin? In other words, am I doing things contrary to God's will? These are questions the Bible raises. My life changes dramatically due to that new sensitivity for how God wants me to live. It's a continual struggle between my will and God's. Two steps forward and one back. Isn't that the way it goes? Pastor Joe goes into detail after each question. The next week, he asks, "Do you have a new understanding of God's Word?" Without an encounter or relationship with Christ, reading Scripture is like reading any other history book, a bunch of interesting thoughts without life application.

The third week, he asks, "Do you have a new love for God's people?" That is a great question. I'm now hanging around a bunch of people I never would have hung out with four years ago. A healthy church environment won't look like a cookie cutter. Even the twelve men, called His disciples, that Christ picked to hang out with were extremely different. James and John, fishermen, were called the "Sons of Thunder" for good reason. Simon the Zealot walked around sporting a dagger. Matthew, a tax collector, was most hated by the Jews. They each encountered Christ, the living God, which radically changed the way they thought and lived, permanently.

The fourth week, Pastor Joe asks, "Do you have a new desire to talk about Christ to others (share your faith)?" Boy, have I been overcooking that one! I'm grabbing these guys out of their delivery trucks at work and telling them they need Jesus now, not later. I am a bit heavy-handed the first half-dozen years. Intense is a better description for some of my conversations with friends, relatives, and strangers. I'm head over heels in love with Jesus. With the help of God, Rosie, and Pastor Joe, I find that forming good relationships with people first is a more fruitful route. Sometimes I come across as judgmental when my spiritual maturity still needs work. Running my own businesses, I'm used to taking charge and telling others what to do.

Joe and I finish our twelve-week study. I feel like it puts me on more solid ground and develops a deep appreciation for the pastor's faith, too. If a spiritual leader does not match God's Word, beware.

BUSY SUMMER

In April of 1996, I am back at the Kingdome for another Promise Keepers. This time I'm there with Pastor Joe and other men from the Baptist church. Dr. E.V. Hill delivers a powerful talk about Joshua and Moses in a war. Above the battle is Moses with two men, Aaron and Hur, at his side. While Moses holds his staff in the air, Joshua and the Israelites prevail. When his arms tire and he lowers his staff, the enemy wins. Realizing this, Aaron and Hur sit Moses on a stone. When his arms grow weary holding the staff up to God, Aaron and Hur support him.

After Pastor Hill finishes, it strikes me that every Sunday during Pastor Joe's sermons, he wages a spiritual battle for people's souls. We talk more about supporting him with intercessory prayer during his preaching with volunteer prayer warriors. From there we launch *The Intercessor,* which quickly expands into a monthly newsletter that contains prayer requests for all three of our pastors. From there *The Intercessor* begins adding long-term prayer requests. Unlike our daily e-prayer that tends toward short-term prayer needs, *The Intercessor* lists people to pray for who may have struggled for months and sometimes years. We normally run about fifty volunteer prayer warriors.

SUNRIVER

For several years, I work for Alice, a wonderful lady who owns the Toledo Telephone Company. Because of her kindness, our family is given the use of the company condo at Sunriver, Oregon, for a week. Sunriver is a large development with a small family-friendly square full of shops, all this built around a beautiful golf course with adjacent tennis courts and a big swimming pool. We seldom play on the expensive Sunriver golf course, instead opting for Quail Run, a beautiful but somewhat less expensive course. Occasionally an hour before dusk, Sunriver allows people to play golf for half price, which encourages us to invent a new game called polo-golf. Each person rents a cart and stays in it while thrashing a golf ball around the course similar to polo. First person to the ninth hole wins.

Sunriver Resort

Between Bend and Sunriver is a three-mile stretch of the Deschutes River, which offers whitewater rafting and includes a series of several Class II rapids and four Class III rapids. Six of us book a rafting trip. A short time before boarding the bus for the Deschutes, my blood pressure skyrockets to 198 over 100. Everyone wants me to go to the hospital immediately. Instead, I tell them once I'm in the raft, I'll be fine. No, I don't know what I'm thinking. By the time we pass through the first rapid, my blood pressure is back to normal. Go figure. I know the Lord watches over me, but that's pushing the situation a bit, right?

Rafting the Deschutes River

251

CHAPTER 39
TRINITY ESTATES I

PART TIME

TEACHING GROWS MORE STRESSFUL FOR ROSE. She is concerned for her health and our finances. The doors open and shut numerous times over this, but finally they open and her request to work part time is approved.

The Lord is always way ahead of us when it comes to our problems. We are not sure what financial strain will come of going part time. Rosie's health is more important than our finances, so something has to give.

I'm looking at our construction company's first-quarter report, which appears to have an unusually high profit. I think this is due to outstanding bills. Without thinking much more about it, a few weeks later, I receive the second quarter totals, and I'm stunned. We earned more the last six months than all last year. This removes any doubt about our decision to curtail Rose's work hours.

Since I placed my faith in God, I understand through Scripture how He works and realize He is the one in control, not us. God has the full ability to add or subtract, bless or curse. In our case, the Lord sees to it that our business is two steps forward and none back. I may still feel and act like a young Christian, but I clearly see God working in me and through me, for which I'm so grateful.

RISKY

I'm still not sure how or why I become a developer, but being a bit of a risk-taker, we decide to approach Dad to purchase enough property to construct a small twelve-lot development. I have no clue as to the amount of red tape involved, but I move forward and quickly learn. To become a more patient person, try developing property for the first time. Like anything else, it becomes somewhat easier the more you do it.

By August, seventy-eight-year-old Ray Wallace artfully constructs what will be called Trinity Drive down the center of the planned development.

We have four generations working on our

Ray with Michael and Austin

project—Ray, Michael, Taylor (who pitched in periodically), and Austin, my grandson, who plays his part picking up sticks off Great-Grandpa's new road, offering a flashback for me to my first paying job for Dad and Uncle Wilbur.

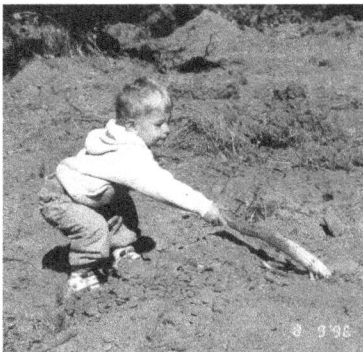

Austin

All goes reasonably well with the engineers, surveyors, and state and county inspectors. After Dad punches in the main road, it's up to me and two hired hands to finish the work.

The only big hiccup comes when I have the skidder at the far end of the development. Always carrying a chainsaw on the skidder, I grab the saw, climb down from the skidder, and begin sawing tops or limbs off the downed trees I plan to pull to the landing with the skidder. My right wrist bothers me. So when I run the saw, I continue to switch from my left hand to my right hand.

The landing

I approach a fallen tree off the ground about waist high. The top section looks like it's hung up in brush. I don't realize the top is in a bind, bent and taut like the string on a hunting bow. With the saw running, I hold it to my right side and walk to the tree, where I intend to make my cut. The top is to my left.

When I touch the saw to the log, I hear a loud snap. The right portion of the log strikes me. I find myself on my knees in a great deal of pain. I know I'm in trouble. I don't see any blood, so I eyeball the skidder. I'm too far away for anyone to hear me.

My only option is to reach the skidder and drive to the landing for help. I can't stand for some reason, but I crawl to the skidder about forty feet away. I

South Edition

Wednesday

September 17, 1997

Volume 32
Number 38

Households Courtesy of our Advertisers

Mike, his father Ray, and son Taylor have logging work to do; and they do it together. Photo by Victoria Stewart

Three generations work together as loggers

pull myself up onto the seat. From there I drive to the landing and wave over one of the guys. After explaining my situation, I ask him to grab my phone so I can call Rosie. She is at home, which is at the bottom of the hill. Still in shock, I say, "Honey, I got hit by a tree. What do you think I should do?"

Pastor Joe happens to be at the house when my guys bring me down in my truck. I don't want to wait for an ambulance. As Rose starts to pull out, Pastor Joe and Taylor pray. Rose yells out the window, "One of you call the hospital and tell them I'm bringing in someone who was hit by a tree." Soon we are on the freeway heading south to Longview at ninety-five miles per hour.

On the way, I struggle to breathe and keep telling Rose, "I'm okay. I'm okay." At the hospital, now with morphine in me and X-rays out of the way, I'm told that fortunately I have only broken ribs, a punctured lung, and a bleeding liver. The irony is that if I had held that saw to my left side, the tree would have struck me full on, and I probably wouldn't have survived.

After the accident, all is mostly downhill except my learning curve regarding the development, which continues to be a sharp uphill climb.

A DEPARTURE

I had left the church at about age seventeen without ever having an encounter with Christ. What faith I had was probably from my parents.

I notice a streak of reminders from Taylor about my past wrongdoings, which seems a little different coming from him. Each thing he mentions is mostly true, but I'm not the same person.

The situation becomes clear when, at sixteen, Taylor reminds me of my sinful past and informs me he will no longer go to church with us. During that conversation, I ask Taylor if he remembers ever hearing the word forgiveness while attending one of Pastor Danny's classes the past three years. He answers, "Yes." I say to Taylor, "Well, I have been forgiven of all my past sins and absolutely no one can ever condemn me for them." Taylor says, "Well, if I'm anything like you, I'll be back." We never broach the subject of my wrongdoings again.

The downside is sadness. The upside is not until this point in my walk with Christ have I so fully realized the importance of forgiveness. Not just toward others but toward myself. Without forgiveness I am hopelessly chained to the past. This realization turns out to be an enormous benefit for me.

COPPER HEADS

No, I'm not referring to snakes. On her way home from her part-time teaching job, Rosie listens to our favorite radio station, out of Portland, where a doctor from a health clinic is being interviewed. She describes a medical condition that includes severe chronic fatigue and memory loss. Rosie tells me about the interview. She has all the symptoms the doctor describes and begins connecting the dots. We noted the green hue in a pot of boiling potatoes and soon find out the green hue indicates the presence of copper in the water.

Rosie's symptoms are associated with metal poisoning. When we call the Portland clinic, we learn it is involved with an experimental chelation process with five hundred volunteers all over the United States. Rosie is called in immediately. After blood, fecal, urine, and hair samples are rushed to the

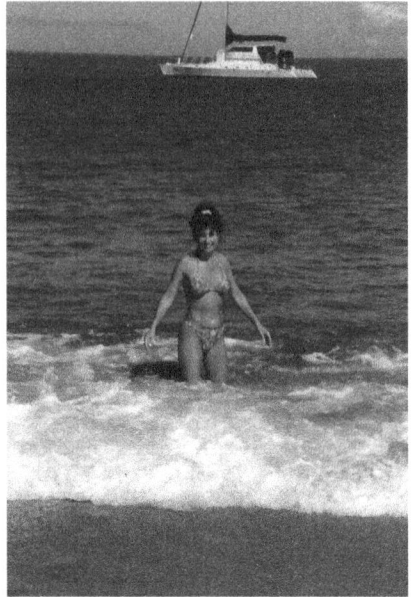

Enjoying better health in 1999

Mayo Clinic in Minnesota, the results come back quickly. Rose has so much copper and mercury in her system that her results are off the charts. They advise her to come to Portland right away before she suffers a severe case of cancer. It is recommended I follow suit.

Things start to make sense as I understand why I struggle to put in a full day's work. For a year, once a month, we go in for four-hour IVs. We are hooked to a large bag of fluid that draws toxic metals from our bodies. A couple of days later, we go back for a second four-hour IV to replenish any good metals removed with the toxins. We find out my body can chelate toxins quickly. Unfortunately, Rose's body cannot, probably due to defective chelating genes. I tease her about being my "toxometer" because of her body's hypersensitivity to anything harmful to our bodies.

While we sit taking our IVs, we receive reams of information to read concerning metal toxicity. The most critical information is the sources of copper toxins. We quickly learn the source of ours. We live in the country with a private well.

Commonly, well water is acidic, so the well is not the problem, nor is the acidity of our water. The problem comes when you run water through copper pipes. The longer the acidic water sits dormant in copper pipes, the more copper leaches into your water. Just sitting there overnight produces copper soup if the pipes are not flushed first. Even sitting there all day while at work is a problem. You can also acquire copper toxins from food sources, birth control pills, swimming pool algaecides, and other sources.

Being a builder I immediately talk with my plumber about the problem with using copper pipes. He refuses to use anything other than copper. I can't find a plumber reasonably close who uses anything other than copper. After some research, I discover PEX pipe, which is a high-density polyethylene. We start installing PEX immediately and find I can put in PEX twice as fast for half the cost and not risk the health of any homeowner. My company, Greenbelt Construction, refuses to use copper even if a client insists. Needless to say, we rip the copper pipes out of our home and replace them with PEX.

After a year, we discontinue our chelation treatments. First, this particular chelation process is taxing on Rose's body. My body handles it quite well. Second, they are extremely expensive. Our health insurance, as good as it is, won't cover experimental procedures, even though these procedures prove life-saving. Europe is way ahead of the United States on this medical issue.

UNSETTLING

I receive an unpleasant piece of news about my cousin Mick, who at fifty-five years old just suffered a fatal heart attack while playing basketball with friends. Mickey was a premier home builder in Portland, Oregon. Big money and the stress that comes with his position may have been the cause. To me, Mickey was so much like his wonderful father, Uncle Les. I loved everything about those two, especially their humility.

After contemplating Mick's passing, I find my prayer somewhat tweaked. I'm often asking, "Lord, don't give me too much or too little; give only what You know I can handle."

From this point on, I have no desire for my business to grow big or make crazy amounts of money. I'm going to design one house at a time, put on my tool belt, and build it.

CHAPTER 40
TRINITY II

SECOND TIME AROUND

OUR FIRST DEVELOPMENT ISN'T EASY by any stretch of the imagination. But here we are considering a second round. Being 1999, the US economy is having one of the best peacetime years in its history.

Rose and I decide to work out a deal with Ray and Elna on seventy-five acres they own. I have no problem with the asking price, which is the going rate at this time, but the payments are high. I agree with what Dad wants, but two months go by, and Rosie sees my stress and suggests we renegotiate for lower payments. Our chances of failure are high with only one income. Mom and Dad agree to lower the payments, not the price. It is a good thing since this is only the first of many bumps.

WORK BEGINS

After applications, surveying, and engineering, I begin creating the main road. Brother Rick stops by to see what I'm doing and informs me I seriously need an excavator if I ever plan to finish the development. After he explains all the advantages of excavators over dozers, I am convinced. We head to the equipment auction where Rick inspects and picks out the right one. Rick gives good advice. I have never enjoyed running any piece of machinery as much as what I now call "The Orange Pumpkin." She is a Hitachi Ex 120, mid-size excavator. Calling her a "she" now, right? Her radio plays only one station, a local country music station. Those songs remind me of being two years old in that logging camp and losing my little kitty and the diamond ring to that cute little two-year-old blonde.

Our vision for Trinity Estates II is similar to that of Trinity I. The only difference is lots in Trinity II will be five acres instead of two and a half. We want Trinity II to look like living in a park. The idea is to clear most of the brush but limit tree removal to areas suited for building homes.

The Orange Pumpkin, above, and Wayne Pedersen

Like Dad had his irreplaceable Frosty Clark, I have my Wayne Pedersen, an operator and mechanic who is an ace at keeping our used equipment running. Like Frosty, he is also a good equipment operator. He hints that he favors problem solving breakdowns, and we had plenty of those.

UGLY BUMP

Trinity II is situated on a flat seventy-five-acre piece with the west half overlooking the Cowlitz Valley fifty feet below. This creates a hillside that runs the length of the property. The plan is to cut the timber and leave a beautiful view of the Cowlitz River winding its way through the valley. This will also provide about $70,000 in funds badly needed for rock and road paving and bringing in power.

I am told state employees must inspect the wetlands below us, a small swampy area with a few ponds that all drain into a quarter mile south of Trinity II. This pond in front of our home dries up most summers. While living on this spot, I discover over the years that it's beneath the flight path of eagles. The eagles' aerie is about a half mile south of our house. They fly from the aerie, over our house and pond, and head to the Cowlitz River to fish. The state inspector sees a smolt (baby fish) belly up on the pond below us and immediately designates the entire western slope of our development a Class A salmon-rearing habitat, which negates any logging at the far end of the swamp. My theory is that the smolt was dropped there by a hungry eagle with slippery talons. I can't prove my theory, and state officials don't need to prove theirs. That decision wipes out $70,000, plus a beautiful view of the valley.

A couple of days later I find myself sitting in the orange pumpkin with the motor off and my head hanging down, wondering what in the world I am doing.

SUCK IT UP

I can do nothing but pray and move forward. We scrape the financial bottom of the barrel. I'm overwhelmed. During countless trips to county offices, I observe my share of angry and upset individuals waiting in line. Over the past year and a half, I discover that expressing my hot displeasure over a ridiculous state regulation to the person at the counter does no good. I quickly learn patience, a smile, and a prayer works wonders.

While picking up my final approval documents, the gentleman I have dealt with at the county lets me know he deals with far more angry people than he cares to. He then says, "I have been thinking about getting you a desk here because you've been patient." That melts away many of my worries that day. I thank the Lord for growing patience in me and giving me the ability to treat people with respect. I'm not always good with that, but I'm working in the right direction with God's help.

PRAYER CLOSET

Being in serious need of funds is now a recurring theme. So I'm calling Pastor Joe to come pray with me in my old green flatbed for the sale of a lot. Not more than a week later, we have a buyer. I don't remember how many times that happens, but pretty soon one sale leads to another, and we never miss a payment to Mom and Dad. Our first sale comes from a high school classmate looking for a piece of property for his son. They end up with a bargain basement deal and make great neighbors.

TERRY

After finishing Trinity Estates II, I am back to building again, thank you, Lord! This new guy I meet in church is looking for employment, so we give it a try. This fellow can outwork two guys, sometimes three, in his sleep. He is also pretty smart, but he lacks patience and seems a little gruff at times. Every day, the Lord tells me to just keep being patient with him. I won't regret it. Keep materials in front of him. Just be patient. The Lord is always right. Terry wants nothing to do with the business end of things, which I'm doing. Our differences complement each other to the point I feel we can accomplish much. Thank you, Lord, again. I won't trade this guy for a dozen good men. By the way, he drives fifty on the freeway. Terry says he gets much better mileage at lower speeds. Being a Type A personality, I have a hard time not losing him on the freeway on our way to a job. Patience, patience, patience.

Glacier Calving

GLACIER CALVING

At the end of the school year, Rosie is chosen along with another teacher to participate in a seminar onboard the Westerdam, a ship bound for Alaska's Inland Passage. Her food and passage is free. For the price of a ticket, I can accompany her, so I do. This is not as much fun for Rosie as it is for me. She attends mandatory meetings and misses incredible sights.

The high point is coming upon Hubbard Glacier, which is well-known for its spectacular calving events as enormous chunks of ice break free and fall a great distance into the water. As the captain navigates toward the glacier, a calving event takes place. We see this giant chunk of ice just as it strikes the water. Immediately we hear what sounds like a loud explosion. Over the loudspeaker, the captain informs us we just witnessed one of the larger and more rare calving events. Impressive is a fitting term for what we witness. When it comes to calving, I think poor old Mother Hubbard is way past her due date. That was an enormous calf.

CAUGHT OFF GUARD

Terry and I are building another home on Trinity Estate II. I wake up early, feeling a little strange. Rosie has left for work, and I call Terry to let him know I'm not feeling right. I find myself hours later, still lying on the couch, feeling like someone put five hundred pounds on my chest. The phone rings. It's the pastor. Before I can say hello, he asks me if I'm okay. My response is, "I think so." Our conversation doesn't last long. I try to sort out what has just occurred. It doesn't take long to figure that out. The Lord has just given me a glimpse of my sins (things I still need to work on). I meet with Joe the following day to thank him for the call and explain what is going on. He says, "I felt something going on with you and was prompted to call."

CHAPTER 41
BIGFOOT RESTS

LOSING GROUND

Dad's last Christmas, and he loved Elna's buns to the end

DAD'S LAST CHRISTMAS with us is in December 2001. For the next ten months, his health declines to the point he needs a care center. His mind is still sharp, but his body refuses to keep up. Ray is a character to the end. One evening after work, I drive Mom to visit him in Centralia. I'm at the end of his bed and Mom stands at his side. With a concerned look on his face, Dad says in a soft caring voice, "Elna?" She responds with, "What, Ray?" He says, "You know I'm not gettin' any!" Elna, very matter-of-factly, says, "Well, you know, I'm not either." Ray, softly and slowly, says, "Oh!" Elna asks him, "Do you really think you need any, Ray?" Dad, with a disappointed voice, says, "Well, Kitty, I guess not."

Mom is visiting Dad again; it's November 23, 2002. Before she leaves, Dad tells her, "Jesus is coming to get me in three days." Mom repeated that to us.

Three days later, the day after Thanksgiving, I leave my jobsite southeast of Chehalis and see a bizarre sunset as I head west to Interstate 5, then home. The entire sky is full of soft billowy clouds with a reddish hue, the likes of which I've never seen. While taking in this unusual sight, I receive a call from the Riverside Nursing and Rehab Facility in Centralia, letting me know Dad had just passed away. Isn't it just like Jesus to keep His word? He told Dad it would be three days.

The November 26, 2002, afternoon sky

BIG NEWS

Only a couple of days after Dad's passing, the phone rings off the hook. We are totally caught off guard. I'm not keeping track of the constant flow of condolences. I'm not surprised about the local calls. The surprise is the stream of radio talk show hosts; reporters from the *LA Times*, *New York Times*, and *Seattle Post-Intelligencer*; then Northwest television reporters. Dan Springer of Fox News in Seattle contacts us. Radio talk show hosts affiliated with Paul Harvey send their condolences.

A couple of months later, national television networks show up—Bill Whitaker with the CBS network and Chip Reid representing NBC. Before Chip leaves, he thanks us for having so much fun. He says, "I'm normally covering tragic news; this has been so refreshing." Just over a week later, we sit in front of our television, watching Chip ride an armored tank with the 3rd Battalion, 5th Marine regiment toward Baghdad, Iraq, in March 2003.

During all these interviews, I realize our family knows nothing about Sasquatches, Yetis, and the like, but we will testify to the who, what, when, where, why, and how of Bigfoot. We lived in and out of the woods with him for sixty years.

Later, Tom Brokaw, host on *Inside Edition*, covers the Bigfoot story. The episode is well done.

Then *National Geographic* shows up with a custom-made Bigfoot suit that my son Taylor wears to demonstrate Bigfoot track-making methods used by Ray and his adult elves. This takes place on one of cousin Don Wallace's plowed fields close to Toledo.

DEEP VALLEYS

The last couple of months are totally nuts. Despite all this activity, Dad's memorial service goes as expected. The memorial service is standing room only with excited anticipation among the family, friends, and community members in attendance. Ray was a big (foot) personality! I wonder if I'm attending a comedy hour with all the stories people share about Ray. The atmosphere is full of emotion from hilarious laughter to tears at the loss of this man who tried to care for anyone he saw in need. The service in the packed church is a celebration of life. This is a bright spot, but it only defers a small portion of our loss, especially for Mom. After all, they were married for sixty years.

To make matters worse, we watch Rose's big brother, George, suffer with head and neck cancer, which is especially difficult for Rose as she's dealing with Dad's death, the media frenzy, her brother's terminal cancer, and now special guests staying at our house. Although they're a wonderful blessing and great people, she needs to spend precious time with her brother. The people I am referring to are interested in making a movie.

HOLLYWOOD

We now receive calls from Hollywood types interested in making a movie about Dad.

Of all the invitations, we have time to meet with only four companies and return home. Of the four, one in particular has the clout and money. We meet the owner and a couple of others. He recently developed a special program for a major television network that earned him an obscene amount of money. In the boardroom, after shooting a long list of questions at us, these guys are amped up and ready to sign. These young producers make it implicitly clear we have no say in what they choose to do with our story.

Rose sits there thinking, "They have no clue that they're dealing with a gyppo man who will never give up full control no matter how much money is thrown his way. Michael will stand strong to protect his family's character and legacy." Rose and I have a problem. While in the waiting room before our meeting, we saw a half dozen magazines on the table before us. They are not *Good Housekeeping* but skin magazines, which raises more than a few questions. All Rosie and I can think about is whether this will be a PG-13 or

R-rated film. Upon ending our meeting, we tell them that we will discuss this with Elna and get back to them.

Back home we describe our meetings with Mom, particularly the one with the young man with all the money. If we are not careful, once we sign the bottom line, it's all out of our hands. The three of us reach the same conclusion; the risk is not worth the reward. We respectfully decline.

On the heels of everything, we receive another call from Hollywood, this time from Judge Reinhold, the actor, and his wife, Amy, who are poring over the day's news. They tell us later how they decide to call. Amy finds a headline out of *The Los Angeles Times* that reads, "Bigfoot Died." She says, "Honey, you have got to come in here to read this. It's so funny!" They both say, "We have to get in touch with this Michael Wallace!" Then Judge says, "Their father just died. I don't want to be a Hollywood buzzard." Amy responds, "You don't think other people are going to?" Then it broke in *The New York Times*.

In the call from the Reinholds, Judge introduces himself. It quickly becomes evident we share the same faith when Judge asks, "Was your father a Christian?" My reply is, "Ray was a sold-out, rock-bottom, where the rubber meets the road one."

I then comment to Judge, "I'm so thankful for your call. I am dealing with Hollywood and do not know who to trust." Then I say, "Do you know who William Morris is? He keeps calling me." Judge says, "You mean the agency?" I answer, "No some guy named William Morris." Judge again responds, "Oh, my gosh! That's a huge agency, Mike."

After a long pause, I finally say, "Well, brother, you better get up here, because we're not sure who to trust."

Soon after our conversation with Judge, Rosie and I find ourselves picking them up at the airport. On the way home in our used Lexus, they tell us, "We were expecting to ride in a big old pickup." They soon discover we don't live that deep in the woods. After dropping their bags at our place, we head to Mom's. Mom, Rosie, and I feel comfortable with our new acquaintances and decide to trust them to tell the family story, come what may.

A few weeks later, Judge and Amy return to our place for a little over a week. The idea is to interview as many people as possible associated with Bigfoot in the past, in the form of a video. They capture enough information on Ray to fill a small library. The time spent is filled with laughter and smiles.

After days of research, Judge sets me straight on an issue concerning Ray. Through all the interviewing, one thing stands out loud and clear to Judge: That's Ray's heart. He may be loud and boisterous at times. For heaven's sakes, the man worked as a logger all his life. I make a not-so-complimentary analysis about Dad's spiritual life. A bit on the judgmental side, you might say. This is when Judge puts me back on the right track. Now remember, I am a twelve-year-old Christian who still needs a lot of work. "Your dad didn't just talk

Michael with Judge, above, and Amy with her camera

about being a good Christian; he put the boots to the ground and got it done." Gulp! I need to hear that. Judge's retort becomes a game-changer for me. He reminds me, without saying it, that it's not my place to judge. That role alone belongs to the Lord.

Hours are spent compiling information on Ray L. Wallace. There are plenty of stories. Ray had been a busy boy. Amy is busy recording one interview after another with Dad's friends, relatives, and associates. Judge takes notes while I fill him in on Dad's many adventures. We have so much fun rehashing an endless stream of past events. These interviews with Dad's friends and associates are fruitful. Judge says, "We have enough here to do more than one story."

GEORGE

In March we learn the news that brother George won't live much longer. After watching him battle, it's a tough pill to swallow. One very large plus is he gave his heart to the Lord a few months earlier. Knowing where he is now eases the loss. From the time George and Rose were small, he was very protective of his sister. This is a hard loss for her. Dealing with George's passing, and all the craziness surrounding Dad's death, is not easy.

Losing George

268

CHAPTER 42
A NEW NORMAL

THE OLD AND THE NEW

WITH RAY WALLACE'S PASSING, we now live a new normal with a fairly large chunk of our family missing. Living with Ray prepared us for just about anything. It's good Mom is strong, not just from being a Dane but from the challenge of living with Bigfoot. With brother Rick and his wife, Donna, just across the street, Mom feels well taken care of.

SETTLING IN

I have come to know the Vieth brothers, two tall drinks of water, who do an excellent job of dry-walling the homes we build.

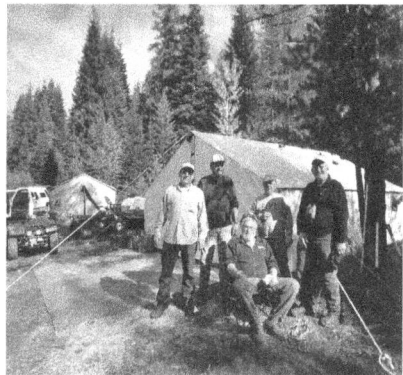

Heads above the rest

In December 2004, they invite me to go with them to Wallace, Idaho, for an elk hunt. Hard to pass on a chance to go camping in the wilderness. Miles out of the small town of Wallace, we set up camp. If you like using a quad and hunting, Idaho is a far more friendly state than most. The crew plans to stay a week, but I must be back for work in four days. Riding the trails out of camp is so much fun, mainly because they are so well kept. Hunting is not going well, but the scenery is outstanding. Hunting suffers partly due to the wolves we hear each night and see signs of during the day.

This is my first time hunting in many years. Being in the wild is so wonderful that even if I don't end up with an animal, I haven't lost anything. I've gained a great experience.

The day comes to leave. The plan is to discontinue the hunt at noon and head down the mountain to camp. Although we work in pairs, this day we split up to cover more ground. After searching for signs of elk all morning, at about eleven in the morning, I remember passing an elk wallow a few days earlier. This is a wet muddy area, often caused by a small spring. Animals like using these to roll in for bathing and scent marking. I find a good location overlooking the wallow and sit on the ground with my back to a large fir tree. I run my eyes over the terrain. Checking my watch, it's 11:45 a.m. I have fifteen minutes before we leave for home. I'm saying in my mind, "Lord you know how much Rosie and I love elk meat. It's so healthy."

Seriously, five minutes later, out of the corner of my eye to the left, I glimpse something move. Quickly rising to my feet, I see movement through a heavy mist. It's an elk moving through heavy timber with little underbrush. I need a better position, so I run uphill about forty yards and find a tree to rest my rifle on. To shoot this elk, I put my crosshairs at a hundred and fifty yards between the next two trees in the elk's path. In the crosshairs, the two trees I chose look like they're about one and a half inches apart.

Timing my shot, I pull the trigger. The elk takes one or two steps and drops. My quad is about a hundred yards uphill, so I retrieve it and park next to the elk. One of the guys hears the shot and helps me dress it. During the process, my friend says, "Do you realize you hit the heart? That's why the elk didn't get far." I have no explanation. I'm fortunate to hit a kill zone, let alone the heart. I know I'm experiencing divine intervention. I waste no time giving thanks for answered prayer.

The following year, we all go back but to a different area in Idaho. We are off the Saint Joe River on the opposite side of the mountains where we hunted last year. We are up so high that often, driving our quads, we find spots where we can see into Montana amid spectacular scenery in every direction. Three days into our hunt, an hour before sunset, we head for camp. On the way, we come to a crossroads.

Standing there is a young man in his mid-thirties, a bit out of shape, holding a big fancy long-range rifle. He looks down this steep mountainside. We pull up to talk and, wasting no time, he says, "Six hundred yards down

The crossroads

the hill is a large four-point buck. If I hit him, will one of you help me pack it up here?" From behind me, I hear, "Sure." The kid takes aim and fires. The buck runs down the hill about another hundred yards and drops.

After watching all of the action, I turn to find just me and the young fella with the fancy rifle. I say, "Well, it's me and you." In no time, we descend the mountain to the buck and dress it out. My newfound friend has his pack with him, and with each of us on one end of the buck, we hike up the mountain about a hundred and fifty yards. This guy looks like he's about to go into cardiac arrest from the steep climb. Grabbing his backpack, we continue.

About halfway up, walking a ridge to our right, is a bull moose. We freeze, and so does the moose. All I know is they can be unpredictable. When the moose starts moving again, we follow suit. He stops, and we stop. I don't know much about moose, but I'm a little concerned. If he decides to charge us, we have only one lone tree on the hillside for protection, and it's another three hundred yards uphill. If the moose charges us, we are in deep doo. After three rounds of starting and stopping, the moose decides we are not worth the trouble and trails off. By the time we reach the lone tree, it is dark. We decide to leave the deer at the tree and head up to our quads while we still can. At the quad, I hand him his backpack, wish him the best, and head to camp.

Dawn breaks the following morning. Something isn't right. I feel clammy and know right away I am in trouble with my blood pressure. The guys want to take me down the mountain, but in my lack of wisdom, I say, "Just load my quad and gear. I can get down okay." So, they load everything of mine, and I take off. At the bottom of the mountain, I find a restaurant in a tiny town. I think I'll rest and drink water and maybe my blood pressure will calm down. In the next booth are two off-duty emergency medical technicians. One goes out, brings back a blood pressure machine, and takes my blood pressure. It's 195/90. One man says, "The hospital is about twenty miles from here. We'll take you." Here I go again. Steeped in wisdom, I say, "I can make the drive, thanks." About halfway there, I'm faint, and I beg God to forgive me for my stubbornness and help me make it to the hospital. Ten minutes later, I pull into the emergency parking lot. The last thing I remember is reaching for the door.

After I wake up in a hospital bed, the nurse tells me they found me outside on the ground against the emergency door. They put a nitro pill under my tongue, which brought down my blood pressure. Late that afternoon, I am released and driving back home, grateful for another decision that could have gone sideways but didn't. Thank you, God.

CHAPTER 43
DREAMS

A PATH

IF YOU ARE A PRACTICAL DREAMER, like me, you need a plan, a path to follow. I cannot just dream for the sake of dreaming, where dreams do not need to be fulfilled. Some dreamers simply enjoy each idea then move on to the next. Neither way is better than the other. They're simply different.

From boyhood on, Dad reminds me to, "Think big boy, think big." He instills courage in my mind so nothing is too big or too scary to tackle in life. From this I conclude that if I am going to dream, I might as well make it a relatively large one.

Timing is also important. The seeds of my dream home are planted in Dr. Southcott's class my senior year at Western Washington in Bellingham. From there I always pursue different versions of a dream home, but I'm still missing a few important ideas.

One of those is Rose. This is our twelfth year of marriage. During our first year together, I mention how glad I am that she is a strong woman. I'm used to being in charge and I need someone to balance me. After twelve years of learning how to trust and listen to her good advice, I make headway. What gives me the strength to make this happen is my love for Christ, and what He wants for my life and my love for Rose. I am an unquestionable work in progress.

NOW IS THE TIME

All the pieces finally come together. The practical dreamer has his path to completion. I have Rose at my side, the finances, and the time, but one huge piece is still missing. What does God want? I want to build a dream home three times larger than what we need. It is a want, not a need. If I remember correctly, I approach Pastor Joe four or five times, asking if this is something I should do. Joe finally asks me, "If you build this house and sell it, will you make a profit?"

My answer is, "I could probably double my money." His answer is, "So what's your problem?" I have asked God about it, but I'm feeling guilty because I need Joe's advice to clear the pathway. In a very practical way, he does so by asking, "So what's your problem?" It's apparent this is strictly a financial issue, not a spiritual one.

Pastor Joe later clarified "it wasn't the money; it was about expressing your art." He shared with Rosie, if a man has a dream to fulfill in his life, don't stand in his way. Having the means and the ability to create and leave behind a beautiful work of art is a noble endeavor. I realize I don't need to feel guilty for having the means and ability to fulfill this unique dream.

Rose is more of an impractical dreamer because she doesn't always need a plan or even a how. She realizes as a little girl living in a humble home with little money that she is a princess ... the daughter of the King of kings and Lord of lords. There is nothing God can't do.

I'm a couple of months into my slow process of designing our dream home. It's a real struggle designing a house that does not look like a hundred others I've seen. My biggest issue is losing space on the second floor above the entry. After a half dozen attempts and throwing all of them away, I dream. That night I find myself standing in an open Moroccan courtyard, looking up as if in an old movie. I see a walkway on the second floor behind small columns connected by arches. After work the next day, I can't wait to get to my drawing board. It's crazy how all of a sudden the pieces come together. Before I know it, I'm putting the finishing touches to my drawing and making material lists and a final budget.

IN FULL PURSUIT

It takes me four months to complete the plans for "The Dream Home." Keeping Greenbelt Construction thriving didn't leave me with much time to work on my design. I only sneak in a few hours after work when I'm not exhausted. But it is finally completed, and we apply for a building permit.

The plan is to first construct the new two-story garage, buy a fifth-wheel trailer to live in, then list our existing home for sale. With the garage completed, we move in our belongings. Our home sells in a short time.

In the meantime, our granddaughter, Gwen, Taylor's oldest, is

Grandpa's orange "crack hoe"

soon to be three. When she stops by the jobsite, she likes riding on my excavator. On the way home she tells Carey, her mom, she really likes riding on Grandpa's "Crack-hoe." Pretty cute.

Rose and I have a great crew. A bit larger than I normally want, but if we're going to finish this project any time soon, I need extra hands. The timing worked with Ryan and Jarod, Rose's nephews, who become a perfect fit for what we need. Their talents are diverse, and these guys are not afraid of work. Coupling these two with Terry, my extremely talented foreman, we are set. A couple of others come and go but also help a lot.

Other than doing a good job, I have only one other request of each of them. During the framing stage, I ask each man to show up every day with a Bible verse and write it on a beam or stud. Everyone humors me, which I appreciate.

Watching our budget is the biggest challenge. The guys do a great job. Rosie and I go head to head on several aesthetic vs. budget issues. I'm thankful she sticks to her guns. We end up paying three times more for wood windows than for the vinyl ones I budget for. This place cries for them, and I cry for my budget that

Terry

just took a $15,000 hit. Then Rosie informs me I'm going to a class in Seattle where I will learn how to apply American clay on interior walls in place of paint. American clay is hand-troweled on interior walls to create many different effects.

In Seattle, our instructor shows us how to prepare the clay for application and hands each of us a trowel. After demonstrating a few basic methods, and after experimenting for about an hour, I conclude that achieving a smooth finish is the most appealing method. When the clay dries, it has a soft sandy feel and the surface sparkles. Rose has made another excellent choice. The American clay is beautiful!

The exterior, above, and the back deck at right

One day, applying the American clay on the entry walls, I'm near the door of the small balcony above it while Jarod lays block in the patio below. After placing a dozen blocks, he comes upstairs, stands on the little rounded balcony, and inspects his work, making sure the blocks run straight and true. This particular time, he stands on the balcony four feet away from me and starts chuckling. I ask him, "What's so funny?" His reply is, "Every time I walk out on this balcony, I feel like the pope. I want to give a speech." We both had a good laugh.

We are now on the home stretch, doing the finish work. Taylor puts in some time staining for us, which is much appreciated. In a few weeks, after our final inspection, we can move out of the fifth-wheel trailer. Its windows are already starting to ice up.

The kitchen, above, and internal columns, left

BIG SURPRISE

In late September, I receive a call from a contractor friend. We both belong to the Lower Columbia Contractors Association, which covers rural Southwest Washington. He asks if I submitted my project entry form for the 2006 construction excellence awards contest. My response is, "Are you kidding? I'd be wasting my time." He says, "It's only $125 to enter. Don't be a tight butt. Send it in." The notice is still in my office garbage can, so I take his advice and dig it out. In the application, you name your project and give a description. Rosie thinks "Waldschlösschen" (little castle in the woods) is a fitting name, and we go with that.

This is the description. "As you drive up to the sky bridge, which connects the home to the garage, you park and walk up the stone walkway past the rock turret and stone courtyard to large arched double wood doors. You sense a European feel to the home. Entering, you find a unique two-story foyer with American clay walls and a walk-around mezzanine above. Most rooms empty into this focal point. Eyes feast on arches, pillars, and wrought iron pickets with wood hand railings as well as custom wood interior doors by a local artisan. There is a simple elegance and warm Tuscan colors created by the combination of American clay, complementing paint colors, natural stone, and oak flooring."

Boy what a mouthful!

I submit this home in the category, "New residential construction over $250k." I send my check and application and wait. In the meantime, someone is sent out to photograph our new home for a panel of judges to pick a winner. To find out who the winner is, you attend a banquet where awards are given out for each category.

Mike and Rose with Ryan, left, and Jerod, right

We are stunned to find out that the "Little Castle in the Woods" wins first place for best design! Never in my dreams did I think that would happen. The only one missing that night is my ace, Terry. He has a shy streak.

TAKE ME OUT TO THE BALLGAME

To make 2006 even more sweet, I receive a call from one of my favorite salesmen and human beings, Jim Kangas. He informs me that, if I'm so inclined, he has a spot for me along with several other contractors on a lumberman's van heading to a Mariners game. Jim tells me we will sit in the press box suite and enjoy a fancy lunch and all. Who can say no to that?

We start the day having our picture taken on the mound with one of the Mariners. Awesome, the player, a pitcher, turns out to be their closer, J.J. Putz, who is having a good year. The night before, he handles San Francisco's Barry Bonds quite nicely. I stand next to him on the mound, waiting for the photographer, and like my father, not feeling very shy, I ask J.J. "Why did you take a risk in pitching to Bonds toward the end of the game and not just walk him since we were several points ahead?" Folks, let me offer a little advice. If you are not cut out to be a sports reporter or analyst, do not quit your day job. Describing the look on J.J.'s face and his nonresponse, I should no longer be breathing. Back to being an arche-tractor (designer/builder), yup!

Would-be analyst

CHAPTER 44
GROWING!

MORE FAMILY

OUT OF THE BLUE I receive a call from my half-sister, Mary Ann Piltner, whom I met a year earlier for the first time. She wants me to meet Kathy and Lorrie, our other two sisters. My family seems to grow faster each year. We have a wonderful time catching up. They are great ladies. Our mom's sister, Rosie Turner, comes with the girls. If you remember, Rosie is cousin Bob's mom. Having Rosie Turner there triggers memories of my childhood, which is great.

Kathy, Mary Ann, Mike, and Lorrie

OUR GREAT MOMS

If I have not mentioned it yet, I happen to have not only a wonderful mother in Elna but also a fine mother-in-law. Elna certainly has a rich history, and so does Rose's mom, Gisela. We call her Bobbie.

Elna with Gisela

Gisela, the youngest of eight children, grew up in Wiesbaden, Germany. Her parents, being semi-retired, ran a small restaurant on the edge of the woods. Gissi, as her family called her, loved working there from the time her eyes could see above the table rim. When she was a teen, World War II broke out. Everyone had to serve their country. Gissi stayed home as her father's personal nurse. In WWI, he was impaled by a bayonet and lost a lung. He had emphysema in his one good lung and needed medication and a shot each day to breathe. Georg, her father, never joined the Nazi party.

Gissi often could be seen walking down the aarstrasse (street in front of her house) with her aktentasche (briefcase) in hand. She was savvy at procuring what the

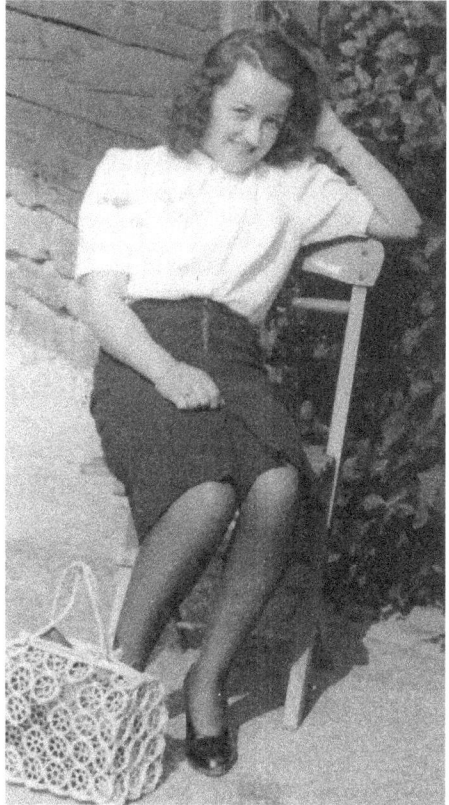

Gissi

family needed during wartime. I'm sure that aktentashe contained a few bottles of wine for barter. A bottle of wine would get you almost anything. Fortunately, they had a full wine cellar. Gissi would do whatever it took to obtain food and medicine for her family and pain medication for a neighbor lady in tremendous pain with open sores (probably cancer). A few times at night during complete blackouts, Gissi walked several miles to get her father's medication.

During this time, her father helped save a Jewish family, which put all of their lives at risk. The Jewish family hid in the woods during the day and entered their house at night through an open window facing the forest. One fateful night, a group of SS officers entered their restaurant and informed them they were commandeering their house for the night. Gissi glimpsed her parents sitting at the kitchen table, trembling. As Gissi saw one officer going toward the door to the room hiding the Jewish family, she quickly stepped in front of the door. She used her feminine wiles to convince the officer the room was full of extra outdoor furniture for the restaurant. "Follow me upstairs, and I will show you great accommodations for you and the other officers." Gissi was welcoming and fearless, which saved all of their lives.

Not long after, an errant bomb was dropped at the end of their street. Gissi insisted her parents let her go and help the wounded. She had a natural inclination for healing. Gissi scurried toward the chaos. She arrived just as the dead bodies were brought out. She collapsed to the ground; these were her neighbors.

Later, during the American occupation, Gissi again walked down aarstrasse with her aktentasche. The street from top to bottom and beyond was filled with an all-Black American regiment. There was no one else around except a few eyes peering from a house window behind a curtain. It was a little eerie when three officers peeled off and advanced toward Gissi. She felt so small, standing next to these three tall soldiers. They asked, "Do you know where we can get some wine?" Of course, Gissi had some in her aktentashe. She says, "I live just up the street. Perhaps my dad can help you out." She brings the officers to her father who traded wine for food. She headed back down aarstrasse with her aktentasche to complete her mission.

OUR OTHER FAMILY

Over the past thirteen years at our church, I've been involved with the men's ministry, teaching, monthly intercessor, and more recently the finance committee. Working around many wonderful people always makes what I'm involved in feel like a "want to," not a "have to." Our pastors are incredibly gifted, great to work with, and teachable when it comes to what the Lord wants of us. Pastor Joe is in his twenty-eighth year as a pastor with no plans to go anywhere but TFBC. This is his church family; it is way beyond just a job, which pastoring should never be. In his seminary days, he is gifted with an amazing mentor, Dr. Henry Blackaby, the founder of Blackaby Ministries International and most noted for his best-selling book, *Experiencing God.* Henry sets the bar pretty high when it comes to leadership. This is reflected in Joe's preaching and teaching. We enjoy hearing from other Blackaby associates, such as Dr. Calvin Miller, Dr. T.W. Hunt, and Dr. Kerry Skinner.

In 2008, Rose and I host Dr. Miller during his weeklong visit at our church. The first couple of days he speaks to our men's group during a retreat at the coast. Calvin is a gifted man in so many different ways. He is a pastor, author of more than sixty books, a painter, a poet, and later a seminary professor.

Upon returning from our retreat, we walk through the door at home to be greeted by Rosie. Calvin asks her, "What have you been doing while we were gone?" Rosie replies, "Cooking for you." After naming off quite a few things she has prepared, she asks him, "What do you want to eat?" With a big smile, he says, "All of it."

Calvin Miller

Rosie and I are so thankful for the extra time he stays with us. Rosie is way ahead of me in seeing the depth of giftedness in this man, which I'm rather glad I didn't see at the time. If I had realized his talents, knowing me, I would have treated him like a rock star. I'm thankful for that lack of knowledge. Calvin just wants to be treated like a friend. Before leaving our home, he gifted us with several of his paintings and books, among them his best-selling book, *Life is Mostly Edges*, an autobiography. He wrote, "To Michael and Rosie whose love for Christ and hospitality are the two rich gifts they offer all." He signed his name, Calvin Miller, and the date, 10-4-08. Four years later, he passes away.

Another special man, Dr. T.W. Hunt, came to speak at TFBC and stayed with us. He has the greatest of all gifts, the gift of love. T.W. is also an accomplished author, seminary professor, and speaker most noted for the book *The Mind of Christ*. The majority of his writing concerns prayer. While in our living room one evening, our conversation led to Rose's heritage, then to the German language. This prompted T.W. to describe an old extinct German language that to him is one of the most beautiful and romantic languages we know of. After his description, I thought for a moment, then asked to be excused.

In my office I have a few old Bibles that Uncle Aage Sorensen gave me. I grabbed a German one. Taking it back downstairs, I handed it to T.W. His eyes widen, and he says, "Do you realize what you have here?" The Bible is written in, I believe he said, "the Moselle romance dialect." I say, "Take it; it's yours." T.W. says, "Oh, no, you don't realize what this is worth." My comment is, "You obviously do. Don't tell me; just take it." What he has given us in his short week here is worth a box of those Bibles. This man is special.

Through our God-given gifts and abilities, we live in this beautiful home until the Lord says otherwise. We hold on to this place loosely and enjoy every day we spend

Christmas

Mom's Christmas display

here. Rosie's touch inside keeps it warm and cozy. Outside, during Christmas, I love displaying Mom's manger scene that has been in our family since the 1960s. The figures remind me of her.

OFF TO SEE BIGFOOT

Elna Lillian Wallace left us on April 9, 2012, for the mansion Jesus prepared for her. Toledo First Baptist Church was packed with community, friends, and family to celebrate the life of a very well-loved woman. Elna was steadfast, and people could trust her with their hearts. Bagpipers playing "Amazing Grace" followed the beautiful casket adorned with painted flowers. Numerous stories were shared of how she touched lives. The songs reflected her deep faith in Jesus. For forty-some years, she prayed over me and for me. I am forever grateful for her persistent prayers and patience. I fight daily to put the old man away and grow the new one in me. If it isn't my actions I struggle with, it's my thoughts. God sets the bar high. With what I now know, I wouldn't want it any other way.

CHAPTER 45
MORE ADVENTURES

CLOSER

THE NEXT EIGHT YEARS ARE FULL OF ADVENTURES. One is always working with Terry. We work out the bugs in our relationship and grow closer year by year. It's so much fun watching what we accomplish together during a week's work. Then, on Sunday, I watch him put smiles on people's faces while he cuts it up playing his drums for church services. I've been around a fair number of drummers in my hippie-dippie days, and Terry is up there with the best of them. Occasionally, some do not see his drum playing as "making a joyful noise unto the Lord." But most of us at TFBC do. Thanks, Terry!

FISH AND GAME

For about an eight-year period, maybe a little longer, I enjoy fishing with a wonderful man, Mike Genson, a retired educator from the Ellensburg area in Central Washington. He and his family moved to the Toledo area and attend Toledo First Baptist. Mike uses a nice salmon sled (boat) and is quite proficient at catching salmon and steelhead. A portion of his proficiency is due to one Clancy Holt who also goes to TFBC. Clancy's guided sport fishing is one of the Pacific Northwest's premiere fishing guide services. Clancy occasionally drops little tips to Mike. This gives Mike quite an advantage, considering the knowledge he already has. Now, with this said, we will not soon forget the year 2012–2013. The spring chinook run is healthy, and we find "The Spot" in the river producing one of the finest meals a fisherman could ever want. The only problem is we are not the only ones aware of this particular fishing hole. To be positioned correctly on the hole above the rapids, there is only room for one boat. You can fit two in there, but it becomes a tangled mess.

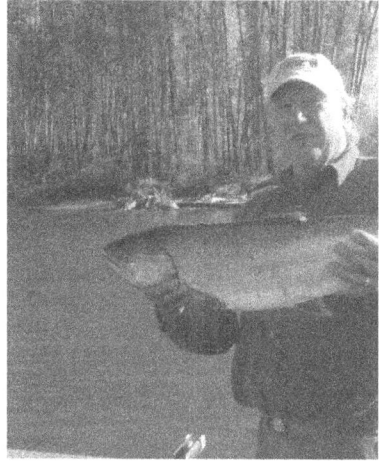

Few men try to do it because that scenario ends in failure for everyone. The solution is evident. To acquire "The Spot," we must get there before anyone else. It is April, and we leave Mike's at 5:30 a.m. for a short drive to the launch area and a fifteen-minute boat ride to "The Spot." We arrive at sunrise, 6:30 a.m., but there sits another boat where we want to be. The rest of the day we fish a lot without catching much.

I can't go every day because I still work. When we go fishing the next time, we leave Mike's at four in the morning and obtain "The Spot." Then, a couple of trips later, another boat beats us to The Spot. We now decide to leave for the Cowlitz River at three in the morning. We no longer settle for second best and discover no one else is crazy enough to anchor on the Cowlitz at three in the morning. This gives us plenty of time to explore a universe full of stars, in between snoozing.

Mike Genson, above, and Mike Wallace

Mike set a personal record for his boat that year. We caught sixty-two delightfully delicious springers. Thanks, Mike Genson.

THE GAME PORTION

I'm doing remodeling for my optometrist and his wife, great people. In one of our conversations, I brag about our church and pastors and challenge them to check it out, which they do. While getting to know Greg Webster better, I learn he is a marksman with a compound bow who at one time reigned as national champion in the over-sixty category. Greg, an excellent instructor, soon teaches me how to use a compound bow for elk and deer. This process also involves learning how to recreate elk calls that draw the critters toward you. This, almost more exciting than the shooting, captivates me.

I'll never forget the first time I call in a bull elk. We walk down an old logging spur, which is usually a short dead-end road. We position ourselves about twenty yards apart, both behind jack firs, smaller fir trees with branches about fifteen feet wide, tip to tip. I use my bull call and get a response right away. The bull continues to respond and draw closer until he stands on the opposite side of the same tree where I stand. I hear him breathing. By this time, my adrenaline soars through the roof, and I'm shaking like a leaf in a windstorm. I'm not sure what happens. Maybe he winds me or hears me trembling. Whatever happens, he simply disappears. That experience has me hooked. That becomes the best part of elk hunting next to the scenery we enjoy.

GAME PHASE 2

Another skill Greg Webster shares with me is his ability with rifles. Greg, already a good shot with his rifle, gets wind of a special class offered in Idaho. It's spendy, but he feels it's worth taking the four-day class, a long-range shooting seminar offered by a SWAT instructor who has trained Seal Team Six members. He is proficient with firearms, period. Greg signs up and heads for Idaho for the intense course with fairly long hours. They are shooting out fifteen hundred yards and more. When he returns, Greg tells me his instructor set up a monitor that tracks their shots. Greg could fire a shot, move from his sitting position to the monitor behind him, and see his bullet hit the target in real time.

Greg offers to pass along to me what he learned, and I waste no time accepting his offer. He gives me eighty-three pages to study for a month before we do anything. The next step is the procurement of a rifle for me to use. Then I learn about manufacturing precision bullets, which is vital for long-range shooting. Months later, we are on the power line west of town, one of the few places in Western Washington where we can make a thousand-yard shot with no bush or trees in the way.

I call this my final exam. I am given five one thousand-yard shots at a ten-inch

Greg Webster

diameter target stuck to a thick metal plate. A soft crosswind runs right to left. When I finish my last shot, we retrieve the target. I shot what looks like an eyebrow over the top of the ten-inch target with a height variation of about two and a half inches. Quite frankly, I'm thrilled with what Greg is patiently teaching me. To make these shots, I enter seven pieces of information into a special phone app: range, temperature, barometric pressure, angle, wind speed, wind direction, and altitude. This is for a beginner.

I have at least a beginning knowledge of how snipers make incredibly long shots. Going through this process is special, and I'm grateful to Greg for the opportunity.

PACKWOOD

Jerry Kuzminsky, another good friend from TFBC, is a Washington State patrolman who enjoys the wilderness and hunting. Jerry has a special area he hunts high on top of the Cascade Range near the Pacific Crest Trail. He invites me to this rugged area with stunning views that he has used for years. I'm now in my late sixties, and hiking to this place with a fifty-pound pack and my gun or bow is a nine-and-a-half mile trek on foot. The first two-thirds of the journey is up and down but nothing severe. The last third is brutal for anyone out of shape. Reaching the top is more than worth the steep climb.

Over the years I hunt with Jerry, we use compound bows, modern firearms, and old-fashioned black powder. Jerry most often goes in early with extra supplies. One year my son, Shane, and I help Jerry and get caught in an unexpected rainstorm. By the time we reach camp, we are soaked and exhausted. It's late, and we put up a tarp to keep off the rain. Halfway through the night, shivering, I truly do not think we will survive the night, yet we do. Just before dawn, the weather breaks, and we start a fire to dry our clothes and gain our strength. I'm not looking to repeat this incident. Fortunately, we do not.

Recalling one particular time always puts a smile on my face. We set up in a comfortable outfitter's tent, spacious for two guys and a woodstove. We settle in for a good night in our sleeping bags on Army cots. Jerry nibbles on one of his favorite munchies, chocolate-covered coffee beans, from a small plastic baggie. In the middle of the night, something else loves his beans. Jerry wakes up startled

Tarp shelter

Drying clothes

to see several mice using his body as an Indianapolis 500 racetrack. These little critters easily chew through the baggie, and now higher than a kite, run it off on top of Jerry. At the time, the loss of sleep steals only a small amount of humor from the situation. The following day, after our hunt, I construct a homemade mousetrap from a bucket, a small aluminum can, a stick, string, and a little peanut butter. We catch six mice later in the night. Somebody always wants a free lunch.

A few years later, Jerry and I hunt with black powder rifles. Our camp is on the east side of a steep ridge. We usually hunt the west side, which is far less difficult to navigate and opens on more flat areas. This is also where elk like to feed during early mornings and evenings.

This particular evening, we try a somewhat different strategy. We decide this time Jerry will go up the east side and over the top while I hang out in our tent to give him enough time to reach his destination. Then I go around

Snow tent

the end of the ridge to the trails we use on the west side. The idea is that Jerry will flush any elk out on top, sending them in my direction. Sounds like a great idea. After making our plan, we hit the sack. It is exceptionally cold throughout the night and, gracious as Jerry is, he wakes up numerous times to stoke the fire, keeping the temperature reasonable in the tent.

Without much sleep and unfamiliar with the east side climb, Jerry heads for the ridge as he sets out. I wait thirty minutes to leave, which should give Jerry time to reach the top and for me to position myself on the westside trail to wait for those big, impressive bull elks to saunter my way.

I'm lying on my cot with ten more minutes before I head out. I decide to step outside to stretch and smell the fresh crisp air. I faintly hear a weird sound. I can't tell if it's an animal or something else, but it unsettles me. The sound is so faint I can hardly tell the direction it comes from. I jog toward where I think I hear the sound. After about a hundred-yard jog, I stop to listen. I look to my right about five hundred feet above me and see what looks like Jerry on a vertical cliff. I still can't hear him or tell what's going on.

I run to the tent, strip about thirty feet of 1,000-pound test mule tape, and stuff it in my belt. He looks like he's in trouble. I don't have time to go around the west side if Jerry is in trouble. Instead, I head directly up the north end of the steep ridge. I pull myself up by bushes and small trees. I am about halfway up when I reach a vantage point where I can see his body with fully extended arms, as far as they can reach, barely holding on to a vertical rock surface. I yell for him to not let go and tell him, "I'm on my way."

I don't realize when I reach the top that the vertical surface Jerry sprawls on is like an exaggerated washboard that comes in then juts out, which creates a large issue. Exhausted by my climb, I walk as fast as I can and yell for him. It is so steep I can't see over the edge in most places. So I continue yelling. I don't realize, at this time, that because of the washboarding, I must be right over Jerry for him to hear me. Most of the time in life it's three strikes and you're out. Well, I'm about to face a third problem. I'm so frantic over the time it's taking to locate Jerry, I never notice a thick fog now covering the entire ridge. I have no clue if I walked past Jerry or haven't gone nearly far enough. I realize this and stop. Standing there, picturing Jerry clinging to that vertical cliff, freaks me out. If he can't hold on any longer, the vertical drop will finish him. I peer into the fog and say to God, "I have to save Jerry; I don't know where he is. I can't be responsible for him not making it. I don't know if he is to the left of me or to the right. Please."

About a minute later, I creep to the edge and walk about fifteen yards to my left as the fog clears. Without saying a word, I look down and see Jerry twenty feet below me. Next to me is a boulder about three feet in diameter with nothing else around it for some distance. I don't believe in luck, but I do believe in divine intervention. Quickly, I tie the mule tape around the boulder and have just enough left to tie a small loop that can wrap around Jerry's wrist and be tightened. With both ends now secure, I slowly pull him up to where I am. Jerry and I sit for a while before moving. We are both totally exhausted and extremely thankful. The alternative is unimaginable.

For those who believe in coincidences, here is one more to add to the mix. The following morning, my body should be getting clammy and in need of a hospital because of my hypertension and pulling myself up the mountain. But I don't need any medical attention; unlike in the previous hunting trip when I end up clammy and unconscious from overexertion in front of the hospital door. The climb to get Jerry is so much more extreme in terms of elevation and difficulty. Back at the tent, after Jerry tells me his side of the story, and knowing mine, it's clear to us outside intervention saved us both.

CHAPTER 46
A TRIP OR TWO

THE COFFEE SHOP

WHILE BUSY AT WORK, I get a call from a man with an accent from India. With a kind voice, he says, "I want you to build a coffee shop for me next to our motel." I inform him I am semi-retired without an active license, end of conversation. Three days later, the same man, same voice, says, "I need your help with the coffee shop." My response is the same as the first time we talked.

Less than a week later, I receive a third call, this time with a twist to his request. He says, "God told me to call you for help." I pause. He most definitely has my attention. I've never heard that one from a potential client, and I'm unsure how to respond. After I explain the retired/license thing again, I say, "Let me think about it, and I'll call you back."

After contemplating for several days, I think of a man with commercial experience. Maybe we could tag team. After calling him, I find he is willing to help.

Calling my now-potential client, Hiten Patel, I let him know we can put a proposal together for him. Since this is a commercial job, I ask my partner with commercial experience to put together the budget, and we proceed with construction.

Hiten's comment, "God told me to call you for help," has me asking him many questions before and after work to figure out where he comes from spiritually. Within a couple of months, I know what an incredibly wonderful family the Patels are. They have a rich history of hospitality going back centuries in the Gujarat region of India. The Patel family dominates the hotel/motel landscape in the United States, beginning in the mid-1900s. Migrating from Gujarat, they carry a trait to the United States where the sky is the limit.

Speaking of hospitality, Rosie and I accept an invitation for dinner with Hiten, Sangita, his wife, and children. Sangita is an amazing cook. After four hours we lose track of how many courses we are served. Wow! This is their normal with guests.

Hiten begins showing up occasionally for church services. After a few, he tells me he likes what Pastor Joe has to say each Sunday. Sangita, one of the sweetest ladies I've ever met, continues to hold to her Hindu beliefs.

Toward the end of constructing the coffee shop, I find we have underestimated our bid. My partner has other obligations to meet, and I end up spending three more weeks working pro bono. We have no official contract. We simply must keep our word and finish the job. It is a tough finish, but I end up with two new wonderful friends and free coffee for as long as they own the place.

ATHENS

We know a delightful couple living in Athens, Greece. Tim and Joan Gillihan, missionaries throughout the Middle East and Africa for about thirty years, are involved in helping refugees. It's 2016, and millions of immigrants from Iraq, Iran, Africa, Afghanistan, and Syria flee their nations

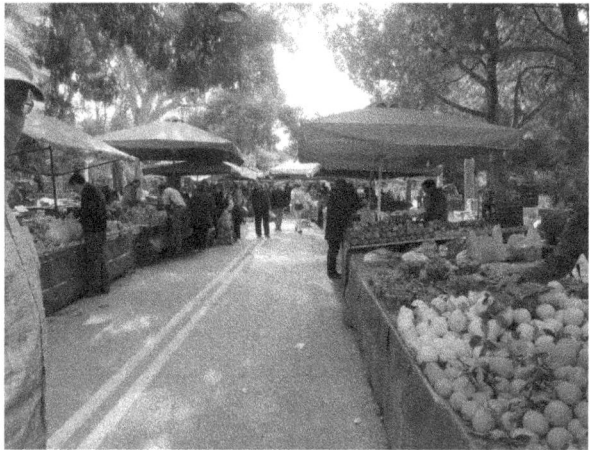

Vrilissia

because of hunger, poverty, persecution, violence, or conflicts. One of the main refugee centers is in Athens. Tim is in charge of refugees in southern Europe but maintains a low profile for fear of Muslim reprisals. Very few at the center in Athens know his position. Most of those working at the center are Iranian with some from Africa, Afghanistan, and other nations. They meet refugees as they arrive on the shore and provide them with food, clothes, and supplies. Most arrive via Turkey and the north coast of Africa.

Rosie and I fly to Greece and end up staying at Tim and Joan's condo in the northern part of Athens called the Vrilissia. Unfortunately for us, Joan is off visiting one of their four daughters who are all involved in missions in different parts of the world.

The first few days, Tim takes us on an extraordinary tour of history. First we visit the Acropolis on which the Parthenon, temple of Athena Nike, Theater of Dionysus, and other ancient structures are perched. Just below the entrance to the Acropolis is the Areopagus (Mars Hill), a rocky hill with crude steps carved into it. On top of this rough rock the apostle Paul met with Athenian philosophers. At the base of the rock is a sign in Greek explaining Paul's visit around AD 50.

Acropolis, above, and Agora

This is one of Tim's favorite places to hang out. When someone who can't understand Greek steps up to read the sign, Tim politely shares Paul's reason for being there 1,966 years ago. Tim has many opportunities to share his faith. As Paul did, Tim also shares what he knows to be true in the agora (marketplace) at the bottom of the hill.

The next few days our visit grows even more interesting. Rosie, Tim, and I head to the "Oasis" refugee center to meet the staff and listen to many refugees tell their stories. Two young men in their twenties from Ghana—Jean Michelle and Samuel, his brother—tell of human sacrifice, idol worship, and the chasm between the rich and those in poverty. We spend time with two young men from Iran. One is heartbroken after leaving his sister behind in a recently arranged, oppressive marriage. She used to be such a happy person, he says, but no longer is.

Areopagus, above; Bema Seat, center; and Oasis

Men, women, and children speak of being crammed onto boats so tightly they can't move. More bodies means more money for the men supplying the boats. They cram as many as they can in the dark and point them in a general direction. Women and children weep as they are shoved off into the dark, dangerous Aegean Sea. We hear so many horror stories, all with a similar theme—each refugee appears to be an independent thinker, willing to fight and take risks.

We meet Americans D.B. and his wife and two little girls. D.B. is the director of "Oasis." After 9/11, instead of wanting to fight, D.B. dedicates himself to learning Farsi and whatever else he needs to know to share Jesus

The village of Oia, above; stone streets at right; sunset, lower right; and below, Aegean Rose

with the Afghani people. He later ends up with his wife, who also learns Farsi, in an Afghani village. The local women ask his wife if she loves her husband. She says, "Yes, I love my husband." The ladies share with her that it is not so with them. They cannot choose who they marry. The international missions board pulls D.B., his wife, and two young girls out of Afghanistan because it becomes too dangerous. He is transferred to the "Oasis" in Athens.

Tim and D.B. take Rosie and me to a special two-story building with a secret entrance. The first floor is a workshop for training refugees in certain usable work skills. Those interested in learning more about Jesus meet in the "upper room" on the second floor. The reason for the secrecy is to protect those wanting to learn about Jesus from Muslim retribution.

The situation is so hard for the refugees living in overcrowded camps with patience wearing thin. But in Athens at the Oasis, on a Monday, we close up early at 2 p.m. and go around the corner for a late lunch. Weekly Javad, from the Oasis, sees this sad, elderly Afghan woman walk in, clearly overwhelmed with the troubles in her world. Javad has prayed with her many times and explains that the answer to all of her troubles is King Jesus. Like many Afghans, she is a hard Muslim and not easily open to hearing about Jesus. Javad asks her, "If God reveals Himself to you and shows you the truth, will you follow Him?" She just laughs.

After we leave for lunch, the elderly lady walks to the Oasis, but the door is closed. A day later, she describes to Javad what happens next. "I sit down on the curb; I am tired. Suddenly, I see a bright light coming from behind me, so bright that I cover my eyes. The light is shining brighter than the sun. In front of me, I see a shadow. Then, I heard a voice speaking in my own language, saying, 'My daughter, my daughter, the door is open for you. Come!' I replied, 'The door is closed!' Again the voice called to me, 'I am the son of God, Jesus. The door is open for you, my daughter. I am the door!'"

I tremble and my heart beats wildly. As the lady recalls this story later to Javad, she proclaims the peace and joy she has experienced every day since hearing Jesus speak to her. Javad says, "I have never seen her so full of life as I have this week. Praise God, she has accepted Jesus as her savior." She says, "Many times you (Javad) have encouraged me to pray that God would speak to me and talk to me. I thought it was blasphemy! But now ... I know, Jesus is alive!"

Tim and Joan Gillihan, like most seasoned missionaries, have discovered that throughout Europe there are four commonalities to Muslims converting to Christ.

1) Contact with a Christian
2) Hearing the Word of God (Bible)
3) Hearing prayer in the name of Jesus
4) Having a dream or vision

Number four is interesting in that dreams or visions are common in a shame/honor society such as Persian and Arab cultures. Historically, westerners, being a guilt/innocence society, often fail to appeal to another group. Also, approaching Arabs or Persians from a fear/power basis, which works better for African or South American cultures, can also fail.

Simply present Christ in a way each different people group can relate to and let God do the rest.

LARRY

Months later, back home, we receive news that brother Larry passed away. I always maintained a good relationship with Larry. Being a twin, he enjoyed a special closeness with Gary, even though Gary was a teaser and Larry had a short temper. The two of them always maintained a good relationship. After Gary's death, Larry missed that special bond most twins have, which is not difficult to understand. He pretty much kept to himself and maintained a private lifestyle.

Brother Larry

OUR EXTRA LOT

In early 2019, with the housing market looking good, Rosie and I conclude it's a good time to build a nice home on the one lot we held back in our development. For six months, with a good crew and my toolbelt on, we go for it.

With this building experience, I find it amusing to observe my grandson and a couple of his buddies attempt to simulate a carpenter, especially while roofing. Their cell phones sometimes serve as a diversion. At other times their dreams of a better future suffice as a diversion.

512 Rosy Drive

Please don't get me wrong; these are great young men. They just belong somewhere else, and eventually they do find work elsewhere. One becomes a deputy, another an accountant, and Austin works a tech job while launching a career as a comedian. I appreciate each of these guys and their time helping me. Each is a fine young man and, if nothing else, they learn a little more about taking care of homes they'll someday own. The kicker to this project is someone else had different ideas as to what would happen with our extra lot. With the home and shop finished, we list the property. I am on my excavator, finishing the ground work around the home. It's noon, and I am totally exhausted. I shut off the excavator and take a break. While sitting there, my thoughts say, "You need to consider this."

Over the next three days, I'm getting the idea that God is prompting Rosie and me to move into this place, which has never been the plan. The perfect scenario is to pass away peacefully in our dream home. But I need to share these thoughts with Rosie. I never feel for a moment God is commanding me to move, simply suggesting it. God's desires for our life are always the best. Being omnipresent, He knows past, present, and future all at the same time. On the third day, I finally share with Rosie what I'm thinking. With a bit of shock and not much awe, she patiently listens. Like her, I've always pictured a team of horses not being able to drag me out of our dream home. Then Rose, being a questioner, thoroughly explores the word "consider" up one side and down the other.

Two weeks later, Rosie goes out the back door to retrieve something from her car. At the top of the steps her body, all of a sudden, feels strange. She pivots a bit to the top of the steps and, in a semiconscious state with her arms at her side, falls from the stone steps face down in the gravel with her face taking the full brunt of the fall. She immediately becomes fully conscious and in pain. As soon as she can stand, she hears a voice in her head, saying, "Get on board quickly, for Michael's sake." She knows immediately what this means. Needless to say Rosie has no desire to further question me and what the Lord wants. We pick gravel out of her face for a month and the broken cartilage on top of her nose takes care of itself.

COVID

Never anticipating the Covid-19 pandemic shutdown is a week away, I ask Pastor Joe if I can put out the word at church asking if anyone is willing to help us move. The thought of moving to our new home seems daunting, as exhausted as I am. If I can get at least six people to help, I tell Joe, I can make it work. The move is planned for Saturday with plans to finish during the week. On Saturday morning, sixteen smiling faces show up, and we completely move in eight hours. "Thank you, God; and thank you, fellow believers."

It is so bizarre how we go from normal one moment to lockdown the next. In a short time, harsh divisions form, vaccinated versus unvaccinated, masked against unmasked. Just like politics nowadays, the lines get drawn, with churches definitely not immune to any of this. Division in the church is nothing new. Humans are humans, but let me make one thing abundantly clear: do not blame this on Jesus; it's humans being human. Churches during the Inquisition and the Crusades should have known better but obviously did not. Greed and power steers the wheel again, not Christ.

During Covid, we all have our list of priorities, and we all begin to show signs of hypocrisy. Our preferences surface, good or bad, for others to see. Fear drives people to shameful acts even with those close to them.

As a whole, we fail the test with Covid, and we fail it with politics in loving each other.

As much damage as Covid does to our church, we persist. Our pastor goes online with church services, and a hardcore element dons long johns in the winter and gathers in the Toledo High School stadium. Quite frankly, being outside and gazing over the forest and landscape while Joe preaches works great for me.

The thing I miss the most during Covid is two years of Man Camp. For the past eight years, we have taken a large group into the wilderness for a week to hike, fish or simply rest in a beautiful environment. Guys come and go to fit their schedules. We have an amazing camp cook, Dave Griffis, in his eighties. I am in charge of logistics and supply Dave with a condensed kitchen where he performs his magic, even baking cakes for dessert. The best part of Man Camp is spending quality time with old and new friends, getting to know them on a deeper level. With all the men coming and going, we normally average six to ten a night.

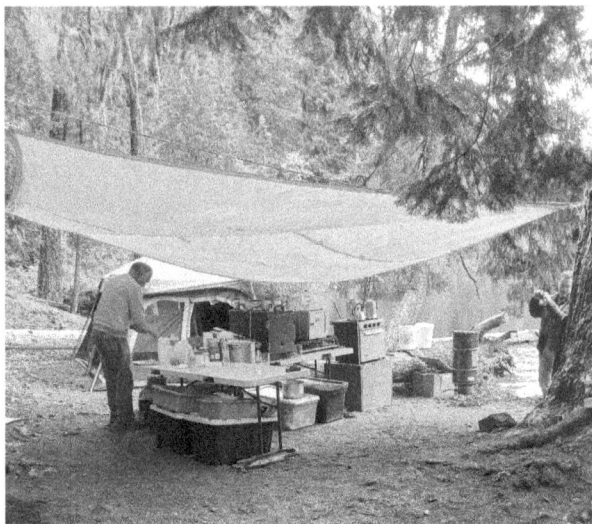

Dave, camp cook, above, and Kona Reef, below

A TRIP WITH FRIENDS

Thanks to a dear couple, Larry and Barb, we enjoy Hawaii on a yearly basis. We stay at the Kona Reef Resort for a couple of weeks. We each kick back in our own unit at their time-share.

CHAPTER 47
LIKE A CHILD

SIMPLICITY

R AY WALLACE IS LIVING PROOF that God has a sense of humor. He sees nothing complicated in his approach to life—with one exception. At times a certain "twinkle" in his eye sparks the thought, "Okay, what is he up to now?" Other than that, with Ray, what you see is what you get.

When it comes to where he put his faith, that is simple also. He put it not in himself but in Christ. He did not philosophize about Christ with words but with action.

Although far from perfect, as none of us are, he cares for others. When others are in need, he tries to help. He loves sharing his time and stories with

Bigfoot filling his diaper with pranks

children. Not just his heart but also his hand goes out to the downtrodden. Again, while not perfect, he does the best he can with who he is and what he has, a logger with a big heart.

Looking back, I see a thread of influence from Dad throughout my adult life that consists of timely conversations in the form of a phone call that changes my life's path multiple times. As much as we butt heads from time to time, the love is always there.

Elna, a polar opposite from Ray L. Wallace, offers her own style of simplicity. She is an expert listener with a heart that does not judge others. She's not a complainer or talebearer. The woman puts God first in all she does. Like Dad, she knows how to care for others.

Her influence in my life continues to pay great dividends to this day. Watching her live out her faith and seeing how that attracts so many others to her is something I appreciate now more than ever.

Christianity, from the very beginning, is never meant to be complicated. Mom is always

Mrs. Bigfoot with clean diapers

straightforward and uncomplicated with a faith meant not only for adults but also for children. Mom's faith resembles Rosie's; they both discovered Jesus at an early age. I've been fortunate to have the influence of both these fine ladies in my life. Jesus wants us to come with a humble, vulnerable, child-like trust. Then He will give us the resources to understand His desires for our lives. A childlike faith is what Christ wants most from us.

The middle ages of my life are similar to the world's with crusades I had no business launching. I passed through my own dark ages. Simplicity is not a word to describe that period. Complicated is more accurate. This made living for Christ, instead of myself, a more difficult road to travel. The more I turn from my past, the freer I am. Nothing can now hold me back other than myself.

ANSELM'S PROSLOGION

Of all the early church fathers, Anselm helps clarify what I can best refer to as an "encounter" with Christ and how it comes about. In short, Anselm says, "First we believe, then we understand." In other words, we first take a step of faith, and then God fills in the blanks. It's not complicated. The problem is not allowing ourselves to take that step of faith. All God needs is the smallest of openings in a person's heart. He then gives us all the evidence we will ever need, one piece at a time.

To further understand the depth of an "encounter," a later church father, Dietrich Bonhoeffer, while imprisoned by the Nazis, wrote, "It is true that encounter with Jesus meant the reversal of all human value." When it comes to the spiritual side of our lives, humans are used to operating in the exact opposite way of how God wants us to: We gather information then decide whether we believe something to be true. This works with everything except coming to Jesus. Faith (belief) comes first, then understanding.

CHOICE

From the very beginning, God gives humans free choice. He is not interested in relationships with robots. We are free to follow our standards or God's, which are much higher. We're free to love or hate, sink or swim.

All I know is that for the past thirty-five years, God's ways have been vastly superior to the twenty years prior without Him. Free choice can be a curse or a blessing. Use it wisely.

What keeps you from taking that step to see if there is anything to this Jesus?
1) This God you're talking about is too good to be true.
2) I prefer putting my faith in myself and running my own life.
3) Past hurts—a real God wouldn't allow these bad things to happen.
4) Hypocrisy—a church leader or follower sets a bad example. The only problem with this is, Christ is not to blame. Christ did not cause them to make poor choices, causing them to fall. Hypocrisy is universal, not exhibited only by believers in Christ.
5) I don't believe in God's absolute truth, absolutely.

If given the chance from an honest seeker, God may not choose to answer all concerns, but He will reveal precisely what you need. Over and over for the past thirty-five years, He has met every need, even some occasional wants. God knows ahead of time what's best for our lives.

FINISHING

I've made a choice to believe God is who He says He is. I also believe He has a place for me after I'm finished with this life. I believe the chief end of man is to bring glory to God while here on earth. While I'm here, finishing well is what counts. As a witness for Christ, we tell what we know from our encounters with Jesus. My intention here is to present my encounter with Christ, not prove His existence. It is God's responsibility to reveal Himself to anyone willing to give Him the opportunity.

For twenty years, my theme song was, "I'll do it my way," from Frank Sinatra's 1969 version of "My Way." Replacing Sinatra for the past thirty-five years is "Front Seat, Back Seat" by Dallas Holm. When I do life my way, I'm definitely in the driver's seat. God has since taken the wheel. Now I'm in the back seat, being chauffeured and enjoying the ride.

I start like a child. I shall finish like one!

ACKNOWLEDGMENTS

Writing and publishing a book is no easy feat. It takes a team, and I'm grateful to the following people for their help.

My loving and patient wife for taking me as her diamond in the rough thirty-two years ago and for her tireless support and help for me to write this book.

As my editor, Julie McDonald Zander went above and beyond with her encouragement and guidance for my first and probably last literary work.

Bob Turner, growing up in the logging camps with you, being five years older, provided depth and insight to my early years.

Don Buswell, at 102 years old with an ironclad memory, provided invaluable recollections for this book.

Kathy Campbell of Inkbooksdesign.com created a cover that illustrates the story of growing up in the shadow of Bigfoot.

Sue Miholer provided eagle-eye proofreading of the manuscript.

Shane Wallace, thank you for starting the idea of a book in the first place.

ABOUT THE AUTHOR

MICHAEL WALLACE earned a bachelor's degree in industrial education from Western Washington University. He spent nine years as a retailer and the last thirty-six as a designer and builder. He and his wife, Rose, who live in Southwest Washington, have two sons, two daughters, and thirteen grandchildren.